POTTERY AND SOCIETY

THE IMPACT OF RECENT STUDIES IN MINOAN POTTERY

POTTERY AND SOCIETY

THE IMPACT OF RECENT STUDIES IN MINOAN POTTERY

Gold Medal Colloquium in Honor of

PHILIP P. BETANCOURT

104th Annual Meeting of the Archaeological Institute of America, New Orleans, Louisiana, 5 January 2003

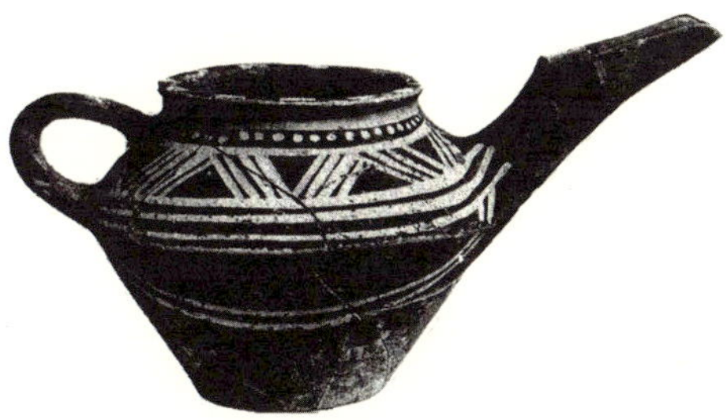

EDITORS

Malcolm H. Wiener

Jayne L. Warner · Janice Polonsky · Erin E. Hayes

with the assistance of Catriona McDonald

ARCHAEOLOGICAL INSTITUTE OF AMERICA
BOSTON
2006

Published by the
Archaeological Institute of America
Boston, Massachusetts 02215-2006

Library of Congress Cataloging-in-Publication Data

Archaeological Institute of America. General Meeting (104th : 2003 : New Orleans, La.)
Pottery and society : the impact of recent studies in Minoan pottery : gold medal colloquium in honor of Philip P. Betancourt : 104th annual meeting of the Archaeological Institute of America, New Orleans, Louisiana, 5 January 2003 / editors, Malcolm H. Wiener . . . [et al.].
p. cm.
Includes bibliographical references.
ISBN 1-931909-14-8 (alk. paper)
1. Crete (Greece)–Antiquities–Congresses. 2. Pottery, Minoan–Greece–Crete–Congresses. I. Betancourt, Philip P., 1936- II. Wiener, Malcolm H. III. Title.

DF221.C8A73 2006
939'.1801–dc22 2006045296

ISBN 1-931909-14-8

TITLE PAGE AND COVER: EM III teapot from Mochlos, HM no. 5473 (Philip P. Betancourt, *East Cretan White-on-Dark Ware. Studies on a Handmade Pottery of the Early to Middle Minoan Periods*. Philadelphia: The University Museum, 1984, pl. 2A).

The paper used in this publication meets the minimum requirements of the American National Standard for Information Sciences – Permanence of Paper for Printed Library Materials, ANSI Z39.48-1984. ∞™

MANUFACTURED IN THE UNITED STATES OF AMERICA

CONTENTS

ARCHAEOLOGICAL INSTITUTE OF AMERICA

GOLD MEDAL AWARD

FOR DISTINGUISHED ARCHAEOLOGICAL ACHIEVEMENT

PHILIP P. BETANCOURT

5 JANUARY 2003

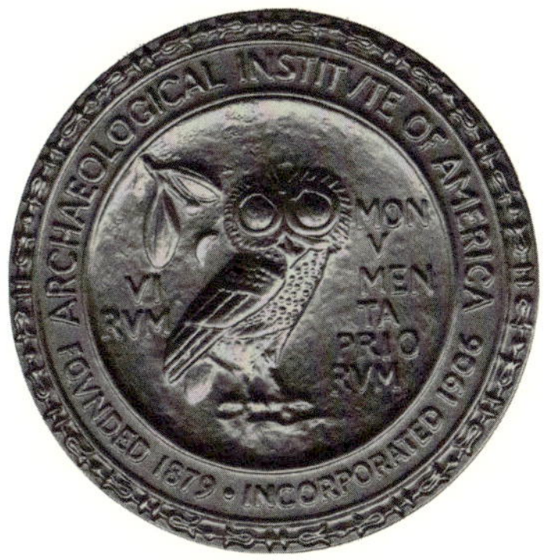

CITATION

PHILIP P. BETANCOURT gets things done. While serving as the Laura H. Carnell Professor of Art History and Archaeology at Temple University, where he has taught since 1970, he also has held the position of Adjunct Professor in the Department of the History of Art at the University of Pennsylvania, and he has served as Acting Dean in the Tyler School of Art of Temple University (1983–1984). In addition, since 1990 he has served as the Executive Director of the Institute for Aegean Prehistory.

His excavation experience began in the United States with work at various sites under the auspices of the University of Missouri and the National Park Service. Thereafter, two field seasons in Italy and a summer at Halieis in Greece preceded his move to Crete, which has been the focus of his research since 1976.

Philip Betancourt has been the author and/or editor of an extensive series of books and other scholarly publications, which since 1965 has grown to number well over 100. Early studies include *The Aeolic Style in Architecture: A Survey of Its Development in Palestine, the Halikarnassos Peninsula and Greece, 1000-500 B.C.* (Princeton 1977), *Vasilike Ware: An Early Bronze Age Pottery Style in Crete* (Göteborg, Sweden 1979), and *East Cretan White-on-Dark Ware: Studies on a Handmade Pottery of the Early to Middle Bronze Age* (Philadelphia 1984). For his basic handbook on *The History of Minoan Pottery* (Princeton 1985), he not only wrote the text but also took all of the photographs himself, working directly from the showcases in the Heraklion Museum. During the same time period he edited 10 volumes in the annual series of the *Temple University Aegean Symposium* (1976–1985) and wrote numerous monographs and journal articles.

He is now completing a series of final reports on his excavations at a number of Minoan sites on Crete, which he began in 1985. To date five volumes on Pseira are published (1995–2001) as well as a multimedia CD-ROM presentation of the site. Chrysokamino has been accepted for publication, Haghia Photia is in the works, and a second excavation season, in 2003, is planned at the new site of Haghios Charalambos. From this record it is clear that we can look forward to many more years of excavation and publication from Philip Betancourt.

But this is only the beginning. Everyone who has had the privilege of working with Philip Betancourt in the field realizes that what sets him apart from all of his colleagues is his dedication to the art of teaching, in the field as well as in the classroom. Every Betancourt field project is a training excavation. All of his students learn how to do things themselves. Although he instructs and gives guidance and encouragement, in the end it is his students who must produce the final product on their own. This holds for training in all aspects of contemporary fieldwork, both traditional methodology and modern scientific technology. Through his efforts and dedication Philip Betancourt is producing students who are qualified to deal with all aspects of Aegean archaeology as it will be practiced in the third millennium A.D.

The Archaeological Institute of America has had, from its founding in 1879, a dual commitment to the promotion of both research and teaching, involving all aspects of that complicated academic enigma that we call archaeology. Today we honor this commitment to its fullest extent by awarding to Professor Philip P. Betancourt the Institute's Gold Medal for Distinguished Archaeological Achievement.

James D. Muhly

Reprinted from *AJA* 107 (2003), 278

PREFACE

JAMES D. MUHLY

AT AN INTERNATIONAL conference far too many years ago, Sinclair Hood pulled me aside to say: "This man Betancourt . . . I think he has a photograph of every known Minoan vase." "Quite possible," I replied. Sinclair went on, "He has interesting things to say about this pottery." Indeed he does, and he has now been saying them for over thirty years. From his first article on Minoan pottery published in the *American Journal of Archaeology* in 1973 to the present day, Philip P. Betancourt's career as an author/editor/publisher, a field archaeologist and a teacher has been closely intertwined with all aspects of the study of Minoan pottery. And, as Sinclair Hood recognized early on, he has always gone about his work in a clear, systematic and productive manner. The accomplishments of his enduring career made Phil Betancourt an obvious candidate for the Archaeological Insititute of America Gold Medal.

A colloquium is traditionally held in conjunction with the presentation of the Institute's Gold Medal. When the medal was awarded to Phil Betancourt at the 2003 annual meeting of the AIA in New Orleans, Louisiana, I had the honor of organizing the Gold Medal Colloquium. The papers published in this volume are expanded versions of the papers delivered.

Organizing a Gold Medal Colloquium is never a simple task, no matter how worthy the honorand. What topics must be included? Which scholars must take part? Phil Betancourt has been a unifying force in a sometimes contentious discipline. Teaching, excavation and publication have always been the cornerstones of that discipline, and Phil has excelled in all three. It was important that these facets of Phil's career be represented in the colloquium.

Phil Betancourt's dedication as a teacher and the way in which he has brought the classroom into the field at each of his excavations deserve emphasis. I have worked with various distinguished American field archaeologists all over the eastern Mediterranean and the Middle East and I have never encountered a field archaeologist more dedicated to working with students, training students and inspiring students than Philip Betancourt. I have been working with Phil on Crete since 1995; every season we have had a great group of student archaeologists, many of whom have continued to come back, year after year.

They have always been treated by Professor Betancourt as future professionals; they were taught how to be scholars, how to work and how to act as professionals.

The way we study Minoan pottery has been transformed in recent years. It is in ceramic studies, perhaps more than in any other branch of archaeological research, that we can see the overwhelming impact of scientific analysis. Today the study of Minoan pottery is conducted in the laboratory as much as in the library. Many scholars today speak of something called "Scientific Archaeology," as if it were a sub-division of the general discipline of Archaeology. Actually, science must now be a part of all archaeology, and Phil Betancourt realized this many years ago. This is very much the future of Aegean Archaeology; Prof. Betancourt is training students qualified to face that future. Obviously, any colloquium devoted to Phil and Minoan pottery must encompass state-of-the-art research in the field.

Phil Betancourt's scholarly output is extensive; I will not try to record it all here, but refer you to his bibliography in this volume. To give an idea of the importance of Phil's contribution to publication in his field, however, I point to his volume on *The History of Minoan Pottery*, published by Princeton University Press in 1985. In order to appreciate fully the impact of this book, it is necessary to turn to Greece and to the Greek translation, published in 1993. So extensive is the use of this volume by the Greek archaeological community, that a new verb has materialized in the spoken language of today. "To betancourt" a vase, as in "I have to betancourt this pithos," means, of course, to look it up in *The History of Minoan Pottery*. What more could any scholar ask for?

How to do justice to all the aspects of his career—to represent achievements in teaching, excavation and publication—in a single colloquium? I decided to bring together distinguished scholars who have worked in areas of special interest to Phil Betancourt with an emphasis on the study of Minoan pottery. I also intended the participants in this colloquium to include former students and young Greek scholars as well as senior scholars from America and abroad. I am grateful to everyone who agreed to take part, and apologize to all the eminent scholars and friends whom I was not able to include because of the tyranny of time.

I wish to thank the Archeological Institute of America for publishing the proceedings of this colloquium. Appreciation is also extended to the archaeologists at INSTAP in Greenwich, Connecticut, for their work in editing this volume and seeing it through all the steps of publication.

PHILIP P. BETANCOURT

BIOGRAPHY

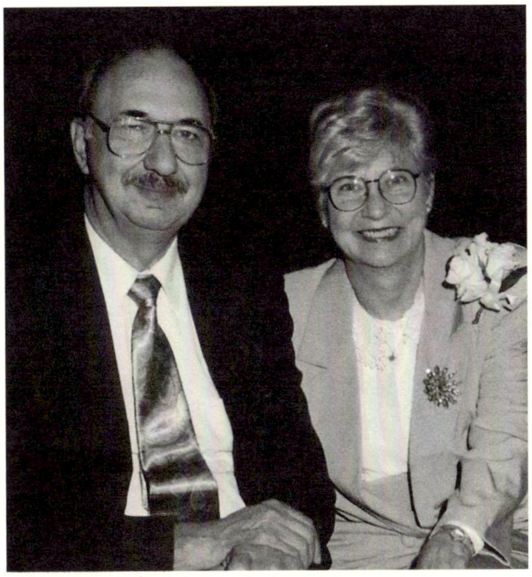

Philip P. Betancourt and his wife Mary.

PHILIP P. BETANCOURT is a leading American authority on the Minoan civilization of Bronze Age Crete, with an exemplary record of teaching, excavation and publication of major archaeological projects. His work has added significantly to our knowledge of the rise of the earliest complex civilization of Europe. Of critical importance has been his creation and direction of important institutions supporting Old World Archaeology.

Since receiving his Ph.D. in Classical Archaeology from the University of Pennsylvania in 1970, Phil Betancourt has served as Professor at Temple University, Adjunct Professor at the University of Pennsylvania, and Chairperson of the Department of Art History at Temple for many years. Among his voluminous articles on all aspects of Minoan archaeology, Phil Betancourt has published indispensable studies of Minoan pottery, painting and metallurgy. They include, in addition to the titles listed in the Gold Medal Citation, *Kommos*, Vol. 2: *The Final Neolithic through Middle Minoan III Pottery* and the two-volume monograph, *The Cretan Collection in the University Museum, University of Pennsylvania.* He has also published nine volumes of excavation reports for Pseira, the important Minoan site off the coast of Crete.

Philip Betancourt, with the invaluable support and assistance of his wife Mary, has directed excavations of several critical Minoan sites, including Pseira, now the most completely studied Bronze Age Cretan town; Eileithyia Cave, where he challenged earlier theories of cult use; and Chrysokamino, the earliest known Cretan metallurgical site. He is currently codirector of the excavations at Hagios Charalambos, an important Middle Bronze Age cave sanctuary and burial site. The publication of his excavations has been prompt and exceptional.

During his tenure as Executive Director of the Institute for Aegean Prehistory, Prof. Betancourt has overseen the grant process providing funding for hundreds of excavations, surveys and research projects throughout the Aegean and the Near East. He is largely responsible for the creation of the Study Center for East Crete, a major state-of-the-art research facility serving over 100 American and other scholars in Greece. He has also spearheaded the formation of publication teams of archaeological scientists, conservators, photographers, draftsmen and editors to facilitate the publication of important material which otherwise would have been delayed, inadequately treated or not published at all.

Philip Betancourt is one of the outstanding archaeologists of his generation. His contributions were duly recognized by his colleagues in the awarding of the Archaeological Institute of America's Gold Medal for Distinguished Archaeological Achievement on January 5, 2003. The proceedings of the Gold Medal Symposium are published here to commemorate this high honor and to pay tribute to his extraordinary contribution to the field of Old World Archaeology.

Malcolm H. Wiener
Editor in Chief

PHILIP P. BETANCOURT: SELECTED BIBLIOGRAPHY

BOOKS

1977

The Aeolic Style in Architecture: A Survey of its Development in Palestine, the Halikarnassos Peninsula and Greece, 1000–500 B.C. Princeton, NJ: Princeton University Press.

1979

(with contributions from T.K. Gaisser, E. Koss, R.F. Lyon, F.R. Matson, S. Montgomery, G.H. Myer and C.P. Swann). *Vasiliki Ware: An Early Bronze Age Pottery Style in Crete. SIMA* 56. Göteborg: Paul Åströms.

1980

Cooking Vessels from Minoan Kommos: A Preliminary Report. Institute of Archaeology Occasional Paper 7. Los Angeles: University of California.

1983

The Cretan Collection in The University Museum, University of Pennsylvania. Vol. 1, *Minoan Objects Excavated From Vasilike, Pseira, Sphoungaras, Priniatikos Pyrgos, and Other Sites.* University Museum Monograph 47. Philadelphia: The University Museum.

1984

(editor). *East Cretan White-on-Dark Ware: Studies on a Handmade Pottery of the Early to Middle Minoan Periods.* University Museum Monograph 51. Philadelphia: The University Museum.

1985

The History of Minoan Pottery. Princeton, NJ: Princeton University Press. (Translated into Greek in 1993: *Η Ιστορία της Μινωικής Κεραμεικής.* Athens: P. Chiotelli.)

1990

Kommos. Vol. 2, *The Final Neolithic through Middle Minoan III Pottery.* Princeton, NJ: Princeton University Press.

1991

(with J.S. Silverman). *The Cretan Collection in the University Museum, University of Pennsylvania.* Vol. 2, *Pottery from Gournia.* University Museum Monograph 72. Philadelphia: The University Museum.

1995

(editor, with C. Davaras). *Pseira.* Vol. 1, *The Minoan Buildings on the West Side of Area A.* University Museum Monograph 90. Philadelphia: The University Museum.

1997

(with M. Becker). *Richard B. Seager: Pioneer Archaeologist and Proper Gentleman.* Philadelphia: University of Pennsylvania Museum.

(editor, with R. Laffineur). *TEXNH: Craftsmen, Craftswomen and Craftsmanship in the Aegean Bronze Age. Proceedings of the 6th International Aegean Conference, Philadelphia, Temple University, 18–21 April 1996. Aegaeum* 16. Liège: Université de Liège.

1998

(editor, with C. Davaras). *Pseira*. Vol. 2, *Building AC (the "Shrine") and Other Buildings in Area A*. University Museum Monograph 94. Philadelphia: The University Museum.

(editor, with C. Davaras). *Pseira*. Vol. 3, *The Plateia Building*. University Museum Monograph 102. Philadelphia: The University Museum.

1999

(editor, with C. Davaras). *Pseira*. Vol. 4, *Minoan Buildings in Areas B, C, D, and F*. University Museum Monograph 105. Philadelphia: The University Museum.

(editor, with V. Karageorghis, R. Laffineur and W.-D. Niemeier). *MELETEMATA: Studies in Aegean Archaeology Presented to Malcolm H. Wiener as He Enters His 65th Year*. *Aegaeum* 20. Liège: Université de Liège.

2001

(editor, with C. Davaras). *Pseira*. Vol. 5, *The Architecture of Pseira*. University Museum Monograph 109. Philadelphia: University of Pennsylvania Museum.

(guest editor). *Aegean Archaeology* 5.

2002

(editor, with C. Davaras). *Pseira*. Vol. 6, *The Pseira Cemetery*. Part 1, *The Surface Survey*. Prehistory Monographs 5. Philadelphia: INSTAP Academic Press.

2003

Greece and Her Neighbors in Historic Postcards: 1895–1920. Athens: Potamos.

(editor, with C. Davaras). *Pseira*. Vol. 7, *The Pseira Cemetery*. Part 2, *Excavation of the Tombs*. Prehistory Monographs 6. Philadelphia: INSTAP Academic Press.

2004

(with C. Davaras). *The Hagia Photia Cemetery*. Vol. 1, *The Tomb Groups and Architecture*. Prehistory Monographs 14. Philadelphia: INSTAP Academic Press.

(editor, with C. Davaras and R. Hope Simpson). *Pseira*. Vol. 8, *The Archaeological Survey of Pseira Island*. Part 1. Prehistory Monographs 11. Philadelphia: INSTAP Academic Press.

2005

(editor, with C. Davaras and R. Hope Simpson). *Pseira*. Vol. 9, *The Archaeological Survey of Pseira Island*. Part 2, *The Intensive Surface Survey*. Prehistory Monographs 12. Philadelphia: INSTAP Academic Press.

ARTICLES

1965

"A Description of Certain Engraved Artifacts from the Utz Oneota Site." *Plains Anthropologist* 10: 256–70.

1969

"The Age of Homer. An Exhibition of Geometric and Orientalizing Greek Art." *Expedition* 12, 1: 2–14.

P.P. BETANCOURT: SELECTED BIBLIOGRAPHY

1970

"The Age of Homer." *Archaeology* 23, 1: 52–4.

"The Maikop Copper Tools and Their Relationship to Cretan Metallurgy." *AJA* 74: 351–8.

1971

"An Aeolic Shrine in Philadelphia." *AJA* 75: 427–8.

"A Hoard of Bronze Coins from Erythrae." *ANSMN* 17: 23–39.

1973

"A Cast Lead Protome from Greece." *Archaeology* 26: 213–6.

"The Polyp Workshop: A Stylistic Group from LM IB." *AJA* 77: 333–4.

1976

"Economic Implications of the Reed Painter's Vases." *TUAS* 1: 15–7.

"The End of the Greek Bronze Age." *Antiquity* 50: 40–7.

(with A. Lengyel, G.T.B. Radan and K. Wright). "The Excavations at Castelliere di S. Fedele in 1975." *Bulletin of Mediterranean Archaeology* 1 (1975–1976): 9–13.

(with G. Weinstein). "Carbon-14 and the Beginning of the Late Bronze Age in the Aegean." *AJA* 80: 329–48.

1977

"Further Observations on the Marine Style." *AJA* 81: 561.

"Marine Life Pottery from the Aegean." *Archaeology* 30: 38–43.

"Perspective and the Third Dimension in Theran Painting." *TUAS* 2: 19–22.

"Some Chronological Problems in the Middle Minoan Dark-on-light Pottery of Eastern Crete." *AJA* 81: 341–53.

(with M.J. Becker). "New Techniques for Analyzing Minoan Stonework." *Archaeology* 30: 276–7.

1978

"LM IA Pottery from Priniatikos Pyrgos." In *Thera and the Aegean World I. Papers Presented at the Second International Scientific Congress, Santorini, Greece, August 1978*, edited by C. Doumas, 381–7. London: Thera and the Aegean World.

"A Middle Minoan Pottery Deposit." *Hesperia* 47: 155–64.

"The Rock-built Chambers at Castelliere di S. Fedele: Report of the Excavations in 1975." *Bulletin of Mediterranean Archaeology* 2 (1977–1978): 13–5.

"Thermoluminescent Dates from Castelliere di S. Fedele." *Bulletin of Mediterranean Archaeology* 2 (1977–1978): 11.

(with H.N. Michael and G.A. Weinstein). "Calibration and the Radiocarbon Chronology of Late Minoan IB." *Archaeometry* 20: 200–3.

(with G.A. Weinstein). "Problems of Interpretation of the Akrotiri Radiocarbon Dates." In *Thera and the Aegean World I. Papers Presented at the Second International Scientific Congress, Santorini, Greece, August 1978*, edited by C. Doumas, 805–14. London: Thera and the Aegean World.

(with T.S. Wheeler, R. Maddin and J.D. Muhly). "Metallurgy at Gournia." *MASCAJ* 1: 7–8.

1979

"Gournia, Crete. The 75th Anniversary of the Excavations, Introduction." *TUAS* 4: 1.

"The Pottery Chronology of Gournia. A Brief Sketch." *TUAS* 4: 7–10.

1981

(with G.H. Myer). "The Composition of Vasilike Ware and the Production of the Mottled Colours of the Slip." In *Scientific Studies in Ancient Ceramics*, edited by M.J. Hughes, 51–5. British Museum Occasional Paper 19. London: British Museum.

1982

"The Crocus and Festoons Motif: Evidence for Traveling Vase-Painters?" *TUAS* 7: 34–7.

"Preliminary Results from the East Cretan White-on-Dark Ware Project." In *Archaeological Ceramics. Papers Presented at a Seminar on Ceramics as Archaeological Material Held at the Smithsonian Institution, Washington, D.C., and the National Bureau of Standards, Gaithersburg, Maryland, 29 September – 1 October 1980*, edited by J.S. Olin and A.D. Franklin, 183–7. Washington, DC: Smithsonian Institution.

1983

(with M.G. Ciaccio, B. Crowell, J.M. Donahoe and R.C. Green). "Ceramic Stands. A Group of Domestic and Ritual Objects from Crete and the Near East." *Expedition* 26, 1: 32–7.

1984

"The Middle Minoan Pottery of Southern Crete and the Question of a Middle Minoan Thalassocracy." In *The Minoan Thalassocracy: Myth and Reality. Proceedings of the Third International Symposium at the Swedish Institute in Athens, 31 May – 5 June, 1982,* edited by R. Hägg and N. Marinatos, 89–92. *SkrAth* 4, 32. Stockholm: Svenska Institutet i Athen.

(with B. Lawn). "The Cyclades and Radiocarbon Chronology." In *The Prehistoric Cyclades: Contributions to a Workshop on Cycladic Chronology*, edited by J.A. MacGillivray and R.L.N. Barber, 277–95. Edinburgh: Department of Classical Archaeology, University of Edinburgh.

(with T.G. Palaima and G.H. Myer). "An Inscribed Stirrup Jar of Cretan Origin from Bamboula, Cyprus." *Kadmos* 23: 65–73.

1985

"A Great Minoan Triangle: The Changing Characters of Phaistos, Hagia Triadha, and Kommos during the Middle Minoan III–Late Minoan III Periods." *Scripta Mediterranea* 6: 31–43.

"The Mediterranean World." In *Introduction to the Collections of the University Museum*, edited by L. Horne, 28–31. Philadelphia: The University Museum.

"The Middle Minoan Pottery at Kommos. " *Hydra* 1: 3–10.

1986

"The Chronology of Middle Minoan Plain Cups in Southern Crete." In *Φίλια Ἔπη εἰς Γεώργιον Ε. Μυλωνᾶν Διὰ τὰ 60 ἔτη τοῦ Ἀνασκαφικοῦ του Ἔργου*, Vol. Α΄, 284–92. Βιβλιοθήκη τῆς ἐν Ἀθήναις Ἀρχαιολογικῆς Ἑταιρείας 103. Athens: En Athenais Archaiologikes Hetaireias.

(with C. Davaras). " Ἀνασκαφική Ἔρευνα Ψείρας: Περίοδοι 1985 καὶ 1986." *Ἀμάλθεια* 68–69: 183–200.

(with G.H. Myer). "Mineralogy of Minoan Pottery from Kommos as an Indicator of Provenience." In *Proceedings of the 24th International Archaeometry Symposium*, edited by J.S. Olin and M.J. Blackman, 377–80. Washington, DC: Smithsonian Institution.

1987

"Dating the Aegean Late Bronze Age with Radiocarbon." *Archaeometry* 29: 45–9.

(with R.G.V. Hancock). "INAA of Minoan Ceramics from Kommos, Crete." *Journal of Radioanalytical and Nuclear Chemistry, Articles* 114: 393–401.

(with H.N. Michael). "Dating the Aegean Bronze Age with Radiocarbon: Addendum." *Archaeometry* 29: 212–3.

1988

(with C. Davaras). "Excavations at Pseira." *Cretan Studies* 1: 35–7.

(with C. Davaras). "Excavations at Pseira, 1985 and 1986." *Hesperia* 57: 207–25.

(with C. Davaras). "Ψείρα." *ArchDelt* 43, B2 [published 1993]: 579–80.

(with C. Davaras). "Ψείρα." *Κρητική Εστία* 2: 338–40.

(with H.N. Michael). "The Thera Eruption: Continuing Discussion of the Dating. II, Further Arguments for an Early Date" and "IV, Addendum." *Archaeometry* 30: 169–75 and 180–2.

(with G.H. Myer and J.B. Rutter). "The Ceramic Petrography of Early Helladic Pottery from Lerna." In *A Pot for All Reasons: Ceramic Ecology Revisited. Papers Dedicated to Frederick R. Matson, 1986*, edited by C.C. Kolb and L.M. Lackey, 73–80. Philadelphia: Laboratory of Anthropology, Temple University.

1989

(with C.P. Swann). "PIXE Analysis of Middle Minoan Pigments from Kommos." In *Archaeometry. Proceedings of the 25th International Symposium*, edited by Y. Maniatis, 177–81, Amsterdam: Elsevier.

1990

"High Chronology or Low Chronology: The Archaeological Evidence." In *Thera and the Aegean World III. Proceedings of the Third International Congress, Santorini, Greece, 3–9 September 1989*. Vol. 3, *Chronology*, edited by D.A. Hardy and A.C. Renfrew, 19–23. London: The Thera Foundation.

"The Stone Vessels of Pseira." *Expedition* 32, 3: 15–9.

(with L. Berkowitz and R.L. Zaslow). "Evidence for Minoan Baskets from Kommos, Crete." *Cretan Studies* 2: 73–7.

(with C. Davaras). "Ψείρα." *Κρητική Εστία* 3 (1989–1990): 296–7.

(with P. Goldberg, R. Hope Simpson and C. J. Vitaliano). "Excavations at Pseira: The Evidence for the Theran Eruption." In *Thera and the Aegean World III. Proceedings of the Third International Congress, Santorini, Greece, 3–9 September 1989*. Vol. 3, *Chronology*, edited by D.A. Hardy and A.C. Renfrew, 96–9. London: The Thera Foundation.

1991

(with E.S. Banou). "Pseira and Minoan Sea-Trade." In *Thalassa: L'Egee Prehistorique et la Mer. Actes de la troisième Rencontre égéenne internationale de l'Université de Liège (23–25 avril 1990),* edited by R. Laffineur and L. Basch, 107–10. Aegaeum 7. Liège: Université de Liège.

(with C. Davaras). " 'Αρχαιολογικές Ἔρευνες στήν Ψείρα: Περίοδοι 1987–1989." *Ἀμάλθεια* 82–85: 20–37.

(with C. Davaras). "Haven for Minoan Mariners." *Archaeology* 44, 3: 32–5.

1992

(with C. Davaras). "Αμερικανική Σχολή Κλασικών Σπουδών. Ψείρα." *ArchDelt* 47 [published 1997]: 605–6.

(with C. Davaras and W.R. Farrand). "Pseira." In *The Aerial Atlas of Ancient Crete,* edited by J.W. Myers, E.E. Myers and G. Cadogan, 262–7. Berkeley and Los Angeles: University of California Press.

(with R. Hope Simpson). "The Agricultural System of Bronze Age Pseira." *Cretan Studies* 3: 47–54.

1993

(with C. Davaras). "Ψείρα." *Κρητική Εστία* 4 (1991–1993): 304–5.

(with G.H. Myer). "Highly Micaceous/Chloritic Imports into Lerna V: Evidence from Ceramic Petrography." In *Wace and Blegen: Pottery as Evidence for Trade in the Aegean Bronze Age 1939–1989. Proceedings of the International Conference Held at the American School of Classical Studies at Athens, Athens, December 2–3, 1989*, edited by C. Zerner, P. Zerner and J. Windor, 195–6. Amsterdam: J.C. Gieben.

1995

"Pseira, Crete: The Economic Base for a Bronze Age Town." In *POLITEIA: Society and State in the Aegean Bronze Age. Proceedings of the 5th International Aegean Conference, University of Heidelberg, Archäologisches Institut 10–13 April 1994*, edited by R. Laffineur and W.-D. Niemeier, 164–7. *Aegaeum* 12. Liège: Université de Liège.

(with C. Davaras). "Recent Excavations at Pseira, Crete." In *Πεπραγμένα του Ζ΄ Διεθνούς Κρητολογικού Συνεδρίου*. Vol. A1: *Τμήμα Αρχαιολογικό*, edited by N.E. Papadogiannakis, 81–6. Rethymnon: Iera Mitropolis Rethymnis & Aulopotamou.

(with R. Hope Simpson, P.J. Callaghan, D.K. Harlan, J.W. Hayes, J.W. Shaw, M.C. Shaw and L.V. Watrous). "The Archaeological Survey of the Kommos Area." In *Kommos*. Vol. 1, *The Kommos Region and Houses of the Minoan Town*. Part 1, *The Kommos Region, Ecology and Minoan Industries*, edited by J.W. Shaw and M.C. Shaw, 325–402. Princeton, NJ: Princeton University Press.

(with N. Marinatos). "The Minoan Household." In *Πεπραγμένα του Ζ΄ Διεθνούς Κρητολογικού Συνεδρίου*. Vol. A2, *Τμήμα Αρχαιολογικό*, edited by N.E. Papadogiannakis, 591–5. Rethymnon: Iera Mitropolis Rethymnis & Aulopotamou.

(with G.H. Myer). "Phyllite Fabrics in Eastern Crete." In *The Ceramics Cultural Heritage: Proceedings of the International Symposium, The Cermaic Heritage, of the 8th CIMTEC—World Ceramics Congress and Forum on New Materials, Florence, Italy, June 28 – July 2, 1994*, edited by P. Vincenzi, 395–9. Monographs in Materials and Society 2. Faenza: Techna.

(with G.H. Myer and S.J. Vaughan). 1995. "Petrography: Ceramic Petrography of Selected Pottery Samples from Lerna IV." In *Lerna. A Preclassical Site in the Argolid*. Vol. 3, *The Pottery of Lerna IV*, by J.B. Rutter, 666–93. Princeton, NJ: American School of Classical Studies at Athens.

(with C.P. Swann and C.R. Floyd). "East Cretan Middle Minoan and Late Minoan I Dark Slips: PIXE Characterization Studies." In *Materials Issues in Art and Archaeology IV. Symposium Held May 16–21, 1994, Cancun, Mexico*, edited by P.B. Vandiver et al., 673–9. Materials Research Society Symposium Proceedings 352. Pittsburgh, PA: Materials Research Society.

(with S.J. Vaughan and G.H. Myer). "Discussion and Interpretation of the Petrographic Data." In *Lerna. A Preclassical Site in the Argolid*. Vol. 3, *The Pottery of Lerna IV*, by J.B. Rutter, 693–710. Princeton, NJ: American School of Classical Studies at Athens.

1996

"Crete," "Pseira" and "Richard Berry Seager (1882–1925)." In *An Encyclopedia of the History of Classical Archaeology*, edited by N.T. de Grummond, 334–7, 937–8, 1020. Westport, CT: Greenwood.

"Μινωικό εμπόριο λίθου: Τα στοιχεία από τη νήσο Ψείρα." *Κρητική Εστία* 5 (1994–1996): 47–70.

(with C. Davaras). "Αρχαιολογικές έρευνες στην Ψείρα [Reprint]." In *Τα Νησιά της Κρήτης*, edited by K. Papageorgios, 129–43. Herakleion.

1997

"The Copper Smelting Site at Chrysokamino, Crete." In *Αρχαία Ελληνική Τεχνολογία. 1° Διεθνές Συνέδριο*, 51–4. Thessaloniki: Etaireia Meletis Archaias Ellinikis Technologias.

"Relations between the Aegean and the Hyksos at the End of the Middle Bronze Age." In *The Hyksos: New Historical and Archaeological Perspectives*, edited by E.D. Oren, 429–32. University Museum Monograph 96. Philadelphia: The University Museum.

"The Trade Route for Ghyali Obsidian." In *TEXNH: Craftsmen, Craftswomen and Craftsmanship in the Aegean Bronze Age. Proceedings of the 6th International Aegean Conference, Philadelphia, Temple University, 18–21 April 1996*, edited by R. Laffineur and P.P. Betancourt, 171–6. *Aegaeum* 16. Liège: Université de Liège.

(with E.S. Banou and C.R. Floyd). "Provincial LM III at Pseira, Crete." In *Late Minoan III Pottery: Chronology and Terminology. Acts of a Meeting Held at the Danish Institute at Athens August 12–14, 1994*, edited by E. Hallager and B.P. Hallager, 57–81. Monographs of the Danish Institute at Athens 1. Athens: The Danish Institute at Athens.

(with N. Marinatos). "The Minoan Villa." In *The Function of the "Minoan Villa." Proceedings of the Eighth International Symposium at the Swedish Institute at Athens, 6–8 June 1992*, edited by R. Hägg, 91–8. *SkrAth* 4, 46. Stockholm: Svenska Institutet i Athen.

(with C.P. Swann, S. Fleming and C.R. Floyd). "PIXE Analysis of Trojan Gold Jewelry." *Nuclear Instruments and Methods in Physics Research Section B: Beam Interactions with Materials and Atoms* 130: 320–3.

1998

"The Chronology of the Aegean Late Bronze Age: Unanswered Questions." In *Sardinian and Aegean Chronology: Towards the Resolution of Relative and Absolute Dating in the Mediterranean. Proceedings of the International Colloquium 'Sardinian Stratigraphy and Mediterranean Chronology', Tufts University, Medford, Massachusetts, March 17–19, 1995,* edited by M.S. Balmuth and R.H. Tykot, 291–6. Studies in Sardinian Archaeology 5. Oxford: Oxbow.

"The Legged Flask from Pseira." In *Eastern Mediterranean. Cyprus—Dodecanese—Crete, 16th–6th cent. B.C. Proceedings of the International Symposium Held at Rethymnon, Crete in May 1997*, edited by V. Karageorghis and N. Stampolidis, 49–53. Athens: University of Crete and the A.G. Leventis Foundation.

"Middle Minoan Objects in the Near East." In *The Aegean and the Orient in the Second Millennium. Proceedings of the 50th Anniversary Symposium, Cincinnati, 18–20 April 1997*, edited by E.H. Cline and D. Harris-Cline, 5–12. *Aegaeum* 18. Liège: Université de Liège.

(with J.D. Muhly and C.R. Floyd). "Excavations at Chrysokamino, Crete, in 1997." *AJA* 102: 391.

1999

"Discontinuity in the Minoan-Mycenaean Religions: Smooth Development or Disruptions and War?" In *POLEMOS: Le contexte guerrier en Égée à l'Âge du Bronze. Actes de la 7e Rencontre égéenne internationale Université de Liège, 14–17 avril 1998*, edited by R. Laffineur, 219–25. *Aegaeum* 19. Liège: Université de Liège.

"What is Minoan? FN/EM I in the Gulf of Mirabello Region." In *MELETEMATA: Studies in Aegean Archaeology Presented to Malcolm H. Wiener as He Enters His 65th Year*, edited by P.P. Betancourt et al., 33–40. *Aegaeum* 20. Liège: Université de Liège.

(with I.D. Bull and R.P. Evershed). "Chemical Evidence for a Structured Agricultural Manuring Regime on the Island of Pseira, Crete during the Minoan Period." In *MELETEMATA: Studies in Aegean Archaeology Presented to Malcolm H. Wiener as He Enters His 65th Year*, edited by P.P. Betancourt, V. Karageorghis, R. Laffineur, and W.-D. Niemeier, 69–74. *Aegaeum* 20. Liège: Université de Liège.

(with J.D. Muhly, W.R. Farrand, C. Stearns, L. Onyshkevych, W.B. Hafford and D. Evely). "Research and Excavation at Chrysokamino, Crete 1995–1998." *Hesperia* 68: 343–70.

2000

"The Aegean and the Origin of the Sea Peoples." In *The Sea Peoples and Their World: A Reassessment*, edited by E.D. Oren, 297–303. University Museum Monograph 108. University Museum Symposium Series 11. Philadelphia: The University Museum.

"The Concept of Space in Theran Compositional Systemics." In *The Wall Paintings of Thera. Proceedings of the First International Symposium, Petros M. Nomikos Conference Centre, Thera, Hellas, 30 August – 4 September 1997*, edited by S. Sherratt, 359–63. Athens: The Thera Foundation.

"The Household Shrine in the House of the Rhyta at Pseira." *JPR* 14: 12–3.

"New Evidence for Village Life in Minoan Crete." In *Πεπραγμενά Η′ Διεθνούς Κρητολογικού Συνεδρίου. Προϊστορική και Αρχαία Ελληνική Περίοδος*, Vol. A1, edited by A. Karetsou, 91–7. Heraklion: Etairia Kretikon Istorikon Meleton.

"Tourloti," "Ayia Photia Ierapetras," and "Vasiliki." In *Crete 2000: A Centennial Celebration of American Archaeological Work on Crete (1900–2000)*, edited by J.D. Muhly and E. Sikla, 21, 117, 118–21. Athens: American School of Classical Studies at Athens and INSTAP Study Center for East Crete.

(with C. Davaras). "Pseira." In *Crete 2000: A Centennial Celebration of American Archaeological Work on Crete (1900–2000)*, edited by J.D. Muhly and E. Sikla, 38–57. Athens: American School of Classical Studies at Athens and INSTAP Study Center for East Crete.

(with C.R. Floyd and J.D. Muhly). "Chrysokamino." In *Crete 2000: A Centennial Celebration of American Archaeological Work on Crete (1900–2000)*, edited by J.D. Muhly and E. Sikla, 62–74. Athens: American School of Classical Studies at Athens and INSTAP Study Center for East Crete.

(with N. Marinatou, K. Palyvou, S. McPherron, S. German, N. Poulou-Papademetriou and T. Albani). "Το σπήλαιο της Αμνισού. Η έρευνα του 1992." *Archaiologike Ephemeris*, 179–236.

(with C.P. Swann and S. Ferrence). "Analysis of Minoan White Pigments Used on Pottery from Palaikastro." *Nuclear Instruments and Methods in Physics Research* B 161–163: 714–7.

2001

"The Household Shrine in the House of the Rhyta at Pseira." In *POTNIA: Deities and Religion in the Aegean Bronze Age. Proceedings of the 8th International Aegean Conference Göteborg, Göteborg University, 12–15 April 2000*, edited by R. Laffineur and R. Hägg, 145–9. *Aegaeum* 22. Liège: Université de Liège.

"Introduction to the Special Issue on Kamares Ware." *Aegean Archaeology* 5: 7–8.

"A Minoan Stone Quarry from Pseira." *Pseira*. Vol. 5, *The Architecture of Pseira*, edited by P.P. Betancourt and C. Davaras, 89–91. University Museum Monograph 109. Philadelphia: University of Pennsylvania Museum.

(with I.D. Bull and R.P. Evershed). "An Organic Geochemical Investigation of the Practice of Manuring at a Minoan Site on Pseira Island, Crete." *Geoarchaeology* 16: 223–42.

(with S. Ferrence and C.P. Swann). "PIXE Analysis of White Pigments on Pottery from Five Bronze Age Minoan Archaeological Sites." *Aegean Archaeology* 5: 47–54.

(with C.R. Floyd). "Ανασκαφή στο Χρυσοκάμινο." *Κρητική Εστία* 8 (2000–2001): 9–22.

2002

"Who Was in Charge of the Palaces?" In *Monuments of Minos: Rethinking the Minoan Palaces. Proceedings of the International Workshop "Crete of the Hundred Palaces?" Held at the Université Catholique de Louvain, Louvain-la-Neuve, 14–15 December 2001*, edited by J. Driessen, I. Schoep and R. Laffineur, 207–11. *Aegaeum* 23. Liège: Université de Liège.

(with K. Melessanaki, S.C. Ferrence and D. Anglos). "Application of LIBS in the Analysis of Archaeological Objects." In *Optics for the Quality of Life: 19th Congress of the International Commission for Optics, ICO XIX, 25–30 August, 2002, Firenze, Italy*, edited by G.C. Righini and A. Consortini, 79–80. Proceedings of the International Society for Optical Engineering 4829, Part 1. Bellingham, WA: SPIE—International Society for Optical Engineering.

(with K. Melessanaki, M. Mateo, S.C. Ferrence and D. Anglos). "The Application of LIBS for the Analysis of Archaeological Ceramic and Metal Artifacts." *Applied Surface Science* 197–198: 156–63.

2003

"The Impact of Cycladic Settlers on Early Minoan Crete." *Mediterranean Archaeology and Archaeometry* 3: 3–12.

"Interpreting Ceramic Petrography: The Special Product Model, a New Model for Pottery Distribution in the Early Minoan Period." In *METRON: Measuring the Aegean Bronze Age. Proceedings of the 9th International Aegean Conference, New Haven, Yale University, 18–21 April 2002*, edited by K.P. Foster and R. Laffineur, 117–21. *Aegaeum* 24. Liège: Université de Liège.

"Land Use in LM III at the Chrysokamino Estate." In *The Periphery of the Mycenaean World. Proceedings of the 2nd International Interdisciplinary Colloquium 26–30 September, Lamia 1999,* edited by N. Kyparissi-Apostolika and M. Papakonstantinou, 555–60. Athens: Ministry of Culture, 14th Ephorate of Prehistoric and Classical Antiquities.

(with S. Ferrence, K. Melessanaki, M. Mateo and D. Anglos). "Adaptation of Laser-Induced Breakdown Spectroscopy (LIBS) for the Analysis of Archaeological Artifacts." In *METRON: Measuring the Aegean Bronze Age. Proceedings of the 9th International Aegean Conference, New Haven, Yale University, 18–21 April 2002*, edited by K.P. Foster and R. Laffineur, 111–16. *Aegaeum* 24. Liège: Université de Liège.

2004

"Knossian Expansion in Late Minoan IB: The Evidence of the Spirals and Arcading Group." In *Knossos: Palace, City, State. Proceedings of the Conference in Herakleion Organised by the British School at Athens and the 23rd Ephoreia of Prehistoric and Classical Antiquities of Herakleion, in November 2000, for the Centenary of Sir Arthur Evans's Excavations at Knossos*, edited by G. Cadogan, E. Hatzaki and A. Vasilakis, 295–8. *BSA* Studies 12. London: The British School at Athens.

"Pseira and Knossos: The Transformation of an East Cretan Seaport." In *Crete Beyond the Palaces. Proceedings of the Crete 2000 Conference*, edited by L.P. Day, M.S. Mook and J.D. Muhly, 21–8. Philadelphia: INSTAP Academic Press.

(with C. Davaras). "Sitia; Archäologisches Museum: Psíra." *Corpus der Minoischen und Mykenischen Siegel*. Vol. 5, *Kleinere griechische Sammlungen*. Suppl. 3, 2, *Neufunde aus Griechenland und der westlischen Türkei (Nafplion—Volos und westliche Türkei)*, edited by I. Pini, 516, 529–31. Mainz: Philipp von Zabern.

BOOK REVIEWS

1971

Review of *Die geometrische Kunst Griechenlands, Frühe Formenwelt im Zeitalter Homers*, by B. Schweitzer. *AJA* 75: 99–100.

1972

Review of *Bronzi orientali e orientalizzanti a Creta nell' VIII e VII sec. A.C.*, by F. Canciani. *AJA* 76: 230–1.

Review of *Fighting on Land and Sea in Greek Geometric Art*, by G. Ahlberg. *AJA* 76: 336–7.

Review of *The Muses at Work: Arts, Crafts, and Professions in Ancient Greece and Rome*, edited by C.Roebuck. *ArtJ* 31: 350–2.

1976

Review of *Before Civilization*, by C. Renfrew. *Bulletin of Mediterranean Archaeology* 1 (1975–1976): 67.

Review of *The Emergence of Civilisation*, by C. Renfrew. *Bulletin of Mediterranean Archaeology* 1 (1975–1976): 67.

1978

Review of *Aegean Metalwork of the Early and Middle Bronze Age*, by K. Branigan. *Bulletin of Mediterranean Archaeology* 2 (1977–1978): 53.

1981

Review of *The Proto-Aeolic Capital and Israelite Ashlar Masonry*, by Y. Shiloh. *AJA* 85: 96–7.

1982

Review of *Thera and the Aegean World II. Papers and Proceedings of the Second International Scientific Congress, Santorini, Greece, August 1978*, edited by C. Doumas. *AJA* 86: 452.

1984

Review of *Provincial Middle Minoan Pottery*, by G. Walberg. *AJA* 88: 601–2.

Review of *Sanctuaries and Cults in the Aegean Bronze Age. Proceedings of the First International Symposium at the Swedish Institute in Athens 12–13 May, 1980*, edited by R. Hägg and N. Marinatos. *AJA* 88: 74–5.

1986

Review of *Thorikos* VIII. *1972/1976. Rapport préliminaire sur les 9e, 10e, 11e, et 12e campagnes de fouilles*, by H.F. Mussche et al. *AJA* 90: 231.

1989

Review of *Greek and Cypriot Pottery: A Review of Scientific Studies*, by R.E. Jones. *JHS* 109: 263.

1996

Review of *The Absolute Chronology of the Aegean Early Bronze Age: Archaeology, Radiocarbon and History*, by S. Manning. *BASOR* 301: 94–5.

POTS AND POLITIES

MALCOLM H. WIENER

It is a pleasure to serve as discussant for this splendid collection of papers on Minoan pottery, published in honor of Philip Betancourt. Pots and indestructible potsherds, however humble, form the backbone of archaeology. Phil's encyclopedic works on the subject and advice and support for colleagues have played a major role in the advancement of knowledge of Minoan ceramics.

For over a century, Minoan pottery has been studied stylistically and stratigraphically. In recent years, it has been studied scientifically as well. Philip Betancourt's own pioneering work coordinating the technical study of Vasiliki Ware, East Cretan White-on-Dark pottery and the ceramic material from his excavation at Pseira is exemplary in this regard. Several of the papers presented in this colloquium provide the opportunity to assess the significance of the skillful scientific examination of pottery for our understanding of Bronze Age society and history.

Let us consider the papers presented in chronological order, beginning with the important contribution by Peter Day, Maria Relaki and Edward Faber. Their paper raises fundamental questions about the nature and context of Minoan specialized craft production, and hence about Minoan society and Minoan polities. Their discovery of high-skill craft continuity of great specificity in the production of pottery in central Crete from the end of Early Minoan I to the end of the Old Palace Period in Middle Minoan IIB—a span of about 1,000 years—may shed light on such questions as whether palatial society was the product of a steady process of development, as Warren and Branigan have argued, or was instead the result of a quantum leap at the time of the creation of the first palaces, as proposed by Cherry.[1] Does the discovery of complex craft continuity by Day et al. imply a substantial degree of stability in society over this long period, at least in south-central Crete, and perhaps also the protection and support of potters by Prepalatial local or regional authorities, or rather the survival of ongoing local potting practices persisting through changes in the scale and symbolism of

Philip Betancourt, Keith Branigan, Elizabeth French, Sturt Manning, Nicoletta Momigliano, Aleydis Van de Moortel and Peter Warren kindly read drafts of this paper and made many helpful comments, for which I am most grateful. Harriet Blitzer and Karen D. Vitelli provided welcome advice regarding anthropological studies of pottery practices.

1. Warren 1975; Branigan 1970; Cherry 1983.

production, yet otherwise unaffected by major political and organizational changes?

There is no evidence for massive destruction or abandonment of Knossos or Phaistos during the long span of Early Minoan to Middle Minoan before the destructions at Knossos and Phaistos caused by earthquakes at the end of MM IIB/beginning of MM IIIA, which mark the close of the Old Palace Period.[2] Not all areas are so fortunate: Vasiliki, Myrtos-Pyrgos and Phournou Koriphi suffer destructions at the end of EM IIB. In east-central Crete, Malia, Gournia and Mochlos undergo changes at the end of EM or beginning of MM, possibly as a result of an area-wide earthquake that also affects Knossos. Watrous has suggested that EM III saw an island-wide decline; if so, adverse climatic conditions in the Near East, Egypt, mainland Greece, the Cyclades and possibly Crete itself may be among the causes, together with destructions and disturbances in these areas in EM III, perhaps themselves partly related to drought.[3] Knossian imports of pottery from the Mesara appear to decrease in EM IIB–EM III, based on the incomplete evidence available.[4] Many doubt the occurrence of an EM III decline, however. Burials spanning the course of a millennium in individual tholos tombs (such as those at Moni Odigitria in the Mesara Plain to the east of Phaistos) between EM I and MM II suggest the possibility of elite continuity and stability. The Prepalatial appearance in these tombs of foreign imports including Egyptian seals and faience (plus their Minoan imitations using Egyptian techniques) indicates expanding horizons, increasing complexity, and elite interest in luxury products prior to the palaces. In the north, the cemetery at Archanes-Phourni 8 km from Knossos on the slope of Mt. Juktas receives burials from EM II until LM IIIC/Subminoan, a period of over 2,000 years.[5] Toward the end of the Prepalatial in EM III–MM IA, elite burial chambers containing luxury imports, such as Tholos B with its commanding position, appear. (Of course the Archanes-Phourni cemetery may serve only Archanes and not Knossos, where unexplored areas of the Gypsades ridge may hold Pre- as well as Proto- and Neopalatial burials. The site of Archanes-Tourkoyeitonia near Phourni shows evidence of occupation from Early to Late Minoan.[6])

The nature of Prepalatial settlement at the sites of Phaistos and Knossos poses various problems, not least because the Kephala Hill was leveled to permit the building of the palace at

2. Knossos seems to suffer some damage, uncertain in extent and cause, at the end of EM III/beginning of MM I and again at the end of MM IA, as well as some burning in MM IIA. Mackenzie 1906; Momigliano 2000; Macdonald (forthcoming). I am grateful to Nicoletta Momigliano for bringing the Knossian evidence to my attention, to Sandy MacGillivray for further comments on the destruction history of Knossos, and to Philip Betancourt for his comments concerning the EM III destructions in east-central and eastern Crete.
3. Watrous 2001, 179–80; Curtis et al. (forthcoming); Forsén 1992, 241–7.
4. Momigliano 2000.
5. Maggidis 1998, 87.
6. Maggidis 1998, 87.

Knossos.[7] Current excavations near the palace at Phaistos indicate major Prepalatial occupation with all phases represented, including the first great ramp at the palace in EM III and four stratified levels with major building activity in MM IA.[8] Earlier excavations disclosed remains of EM II buildings over an area of 3,400 sq m at Phaistos, and the presence of EM III/MM IA.[9] Nearby Hagia Triada has substantial EM II houses and two EM/MM tholos tombs.[10]

In the final phase of the Prepalatial period during MM IA, tombs at the southern flank of the Mesara Plain in the general vicinity of Phaistos contain both imported early Middle Kingdom Egyptian "white piece" scarabs or scaraboids and Minoan versions utilizing similar material and firing technique, covered with a glaze similar to the Egyptian glaze.[11] A Prepalatial polity capable of exchange with Egypt and skilled craft emulation of its products surely could have provided protection and patronage for potters, particularly those producing vessels used in ritual and feasting. Patrikies, halfway between Phaistos and Hagia Triada, yielded large amounts of fine MM I pottery, with many teapots in particular, suggesting the presence of either a ceramic workshop or an area of large ritual feasting connected to nearby tombs.[12] Carinci believes that the nature and amount of MM I pottery found in the area south of Tholos Tomb A at Hagia Triada may indicate a "priestly" source of demand for such pottery.[13] At Knossos tests in Prepalatial levels have disclosed evidence of extensive terracing in EM IIA, and in EM IIA or B well-built house walls plus a paved ramp leading to the top of the hill at the northwest corner of the later palace.[14] In addition, fragments of Egyptian stone bowls and one probably Egyptian rare obsidian bowl have been found in the EM II house deposits at Knossos.[15] EM III–MM IA witnesses further building activity including the monumental construction at the northwest corner of the palace and the significant extension of occupation, sufficient to cause Warren to conclude that MM IA Knossos could be deemed "urban."[16]

Taken as a whole, the available evidence from central Crete implies the existence of substantial continuing regional or local authorities in the Prepalatial period, capable of maintaining links with ongoing pottery communities. "The articulation of social identities" to which Day et al. refer may have involved elites as well as potters while Day's putative "common consumption strategies" were surely elite strategies in the main. Whether it

7. Evans 1972, 115.
8. La Rosa 2004; Todaro 2003; 2005; (forthcoming).
9. Pernier 1935, 139–42, pls. XIII–XV; Banti 1939–1940.
10. Banti 1930–1931; Stefani 1930–1931.
11. Phillips 2004, 162–4; Pini 1992; 2000; Wiener 1994.
12. Watrous 2001, 185; Warren 1987, 54; Levi 1976, 747–56; Todaro 2003.
13. Carinci 2004.
14. D.E. Wilson 1994, 37–8, cited in Watrous 2001, 171–2.
15. Warren 1981.
16. Warren 1987, 53; see also Momigliano 1991, 269.

is likely that such links between potters and polities controlled by rulers or ruling elites existed in fact is considered below. It should also be noted that Prepalatial evidence of various craft skills, wide foreign contacts and emerging complexity exists in parts of Crete where evidence of a continuing potting tradition of similar specificity and complexity has not been observed. These include Vasiliki, with its houses of many rooms, storage areas, fine small paved court, painted wall plaster, and metal mold for production of double axes (but a site which suffered a destruction at the end of EM IIB as previously noted);[17] Palaikastro with its monumental EM II structure;[18] Mochlos with its impressive tombs containing exotic and luxurious foreign imports;[19] and Malia, where Pelon has reported finding under room IX 1 of the palace an EM IIA wall on the same orientation as the preceding town, followed by EM IIB walls of rooms on the same orientation as the later palace.[20] Moreover, in EM I and EM II, some of the ceramic production in these and other places was based not on household or small village production for local use as might be anticipated, but rather concentrated in a restricted number of areas, from which some vessels were exchanged over long distances, as Day and Wilson have noted.[21] Soles has suggested that by EM II such traffic may be the result of elite gift exchange.[22]

If connections between established elites and groups of potters in central Crete existed from the end of EM I to the end of MM IIB, what was the nature of their interaction? Day et al. note that the principal locations of production and consumption of pottery may be different. Of course the fact that a type of production occurred outside the precincts of a palace or a Prepalatial center does not necessarily mean that the production in question was wholly, largely, or even partially independent. On the other hand, pottery production immediately adjacent to a palace would seem to imply strong palatial interest and influence at the least, and probably palatial control. Kilns of the Old Palace Period exist in the vicinity of the palace of Phaistos, but whether they were used for the production of pottery is unclear,[23] whereas wasters found in the vicinity of the palace indicate some production close at hand, however uncertain its extent and significance. Walberg suggests that Phaistian palatial elites closely controlled the production of the finest Classical Kamares Ware, utilizing the distinctive pure white paint available from the local steatite,[24] while other white paints were used elsewhere in the Mesara.[25] At Malia in MM II a related

17. Watrous 2001, 170–1; Zoes 1976.

18. Bosanquet 1902; Dawkins 1902–1903; 1903–1904; 1904–1905.

19. Seager 1912.

20. Pelon 1993, 545; I am grateful to Alyedis Van de Moortel for reminding me of the results of these soundings.

21. Wilson and Day 1994, 84–5; Day and Wilson 1998, 353–4.

22. Soles 1992, 156–8.

23. Carinci 1997, 318–9, and n. 9.

24. Walberg 2001, 14.

25. Faber et al. 2002. I am most grateful to Peter Day for calling my attention to this reference.

polychrome pottery was produced at Quartier Mu, within sight of the palace, although pottery from a wide variety of other sources is found there as well.[26] At Knossos, the closest known kiln lies 3 km south of the palace at an excellent clay source near Archanes.[27]

Day et al. of course acknowledge the striking innovations in pottery production coincident with the beginning of the Old Palace Period, including the dramatic change in vessel decoration, the use of the potter's wheel, and the making of such exceptional products as Eggshell Ware. Some may even consider the pottery created from these innovations a quantum leap in technological and aesthetic ambition. The role of palatial demand—whether stemming from a desire for fine wares for display and feasting, for the affirmation of identity or for items suitable for high-level exchange—in spurring innovation remains a critical question, together with the extent of palatial control of the production.

In the Neopalatial period evidence of ruling/elite interest in pottery available for feasting may be seen in an LM IB Linear A tablet from Hagia Triada [HT 31] listing various vessels including 3,710 conical cups.[28] One area adjacent to the palace at Knossos contained so many LM I conical cups that Evans' workmen called it the "Kapheneion."[29] It seems likely that provision of vessels for feasting was always of ruling/elite interest, from the pouring and drinking sets already prominent in EM I, especially at Knossos, as described in Day and Wilson,[30] to the matching sets of eating and drinking vessels, large numbers of shallow bowls and elaborate pouring vessels of late EM IIA, to the fine sets of Kamares pouring and drinking vessels in the Protopalatial period, to the mass-produced vessels of the Neopalatial. The MM IB "Royal Pottery Stores" at Knossos at the beginning of the Protopalatial period contained both high quality painted polychrome vessels and very roughly modeled and poorly decorated drinking vessels, perhaps reflecting the different classes of society participating in feasts, while in the Neopalatial period even the conical cups of Knossos showed marked differences in competence of manufacture, ranging from ordinary to dreadful, perhaps resulting from the need to provide vessels for large numbers of participants of all classes in ritual feasts.[31] Apart from the provision of feasting equipment, securing a supply of storage and transport vessels would also likely have been a palatial concern. Levi found large numbers of such vessels in the Old Palace at Phaistos. In the Final Palatial Period one fragment of a Linear B tablet from the early IIIA2 destruction at the palace of Knossos lists 1,800 stirrup jars; when whole, the tablet may have listed still more.[32]

26. Knappett 1997.
27. MacGillivray 1987, 276.
28. Godart and Olivier 1976, 58–9.
29. Evans 1928, 308.
30. Day and Wilson 1998, 354.
31. Momigliano 2000; Knappett 1999.
32. I am grateful to Philip Betancourt himself for reminding me of these two references to palatial storage vessels. See Levi 1976, figs. 157–9; Betancourt 1985, 159–60.

Later still, in the different society and administrative system of mainland Greece,[33] Mycenaean Linear B tablets from the palaces of Pylos and Mycenae refer to five potters in all, and in the case of Pylos to a royal potter (*wanakteros kerameu*) who holds land that he can lease. Three other potters at Pylos are mentioned, one by name. At Mycenae one tablet refers to a potter in the dative.[34] It has been suggested that the number of potters mentioned is small in relation to the number of pots found in the palace at Pylos and at Mycenaean sites in general.[35] Whitelaw notes that an estimated 8,450 pots were recorded in the destruction level of the palace, many stacked in pantries and never used; he estimates the total annual requirement of the palace for pots of all types at around 12,000. Given the anthropological evidence from preindustrial societies for the amounts of pottery produced per workshop and individual potter discussed below, the number of vessels proposed as the annual requirement of the Palace of Nestor appears to be within the production capacity of one potting establishment comprising one or two master potters and some apprentices, with enough pots left over to supply the town of Pylos. Detailed study of the pottery by Hruby for her forthcoming dissertation provides important support for the proposition that the pottery found in the palace was produced by one principal potter or pottery, which produced the finer ware, and perhaps several other potters or potteries, which produced three different coarse wares.[36] Moreover, unlike bronzesmiths who received bronze from the palace for the manufacture of weapons and other products or herders placed in charge of flocks of sheep, potters were unlikely to have received anything from the palace that required tracking by scribes, nor were locally made pots suitable subjects for the collection of taxes from the sixteen Pylian districts recorded in the tablets. Accordingly, the argument for the existence of a large private sector within the Mycenaean economy in other areas (such as metallurgy or foreign trade) based on a purported absence of significant palatial interest in pottery production seems misplaced.

The Day et al. paper asks us to consider the likelihood of ongoing communities of potters. How should we envision the nature of the relationship between such potting communities and the ruling elites, Palatial and Prepalatial, given the elite interest discerned above? The question of "attached" versus "independent" potters has acquired a large archaeological literature covering many cultures.[37] For purposes of this discussion I define the term "attached" to include 1) full-time retainers of a palace or Prepalatial polity, par-

33. Wiener (forthcoming).

34. Palaima 1997, 410 n. 23.

35. Whitelaw 2001; see also Knappett 2001. Galaty 1999 suggests that it was likely that all the fine wares used in the Pylos area were made by one pottery establishment while the coarse wares came from various local sources.

36. I am most grateful to Julie Hruby for providing me with a synopsis of her work prior to publication and permission to make reference to it here.

37. Clark 1995; Costin 1991; Lewis 1983.

ticularly when working in the immediate vicinity, 2) those who are given an estate at a clay source and/or wood for fuel to supply pottery primarily to fill the needs of the ruling center, and 3) those who receive necessities in exchange for a major part of their production. Utilizing this definition, it seems likely that many Minoan potting communities were in some sense attached to the palaces and perhaps even to their Prepalatial predecessors. At the least, palaces and Prepalatial centers probably would have guaranteed the potting communities access to raw materials and to exchange networks. Nevertheless there remains the possibility, particularly in the earlier part of EM, that elites obtained pots through exchanges with wholly independent potters. Potters or potteries independent initially could thereafter have been absorbed into the palatial sphere after the rise of the palaces.

The Day et al. paper also reminds us that vessels in the Prepalatial period are already metal-imitating, particularly with regard to late EM IIA high-quality drinking assemblages of Fine Gray Ware (FGW) and Fine Painted Ware (FPW), but with the tendency perhaps beginning already in EM I. The Early Minoan metal prototypes of these vessels, however, are absent. Of course metal in any form has been melted down throughout history. The amount of trade in metal indicated in the Assyrian Trading Colony records is staggering, but the amount of metal found in the *karums* is very small. In the Bayeux tapestry, every warrior is shown clad in mail, but none of it has ever been found, except perhaps for one cheekpiece. In seventeenth-century Portugal, many middle-class households had a silver brazier, but only six have been reported to exist today.[38] There must have been numbers of Minoan Prepalatial metal vessels that have not survived. Such vessels are further evidence of Prepalatial foreign contacts, given the absence of tin and paucity of copper in Crete. Philip Betancourt's own recently completed excavation of the EM III metallurgical site at Chrysokamino shows the precociousness of metallurgy on Crete, as does the evidence of metallurgy at Hagia Photia and Poros in late EM I. Of course there is a strong case to be made that what we see at Hagia Photia, Poros and even at Chrysokamino is in reality Cycladic metallurgy in the hands of Cycladic immigrants, but the EM II metal mold from Vasiliki represents an advanced technique so far unmatched elsewhere in the Aegean, as Branigan has noted.[39] The presumed existence of metal vessels in Prepalatial Crete, or at least detailed knowledge of them, again suggests wide Prepalatial horizons, given the relative scarcity of copper and absence of tin in Crete noted above.

Aleydis Van de Moortel's fine paper on the pottery of the Kamares Cave follows easily upon the contribution by Day et al. She finds, as do Day et al., that pottery travels widely in Crete in the Old Palace Period. Her observation that the Kamares Cave included pot-

38. D.M. Wilson 1985, 221; Gruber 1982, 232.
39. Branigan 1974.

tery from the island of Gavdos, a natural stopping place for Phaistian ships, is intriguing given the fact that polychrome Kamares is found in Egypt and the Levant. Jeremy Rutter's paper, considered below, reports the presence of Gavdiot imports at Kommos in Old Palace, New Palace and LM II contexts. Perhaps Gavdos specialized in pottery production to compensate for a lack of other resources.[40] Van de Moortel notes that Kamares Ware is not limited to the palaces and their related sanctuaries, but rather is also found in the townhouses of Phaistos, Hagia Triada, Kommos and Knossos. Such pottery is not found, however, at ordinary inland houses or farmsteads, nor indeed at Cretan sites other than Phaistos and its immediate vicinity, Knossos, and ports such as Gournia and Palaikastro where ships may have stopped en route to foreign ports.[41] When found abroad in Egypt or the Levant, Kamares Ware appears not in palaces or temples but in what appear to be private houses.[42] Such findspots, however, do not necessarily imply the absence of state involvement. When, for example, Amenhotep III sent the Kassite ruler Burnaburiash in Babylon at least 1,007 stone vessels filled with unguents or other liquids plus 160 empty stone vessels, some of the stone vessels were distributed within Babylon and others were exchanged elsewhere.[43] Vases may also arrive in the context of "captains' trade," for ships' captains and crews often traded for themselves on voyages organized by state authorities or by persons connected to the rulers.

In connection with the appearance of Kamares at sanctuaries, I would note the discovery of a fragment of a fine Kamares polychrome vessel in the cave of Zas on the highest point of Naxos, the largest island of the Cyclades.[44] The vessel in question must have been carried for about six hours from the point on the seashore where it arrived until the bearer reached the cave on the top of the island, which suggests that the cave of Zas was a ritual site, like the Kamares Cave itself, rather than merely a place where shepherds on the adjacent upland plain took shelter. Of course the Kamares Cave deposit was itself a specialized assemblage, as Van de Moortel's study reveals, given the relative infrequency of cups and bowls compared to any normal domestic deposit. Van de Moortel also notes the paucity of lamps from the cave, for which a number of reasons may be suggested, such as the possible presence of a perpetual fire, providing warmth in the cave and/or playing a role in cave cult, perhaps involving the contrast of dark and light. Alternatively, because the cave is not totally dark, celebrants may have relied on guides who knew every step and had no

40. I am grateful to Sturt Manning for this suggestion.

41. Walberg 2001, 17. In one instance at Knossos, polychrome Kamares was found in what the excavator described as the basement of "a substantial building" whose superstructure had disappeared; hence the status of the building is unclear (Popham 1974, 188 and fig. 7; Van de Moortel 2002).

42. Kemp and Merrillees 1980, 235; Van de Moortel, personal communication.

43. Wiener 1991, 327; Moran 1992, 32–3; Knudtzon 1915, 118–9; Lilyquist 1996, 156.

44. Konstantinos Zachos and Angelika Douzougli, personal communication for which I am most grateful.

need of lamps. That the intensive use of the Kamares Cave began not in MM IA but in MM IB at the time of the creation of the first palace at Phaistos, and declined notably after the destruction of the first palace at the end of MM IIB, is a further important discovery of this fine research project.[45]

Next in chronological order is a most interesting paper by Eleni Banou and Eleni Tsivilika describing the results of the current excavations at the MM II–MM III port site of Pera Galenoi, 22 km west of the port of Knossos at Poros, and 29 km east of Stavromenos, the natural northern entrepôt (along with Rethymnon, 12 km farther to the west) for the Amari Valley with its southern anchor at Phaistos. The Amari contains the major sites of Monastiraki and Apodoulou founded at the beginning of the Old Palace Period, whose sealings and pottery (including the storage pithoi discussed in Kostandinos Christakis' paper considered below) among other finds indicate direct links with Phaistos. (The scarcity of occupation in the fertile if remote Amari Valley in the New Palace Period after the intense Phaistian settlement in the Old Palace Period constitutes a major puzzle of Minoan prehistory; relevant factors may include putative climate change leading to improved conditions in the Mesara versus occasional flooding and difficulties of access to the Amari in the New Palace Period and the decline of Phaistos in MM IIIB–LM IA.) Banou and Tsivilika's paper reports that the pottery of Pera Galenoi is influenced by Knossos from its foundation in MM IIA, as it so clearly is after MM IIIA, whereas Van de Moortel remarked in the discussion following the presentation of the paper that in her view the pottery from Pera Galenoi illustrated in the presentation had Phaistian features prior to the end of MM IIB (when Phaistos, Monastiraki and Apodoulou were destroyed). Further examination of the MM II pottery from the site should clarify this question.

In any event, the small port site of Pera Galenoi had wide links, as shown by the excavation of a sherd thought highly likely to be from a Syrian amphora and two sherds with potters' marks known from Hagia Eirene on Kea as described in the paper by Banou and Tsivilika. Warren[46] has noted that the town of Sissi near Pera Galenoi is known today for its production of ladanum, the perfume made from the cistus plant, suggesting the possibility that Pera Galenoi could have been involved in the transport and perhaps the production of ladanum in Minoan times. Recent research on residues has shown that in MM IA oil of iris was produced at Chamalevri on the ridge behind the next port to the west at Stavromenos.[47]

Banou and Tsivilika's excavation revealed that Pera Galenoi was destroyed early in the MM III–LM I transition (perhaps by the same massive earthquake that caused considerable

45. Small amounts of LM from the Kamares Cave are reported in Dawkins and Laistner 1912–1913; Kanta 1980, 112.

46. Personal communication, for which I am most grateful.

47. Tzedakis and Martlew 1999, 50–1 nos. 12–3, 19.

damage elsewhere in central Crete and the early LC I seismic destruction at Akrotiri on Thera) and was never reoccupied. The damaged remains on the hillock of Pera Galenoi would have been difficult to repair or remove. Perhaps the putative Knossian Neopalatial dominance over Crete and the surrounding seas made the site superfluous because it was no longer deemed necessary to occupy every harbor, or at least not this particular harbor near a natural Knossian/Phaistian boundary.

The splendid paper by Kostandinos Christakis on traditions and trends in pithos production and consumption covers both the Proto- and Neopalatial periods. His fine-grained analysis may serve as a warning against facile assumptions regarding pottery production, trade and use. Potters as well as pots move—the paper notes, for example, that itinerant potters from Phaistos may have traveled to Monastiraki and Apodoulou in the Protopalatial period—while large undecorated storage vessels may be shipped long distances, even when local examples are available at the point of destination. Blitzer has shown that this latter phenomenon continued into the twentieth century A.D.; in the 1920s, large pithoi were produced in a village on a low hilltop in Messenia, rolled down the hill to sailing vessels, and shipped as far as Alexandria and Anatolia. (Some were also shipped to Crete, where they were often preferred because the bottoms of the locally produced pithoi could fall out.)[48] The potential complexity of the picture is illustrated by Christakis' discovery that at Galatas Pediados in MM III, pithoi may have been produced by three different potters or groups, two of whom imitated Knossian prototypes, one employing local clays similar to those used in the Knossos-Archanes area and the other the characteristic local red and orange clays. The third pithos-maker followed the local pottery tradition rather than the Knossian in shape and decoration.

Christakis' paper also shows that by LM I a new type of pithos derived from the pottery tradition of north-central Crete (large and ovoid with a wide mouth and decorated with rows of raised bands) appears in both north- and south-central Crete and becomes *par excellence* the storage container favored in palatial and elite contexts. No great care was given to the making of these pithoi, however, as can be seen in their unsmoothed surfaces and irregular appendages. Pithoi as well as conical cups continue to display the low or limited labor-input pottery practices of MM IIIB.

Particularly intriguing in this regard is Christakis' observation that many of the morphological and decorative attributes of these pithoi were adopted by potters on Thera. That Thera followed Knossian practices and examples in this regard even when the Knossian product was hardly worthy of emulation is suggestive, particularly in the context of the simultaneous wholesale adoption of Minoan massive use of conical cups, presumably

48. Blitzer 1990.

in feasting rituals, along with Minoan kitchen ware and Minoan-type loom weights.[49] We must of course allow for the possibility that the pots were produced by Minoan potters, whether immigrant or itinerant, perhaps working alongside natives. (In 1885 the traveler Bent reported that the celebrated potters of Siphnos traveled extensively: "In the springtime they start on their travels far and wide, and settle in towns and villages for days and weeks until the place is supplied with large well-made earthenware amphoras and cooking utensils; and it is an ancient art which has never left the island."[50]) Furumark long ago noted a Cycladic trend in LC I and II toward what he regarded as a " 'soulless and wholesale imitation' of Cretan pottery, culminating in the 'degeneracy and death of local ceramic art.' "[51] Davis and Lewis add that the decline in quality and labor-input per pot begins at the end of Middle Bronze, just as it does in Crete.

Of course high labor-input pots are never entirely lacking in Minoan Crete. Classical Kamares appears to continue at Knossos for about a generation after the MM IIB destruction,[52] and roughly the same pattern may pertain in the Mesara.[53] A post-Kamares phase follows, and is in turn followed by the fine wares of LM IA. Nevertheless, the drastic decline in MM III in the quality of much of the pottery, and particularly that found in the palace of Knossos itself, is striking. Hood describes the pottery in the palace as "unbelievably squalid in character," and notes the contrast to the pottery found in the surrounding houses in MM IIIA.[54] With respect to utilitarian vessels, the decline may begin at Knossos before the end of the Protopalatial period, as Van de Moortel has noted.[55] Indeed, a good part of the explanation for the overall dramatic decline in labor-input per pot by MM IIIB may lie simply in the rise to dominance of Neopalatial Knossos. The New Palace period at Knossos provides abundant evidence of rituals involving mass feasting, requiring enormous numbers of ordinary, low-input vessels, some less costly to make than to wash and keep. In this last respect I am of course thinking of my old favorite, the omnipresent conical cup, capable of holding liquid for only about five minutes before becoming permeated.[56] Warren has estimated Knossian production of conical cups in the Neopalatial period at a minimum of 100,000 per year![57] Knappett has noted that conical cups produced at Malia and Myrtos-Pyrgos in LM I are more uniform than those from Knossos with respect

49. Wiener 1990, 134–40.
50. Bent 1965, 22–3, originally published in 1885, cited in Lewis 1983, 65.
51. Furumark 1950, 199, as quoted in Davis and Lewis 1985, 79.
52. MacGillivray 1998, 95.
53. Walberg 1991, 117.
54. Hood 1996, 10.
55. Personal communication of 8 August 2003.
56. Lewis 1983, 110.
57. Personal communication of 6 August 2003; see generally Wiener 1984.

to such features as the width of side walls, and never descend to the depths of potting carelessness or incompetence displayed by some of the cups produced at Knossos; he suggests that the numbers of cups needed at Knossos for its feasting rituals may account for the difference.[58] It is hard to imagine that the palatial elites used any conical cups in feasting ceremonies; rather it seems likely that they used the metal vessels we see depicted in the Egyptian tomb paintings of arriving Keftiu.

The production of every category of pottery is affected, however. Population growth; changes in numbers of participants and customs involved in feasting rituals requiring mass production of pots for pouring, storing and transporting as well as for eating and drinking; changes in expectations regarding pottery as its use in feasting encompassed significantly broader segments of the populace; new or more widely attended funerary rites requiring masses of conical cups;[59] and Evans and Pendlebury's old favorite, increased elite access to metal vessels in the Neopalatial period,[60] may be invoked as stimuli for the general decline in quality across all pottery shapes (subject to the few exceptions noted) throughout central and east-central Crete, from Malia to Phaistos, beginning in MM IIIA and accelerating in MM IIIB.[61] The mass production necessary to meet greatly expanded demand would itself have required increased routinization of activity and division of labor; whereas an individual master potter may have previously been responsible for all stages of production of a particular pot, now various stages—preparing clay, forming, finishing and firing—may have been in different hands. It seems likely, for example, that apprentices were assigned the tasks of preparing clay cones and slicing conical cups off the hump with string. Less significant factors may have included Neopalatial expansion resulting in Minoan communities living abroad,[62] leading to increasing emigration or itinerant travels of potters, thus thinning the ranks in potting communities, while skilled pot painters may have found expanding employment opportunities in the field of wall-decoration—there are strong similarities, notably on the foliate bands, between the color and motifs of Kamares Ware and the wall paintings of the first palace at Phaistos.[63]

Competition between independent potters resulting in efforts to lower labor costs, presumably in order to be able to offer wares for less in exchange, has sometimes been proposed as an explanation for the change both in Crete and in Kea, particularly in light of the fact that all categories of pottery are affected, notwithstanding the general tendency of

58. Knappett 1999, 416–7.

59. Wiener 1990, 138–40.

60. Evans 1921, 553; Pendlebury 1963, 158. For the large quantities of bronze available in the Neopalatial period, see Wiener 1990, 145–50.

61. Van de Moortel 2002, esp. 204.

62. Wiener 1990.

63. Boulotis 1995, fig. 8, cited in Day and Wilson 1998, 356.

competition to produce quality enhancement rather than decline.[64] In that case it might be expected that at least one of the putative competing independent potters would continue to produce high labor-input pottery to fill an elite demand niche, if such a niche and the requisite skill had continued to exist. Had Neopalatial elites considered it important to display pottery requiring high labor-input and high skills, it seems likely that the means could have been found. (As noted above, some more labor-intensive pottery is produced in MM III, perhaps in the same pottery workshops as the greatly preponderant low labor-intensive wares.[65] Even conical cups came in a better version, smoothed and dipped in paint, perhaps reducing their porosity.[66])

Would Hagia Eirene on Kea, with its estimated population of 300–400 people,[67] have supported competing cost-cutting independent potteries, even considering the masses of locally produced conical cups found there?[68] Curtis[69] reports that potters in remote traditional potting villages using the wheel and working with apprentices who haul wood and prepare clay can produce 500 pots per master potter per day,[70] which for a potting season of 100 working days could mean 50,000 pots per year. Lewis has observed that an individual potter working alone and part-time on Siphnos produced 500 pots per month, or about 2,000 per pottery season, enough to provide five to seven pots per person annually for the estimated population of Hagia Eirene. (Perhaps the potters' marks noted[71] on Keian pots identified the work of individual potters sharing a kiln.) Conical cups cut off the hump can of course be produced by apprentices much more quickly, at a rate of well over 100 per hour.[72]

Not all LM I storage pithoi displayed unsmoothed surfaces and irregular appendages, however, for Christakis reports that the very large pithoi in the Palace of Minos itself, in contrast to those in the surrounding houses, were made with care and covered with original appliqué patterns. Initially it might seem that an explanation should be sought in the cultic function of the palace, since we do not ordinarily think of distinguished visitors observing the furnishings of storerooms. Christakis offers a different explanation, namely that visitors to the palace did indeed visit the West Magazines, where these exceptional

64. Van de Moortel 2002, 203; 2001, 110; Davis and Lewis 1985; see also Rathje 1975. Declines in labor input in pottery during the Ubaid and Uruk periods in the Near East are considered in Falconer 1993.

65. Hood 1996, 10–1; Knappett 1997, 309.

66. Knappett 2001.

67. Wiener 1990, 132.

68. Wiener 1990, 137–8; Schofield 1979.

69. Curtis 1962.

70. Lewis 1983, 53.

71. Bikaki 1984.

72. I am grateful to Veronica Hankey Newman for information concerning her experiments in reproducing conical cups.

pithoi would have formed part of what he suggests was a "scenographic setting" for the display of stored wealth. He observes that the West Magazines had "gypsum floors, walls lined with gypsum slabs, gypsum jamb bases, finely plastered walls with frescoes" and planned patterns of lighting, plus the direct communication to the Central Sanctuary Complex. (Whether the fragments of miniature fresco painting found sealed in the lower stratum of cists in the Thirteenth Magazine by Evans in 1904 were originally attached to any of the walls of the Magazines and, if so, whether the frescoes were in place in LM I or were painted later in the course of a Creto-Mycenaean refurbishing in LM II, has been discussed by Cameron and Immerwahr, among others. Cameron favored an LM II date for the fresco fragments, whereas Immerwahr, who had available as comparanda LC I frescoes from Thera and Kea discovered post-Cameron, considered the fragments from the Thirteenth Magazine cists to be LM I.[73] The entrance to the adjoining Twelfth Magazine was covered with plaster and two painted dado bands of Venetian red over bluish gray at 86 and 147 cm above the floor surface;[74] it is this decoration in particular that Christakis regards as LM I in origin.[75]) The fact noted by Christakis that one of these carefully made Palatial Style pithoi was found at Petras on the east coast of Crete may support his interpretation of conspicuous consumption rather than religious respect as the reason for their production.

Continuing chronologically, we come finally to the important and thought-provoking paper by Jeremy Rutter on "Southwestern Anatolian Pottery from Late Minoan Crete: Evidence for Direct Contacts Between Arzawa and Keftiu?" Rutter reports that at Kommos by far the most common ceramic import in LM II–LM IIIA was pottery from southwest Anatolia. He notes further that a similar number of such jugs have been identified from LM II contexts at Knossos in the pillared hall of the Unexplored Mansion, together with one additional example from the Temple Tomb. His research reveals that the jugs from Kommos and Knossos of this unusual fabric have their closest parallels in jugs common at sites such as Panaztepe, Bayraklı and Limantepe at the eastern end of the Gulf of Izmir.

The 2002 excavations at Limantepe and Çeşme (not far from ancient Erythrai with its Minoan foundation legend) provided evidence of additional Aegean settlements on the Anatolian coast, established earlier but continuing into the fourteenth–thirteenth century B.C. At Miletus what had once been a flourishing Minoan colony, with 95% of its pottery Minoan or Minoan-imitating, in the course of Late Helladic IIIA1 becomes largely Mycenaean, with 95% of its pottery reported by the excavator to be Helladic or Helladic-

73. Immerwahr 1990, 64, 162, 173; Cameron 1975.

74. Evans 1935, 650–1 and fig. 634.

75. Personal communication of 27 August 2003.

imitating, but with evidence of both Mycenaean- and Minoan-type kilns in operation and some Late Minoan IIIA1 imports as well. Pottery evidence from the tombs along the Anatolian coast also suggests an ongoing Creto-Mycenaean presence.[76]

Certainly it would not be surprising to discover that there were Anatolian imports flowing toward Crete in LM II and IIIA1, as Rutter's paper implies. It is interesting to learn that these vessels exist in Kos but have not been found to date in Rhodes, for in "Isles of Crete"[77] I proposed the existence of two LM I Minoan trading networks going toward the east, one leading via the heavily Minoan site of Trianda in Rhodes toward Cyprus and the Levant, the other going from the Seraglio in Kos, also heavily Minoan, to Anatolia. Further evidence of a trade route running from Crete to the coast of Anatolia via Kos in LM/LB I comes in the form of Minoanizing pottery appearing in some quantity at Iasos and Miletus, which petrographic and chemical analysis identifies as Koan. Additional examples of this ware have been found at Kalymnos and Knidos along the same proposed route, and from Akrotiri on Thera and Hagia Eirene on Kea as well. Koan wines were praised in the classical period; perhaps they were also exported in LB I in these containers.[78] Of course Kos would still have been the natural stopping point en route to the Anatolian coast in LM IIIA1, when the jugs from the Gulf of Izmir region appear in Kos and in Crete. LM IIIA1 exports from Crete appear not just in Kos, however, but also in Rhodes, at Ialysos and Trianda.[79] Rutter's paper notes that no examples of the Arzawan jugs of the type found in the Gulf of Izmir region have as yet been recognized from mainland Greece. (Of course unrecognized sherds may be lurking undiscovered in excavation "puzzle boxes," or may have been discarded by excavators.) It is worth noting in this regard that Arzawa reaches the peak of its power around 1370 B.C., when Egyptian texts recognize the land as an important political ally,[80] just as Knossos is destroyed and the importation of Arzawan pottery into Crete appears to end.

We should not assume that the Arzawan jugs found in Crete and the Minoanized sites abroad beginning in LM II or the Minoanizing Koan jugs found in Arzawa traveled on Minoan or Creto-Myceneaean vessels, for the Arzawans were known for their shipbuilding skills. The daily logs at the shipyard at Perunefer, the port city of Memphis during the reign of Tuthmosis III (1479–1425 B.C.) and his successor, Amenophis II (1428–1397 B.C.), record Arzawans at work.[81]

Recent years have seen great advances in our knowledge of the geography of Anatolia

76. Müller-Celka 2005.
77. Wiener 1990.
78. Marthari et al. 1990; Knappett 2003; W.-D. Niemeier, personal communication, for which I am most grateful.
79. Watrous 1992, 173; Mee 2002.
80. Haider 2003, 180.
81. Haider 2003, 177.

in the Late Bronze Age and of Aegean activity in the area.[82] References to the land of Ahhiyawa and its king appear in Hittite texts of the late fifteenth/early fourteenth century B.C. Manning has suggested that the capital of Ahhiyawa at this time may even have been located at Knossos, before moving to the Greek mainland prior to or immediately upon the destruction of Knossos early in LH/LM IIIA2.[83] However that may be, it seems likely that Creto-Mycenaeans played a significant role in Aegean interactions with Anatolia in LM II–IIIA1. (By the time of the Mycenaean maxima of LH IIIA2 through IIIB1, c. 1370–1240 B.C.,[84] following the Knossos destruction early in IIIA2, exchanges between mainland Greece and the East become more prominent, but the presence of at least some Creto-Mycenaean settlers along the Anatolian coast in this period is suggested by tomb types similar to types known from Crete, their lack of Mycenaean mainland-style figurines, and their mixture of inhumation and cremation burials typical of LM IIIA2–IIIB cemeteries in Crete.[85]) Rutter notes that the Anatolian jugs arriving in Crete are again clearly metal-imitating, and that the prototype for their shape may be found in LM I metal vessels. We may accordingly be witnessing a process involving Minoan forms introduced into Anatolia by Neopalatial Minoan settlements such as Miletus influencing later Aegeo-Arzawan output in the late fifteenth and fourteenth centuries B.C., with some of the resulting ceramic output returning to Crete.

Of course the splendid papers presented here, and especially my reflections on them, are open to the objection that we are suffering from a *déformation professionnelle* of pottery specialists in forming sweeping historical conclusions on the basis of ambiguous ceramic evidence. You, gentle reader, must be our judge. In any event, the fact that this Gold Medal Colloquium in honor of Philip Betancourt inspired so fine and important a set of papers on Minoan pottery is itself a fitting tribute to the honorand.

82. See, e.g., Hawkins 1997–1998; Niemeier 1998a; 1998b.

83. Unpublished conference comments and personal communication for which I am most grateful. My thanks are due also to Jerry Rutter for reminding me of this comment.

84. Wiener 2003.

85. See Müller-Celka 2005.

WORKS CITED

Banti, L. 1930–1931. "La grande tomba a tholos de Haghia Triada." *ASAtene* 13–14: 155–251.

———. 1939–1940. "Cronologia e ceramica del palazzo minoico de Festòs." *ASAtene* 17–18 (n.s. 1–2): 9–39.

Bent, J.T. 1965. New ed. *Aegean Islands: The Cyclades, or Life Among the Insular Greeks.* Chicago: Argonaut. Original edition published in 1885 under the title *The Cyclades or Life Among the Insular Greeks.*

Betancourt, P.P. 1985. *The History of Minoan Pottery.* Princeton, NJ: Princeton University Press.

Bikaki, A.H. 1984. *Keos.* Vol. 4, *Ayia Irini: The Potters' Marks.* Mainz on Rhine: Philipp von Zabern.

Blitzer, H. 1990. "Koroneika: Storage-jar Production and Trade in the Traditional Aegean." *Hesperia* 59: 675–711.

Bosanquet, R.C. 1902. "Excavations at Palaikastro I." *BSA* 8: 286–316.

Boulotis, C. 1995. "Αιγαιακές Τοιχογραφίες: Ενας πολύχρωμος αφηγηματικός λόγος." *Αρχαιολογία & Τέχνες* 55: 13–30.

Branigan, K. 1970. *The Foundations of Palatial Crete: A Survey of Crete in the Early Bronze Age.* States and Cities of Ancient Greece. London: Routledge and Kegan Paul.

———. 1974. *Aegean Metalwork of the Early and Middle Bronze Age.* Oxford Monographs on Classical Archaeology. Oxford: Clarendon Press.

Cameron, M.A.S. 1975. "A General Study of Minoan Frescoes, with Particular Reference to Unpublished Wall Paintings from Knossos." Ph.D. diss., University of Newcastle-upon-Tyne.

Carinci, F.M. 1997. "Pottery Workshops at Phaistos and Haghia Triada in the Protopalatial Period." In *TEXNH: Craftsmen, Craftswomen and Craftsmanship in the Aegean Bronze Age. Proceedings of the 6th International Aegean Conference, Philadelphia, Temple University, 18–21 April 1996*, edited by R. Laffineur and P.P. Betancourt, 317–22. *Aegaeum* 16. Liège: Université de Liège.

———. 2004. *"Priests in Action:* considerazioni sulla fine dell'età prepalaziale ad Haghia Triada." *Creta Antica* 5: 25–41.

Cherry, J.F. 1983. "Evolution, Revolution, and the Origins of Complex Society in Minoan Crete." In *Minoan Society. Proceedings of the Cambridge Colloquium 1981,* edited by O. Krzyszkowska and L. Nixon, 33–45. Bristol: Bristol Classical Press.

Clark, J.E. 1995. "Craft Specialization as an Archaeological Category." *Research in Economic Anthropology* 16: 267–94.

Costin, C.L. 1991. "Craft Specialization: Issues in Defining, Documenting, and Explaining the Organization of Production." In *Archaeological Method and Theory* 3, edited by M.B. Schiffer, 1–56. Tucson: University of Arizona Press.

Curtis, F. 1962. "The Utility Pottery Industry of Bailén, Southern Spain." *American Anthropologist*, n.s. 64: 486–503.

Curtis, J., M. Rosenmeier, H. Weiss and K. Willis. Forthcoming. "Holocene Paleoenvironmental Reconstructions from Lake Kournas."

Davis, J.L. and H.B. Lewis. 1985. "Mechanization of Pottery Production: A Case Study from the Cycladic Islands." In *Prehistoric Production and Exchange: The Aegean and Eastern Mediterranean*, edited by A.B. Knapp and T. Stech, 79–92. UCLAMon 25. Los Angeles: Institute of Archaeology, University of California.

Dawkins, R.M. 1902–1903. "Excavations at Palaikastro II." *BSA* 9: 274–328.

———. 1903–1904. "Excavations at Palaikastro III." *BSA* 10: 192–226.

———. 1904–1905. "Excavations at Palaikastro IV." *BSA* 11: 258–92.

Dawkins, R.M. and M.L.W. Laistner. 1912–1913. "The Excavation of the Kamares Cave in Crete." *BSA* 19: 1–34.

Day, P.M. and D.E. Wilson. 1998. "Consuming Power: Kamares Ware in Protopalatial Knossos." *Antiquity* 72: 350–8.

Evans, A. 1921. *The Palace of Minos at Knossos.* Vol. 1. London: Macmillan.

———. 1928. *The Palace of Minos at Knossos.* Vol. 2. London: Macmillan.

———. 1935. *The Palace of Minos at Knossos.* Vol. 4. London: Macmillan.

Evans, J. 1972. "The Early Minoan Occupation of Knossos: A Note on Some New Evidence." *AnatSt* 22: 115–28.

Faber, E.W., V. Kilikoglou, P.M. Day and D.E. Wilson. 2002. "A Technological Study of Middle Minoan Polychrome Pottery from Knossos, Crete." In *Modern Trends in Scientific Studies on Ancient Ceramics. Papers Presented at the 5th European Meeting on Ancient Ceramics, Athens, 1999*, edited by V. Kilikoglou, A. Hein and Y. Maniatis, 129–41. *BAR-IS* 1011. Oxford: Archaeopress.

Falconer, S.E. 1993. Reprint. "Rethinking Ceramic Degeneration: An Ancient Mesopotamian Case Study." In *Arizona Anthropologist: Papers of the University of Arizona Department of Anthropology (formerly Atl Atl)* 2, 54–71. Original edition, Tucson: University of Arizona, 1981.

Forsén, J. 1992. *The Twilight of the Early Helladics: A Study of the Disturbances in East-Central and Southern Greece towards the End of the Early Bronze Age*. Jonsered: Paul Åströms.

Furumark, A. 1950. "The Settlement at Ialysos and Aegean History c. 1550–1400 B.C." *OpArch* 6: 150–271.

Galaty, M.L. 1999. *Nestor's Wine Cups: Investigating Ceramic Manufacture and Exchange in a Late Bronze Age "Mycenaean" State*. *BAR-IS* 766. Oxford: Hadrian Books.

Godart, L., and J.-P. Olivier. 1976. *Recueil des Inscriptions en Linéaire A*. Vol. 1, *Tablettes éditées avant 1970*. *Ét-Crét* 21. Paris: Libraire Orientaliste Paul Geuthner.

Gruber, A.C. 1982. *Silverware*. New York: Rizzoli.

Haider, P.W. 2003. "Westkleinasien nach ägyptischen Quellen des Neuen Reiches." In *Der neue Streit um Troia: Eine Bilanz*, edited by C. Ulf, 174–92. Munich: C.H. Beck.

Hawkins, D. 1997–1998. "Hittites on the Aegean Coast: New Evidence." *BICS* 42: 231–2.

Hood, S. 1996. "Back to Basics with Middle Minoan IIIB." In *Minotaur and Centaur: Studies in the Archaeology of Crete and Euboea Presented to Mervyn Popham*, edited by D. Evely, I.S. Lemos and S. Sherratt, 10–6. *BAR-IS* 638. Oxford: Tempvs Reparatvm.

Immerwahr, S. 1990. *Aegean Painting in the Bronze Age*. University Park, PA: Pennsylvania State University Press.

Kanta, A. 1980. *The Late Minoan III Period in Crete: A Survey of Sites, Pottery and Their Distribution*. *SIMA* 58. Göteborg: Paul Åströms.

Kemp, B.J., and R.S. Merrillees. 1980. *Minoan Pottery in Second Millennium Egypt*. Mainz on Rhine: Philipp von Zabern.

Knappett, C. 1997. "Ceramic Production in the Protopalatial Mallia 'State': Evidence from Quartier Mu and Myrtos Pyrgos." In *TEXNH: Craftsmen, Craftswomen and Craftsmanship in the Aegean Bronze Age. Proceedings of the 6th International Aegean Conference, Philadelphia, Temple University, 18–21 April 1996*, edited by R. Laffineur and P.P. Betancourt, 305–11. *Aegaeum* 16. Liège: Université de Liège.

———. 1999. "Can't Live without Them—Producing and Consuming Minoan Conical Cups." In *MELETEMATA: Studies in Aegean Archaeology Presented to Malcolm H. Wiener as He Enters His 65th Year*, edited by P. Betancourt, V. Karageorghis, R. Laffineur, and W.-D. Niemeier, 415–20. *Aegaeum* 20. Liège: Université de Liège.

———. 2001. "Overseen or Overlooked? Ceramic Production in a Mycenaean Palatial System." In *Economy and Politics in the Mycenaean Palace States. Proceedings of a Conference Held on 1–3 July 1999 in the Faculty of Classics, Cambridge*, edited by S. Voutsaki and J. Killen, 80–95. Cambridge: Cambridge Philological Society.

———. 2003. "Minoanisation in the South-East Aegean: Pottery Fabrics from Miletus and Iasos." Preliminary abstract of paper presented at the Fourth Symposium on Archaeometry, Athens, 28–31 May 2003. http://www.archaeometry.gr/symposium2003/pages_en/abstracts/papers/clays/clay17.htm.

Knudtzon, J.A. 1915. *Die El-Amarna-Tafeln*. Vol. 1. Vorderasiatische Bibliothek. Leipzig: J.C. Hinrichs.

La Rosa, V. 2004. "Perché il Palazzo a Festòs?" *Creta Antica* 5:43–51.

Levi, D. 1976. *Festòs e la civiltà minoica*. Vol. 1. Incunabula Graeca 60. Rome: Edizioni dell'Ateneo.

Lewis, H.B. 1983. "The Manufacture of Early Mycenaean Pottery." Ph.D. diss., University of Minnesota.

Lilyquist, C. 1996. "Stone Vessels at Kāmid el-Lōz: Egyptian, Egyptianizing, or Non-Egyptian. A Question at Sites from the Sudan to Iraq to the Greek Mainland." In *Kāmid el-Lōz*. Vol. 16, *'Schatzhaus'-Studien*, edited by R. Hachmann, 134–73. Bonn: R. Habelt.

Macdonald, C. Forthcoming. "Defining Earthquakes and Identifying Their Consequences in North Central Crete During the Old and New Palace Periods." In *Proceedings of the 9th International Congress of Cretan Studies, Elounda, 1–6 October 2001*.

MacGillivray, J.A. 1987. "Pottery Workshops and the Old Palaces in Crete." In *The Function of the Minoan Palaces. Proceedings of the Fourth International Symposium at the Swedish Institute in Athens, 10–16 June, 1984,* edited by R. Hägg and N. Marinatos, 273–9. *SkrAth* 4, 35. Stockholm: Svenska Institutet i Athen.

———. 1998. *Knossos: Pottery Groups of the Old Palace Period. BSA* Studies 5. London: British School at Athens.

MacKenzie, D. 1906. "The Middle Minoan Pottery of Knossos." *JHS* 26: 243–67.

Maggidis, C. 1998. "From Polis to Necropolis: Social Ranking from Architectural and Mortuary Evidence in the Minoan Cemetery at Phourni, Archanes." In *Cemetery and Society in the Aegean Bronze Age*, edited by K. Branigan, 87–102. Sheffield Studies in Archaeology 1. Sheffield: Sheffield Academic Press.

Marthari, M., T. Marketou, and R.E. Jones. 1990. "LB I Ceramic Connections between Thera and Kos." In *Thera and the Aegean World III. Proceedings of the Third International Congress, Santorini, Greece, 3–9 September 1989*. Vol. 1, *Archaeology*, edited by D.A. Hardy, C.G. Doumas, J.A. Sakellarakis and P.M. Warren, 171–84. London: The Thera Foundation.

Mee, C. 2002. "Mycenaeans Overseas in the Eastern Aegean and Western Anatolia." Paper presented at From Crete and Mycenae to Amarna: Pots, Pictures and Places in the Work of Vronwy Hankey, 25 May 2002, University College London.

Momigliano, N. 1991. "MM IA Pottery from Evans' Excavations at Knossos: A Reassessment." *BSA* 86: 149–271.

———. 2000. "Knossos 1902, 1905: The Prepalatial and Protopalatial Deposits from the Room of the Jars in the Royal Pottery Stores." *BSA* 95: 65–105.

Moran, W.L., ed. 1992. *The Amarna Letters*. Baltimore: Johns Hopkins University Press.

Müller-Celka, S. 2005. "Évaluation de l'élément mycénien en Asie Mineure à travers les données funéraires." In *EMPORIA: Aegeans in the Central and Eastern Mediterranean. Proceedings of the 10th International Aegean Conference, Athens, Italian School of Archaeology, 14–18 April 2004,* edited by R. Laffineur and E. Greco, 247–58. *Aegaeum* 25. Liège: Université de Liège.

Niemeier, W.-D. 1998a. "The Minoans in the South-Eastern Aegean and in Cyprus." In *Eastern Mediterranean: Cyprus-Dodecanese-Crete, 16th–6th Cent. B.C. Proceedings of the International Symposium Organized by the University of Crete, Rethymnon and the Anastasios G. Leventis Foundation, Nicosia, Rethymnon 13–16 May 1997*, edited by V. Karageorghis and N. Stampolidis, 29–47. Athens: University of Crete and the A.G. Leventis Foundation.

———. 1998b. "The Mycenaeans in Western Anatolia and the Problem of the Origins of the Sea Peoples." In *Mediterranean Peoples in Transition: Thirteenth to Early Tenth Centuries BCE. In Honor of Professor Trude Dothan*, edited by S. Gitin, A. Mazar and E. Stern, 17–65. Jerusalem: Israel Exploration Society.

Palaima, T.G. 1997. "Potter and Fuller: The Royal Craftsmen." In *TEXNH: Craftsmen, Craftswomen and Craftsmanship in the Aegean Bronze Age. Proceedings of the 6th International Aegean Conference, Philadelphia, Temple University, 18–21 April 1996*, edited by R. Laffineur and P.P. Betancourt, 407–12. *Aegaeum* 16. Liège: Université de Liège.

Pelon, O. 1993. "La Salle à piliers du Palais de Malia et ses antécédents: recherches complémentaires." *BCH* 117: 523–46.

Pendlebury, J.D.S. 1963. *The Archaeology of Crete: An Introduction*. New York: Biblo and Tannen.

Pernier, L. 1935. *Il palazzo minoico di Festòs*. Vol. 1, *Gli strati più antichi e il primo palazzo*. Rome: Libreria dello stato.

Phillips, Jacke. 2004. "The Odd Man Out: Minoan Scarabs and Scaraboids." In *Scarabs of the Second Millenium BC from Egypt, Nubia, Crete and the Levant: Chronological and Historical Implications. Papers of a Symposium, Vienna 10–13 January 2002*, edited by M. Bietak and E. Czerny, 161–70. Contributions to the Chronology of the Eastern Mediterranean. Vienna: Österreichischen Akademie der Wissenschaften.

Pini, I. 1992. "Seals." In *Minoan and Greek Civilization from the Mitsotakis Collection*, edited by L. Marangou, 200–5. Athens: N.P. Goulandris Foundation-Museum of Cycladic Art.

———. 2000. "Eleven Early Cretan Scarabs." In *Κρήτη–Αίγυπτος. Πολιτισμικοί δεσμοί τριών χιλιετιών. Μελέτες*, edited by A. Karetsou, 107–13. Athens: Archaiologiko Museio Hrakleiou.

Popham, M.R. 1974. "Trial KV (1969), a Middle Minoan Building at Knossos." *BSA* 69: 181–94.

Rathje, W.L. 1975. "The Last Tango in Mayapán: A Tentative Trajectory of Production-Distribution Systems." In *Ancient Civilization and Trade*, edited by J.A. Sabloff and C.C. Lamberg-Karlovsky, 409–48. Albuquerque: University of New Mexico Press.

Schofield, E. 1979. "Kea and Its Aegean Connections in the Late Bronze Age." *BICS* 26: 132.

Seager, R.B. 1912. *Explorations in the Island of Mochlos*. Boston and New York: American School of Classical Studies at Athens.

Soles, J.S. 1992. *The Prepalatial Cemeteries at Mochlos and Gournia and the House Tombs of Bronze Age Crete. Hesperia* Suppl. 24. Princeton, NJ: American School of Classical Studies at Athens.

Stefani, E. 1930–1931. "La grande tomba a tholos de Haghia Triada." *ASAtene* 13–14: 147–54.

Todaro, S. 2003. "Haghia Triada nel periodo Antico Minoico." *Creta Antica* 4: 69–95.

———. 2005. "EM I–MM IA Ceramic Groups at Phaistos: Towards the Definition of a Prepalatial Ceramic Sequence in South Central Crete." *Creta Antica* 6: 11–46.

———. Forthcoming. "Il desposito AM I del Piazzale dei Sacelli di Haghia Triada: I modellini architettonici." *ASAtene* 82 (3rd ser. 3).

Tzedakis, Y. and H. Martlew, eds. 1999. *Minoans and Mycenaeans: Flavours of their Time. National Archaeological Museum, 12 July – 27 November, 1999*. Athens: Greek Ministry of Culture, General Directorate of Antiquities.

Van de Moortel, A. 2001. "The Area Around the Kiln, and the Pottery from the Kiln and the Kiln Dump." In *A LM IA Ceramic Kiln in South-Central Crete*, by J.W. Shaw, A. Van de Moortel, P.M. Day and V. Kilikoglou, 25–110. *Hesperia* Suppl. 30. Princeton, NJ: American School of Classical Studies at Athens.

———. 2002. "Pottery as a Barometer of Economic Change: From the Protopalatial to the Neopalatial Society in Central Crete." In *Labyrinth Revisited: Rethinking 'Minoan' Archaeology*, edited by Y. Hamilakis, 189–211. Oxford: Oxbow Books.

Walberg, G. 1991. "The Finds at Tell el-Daba and Middle Minoan Chronology." *Ägypten und Levante* 2: 115–20.

———. 2001. "The Role and Individuality of Kamares Ware." *Aegean Archaeology* 5: 9–18.

Warren, P.M. 1975. *The Aegean Civilizations*. The Making of the Past. Oxford: Elsevier International Projects.

———. 1981. "Knossos and Its Foreign Relations in the Early Bronze Age." In *Πεπραγμένα του Δ' Διεθνούς Κρητολογικού Συνεδρίου (Ηράκλειο, 29 Αυγούστου–3 Σεπτεμβρίου 1976)*. Vol. A2, *Προϊστορικοί καὶ Αρχαίοι Χρόνοι*, 628–37, Athens: Panepistemion Kretes.

———. 1987. "The Genesis of the Minoan Palace." In *The Function of Minoan Palaces. Proceedings of the Fourth International Symposium at the Swedish Institute of Athens, 10–16 June, 1984*, edited by R. Hägg and N. Marinatos, 47–56. *SkrAth* 4, 35. Stockholm: Svenska Institutet i Athen.

Watrous, L.V. 1992. *Kommos*. Vol. 3, *The Late Bronze Age Pottery*. Princeton, NJ: Princeton University Press.

———. 2001. "Review of Aegean Prehistory III: Crete from the Earliest Prehistory through the Protopalatial Period." In *Aegean Prehistory: A Review*, edited by T. Cullen, 157–223. *AJA* Suppl. 1. Boston: Archaeological Institute of America.

Whitelaw, T. 2001. "Reading Between the Tablets: Assessing Mycenaean Palatial Involvement in Ceramic Production and Consumption." In *Economy and Politics in the Mycenaean Palace States. Proceedings of a Conference Held on 1–3 July 1999 in the Faculty of Classics, Cambridge*, edited by S. Voutsaki and J. Killen, 51–79. *PCPS* Suppl. 27. Cambridge: Cambridge Philological Society.

Wiener, M.H. 1984. "Crete and the Cyclades in LM I: The Tale of the Conical Cups." In *The Minoan Thalassocracy: Myth and Reality. Proceedings of the Third International Symposium at the Swedish Institute in Athens, 31 May – 5 June, 1982*, edited by R. Hägg and N. Marinatos, 17–26. *SkrAth* 4, 32. Stockholm: Svenska Institutet i Athen.

———. 1990. "The Isles of Crete? The Minoan Thalassocracy Revisited." In *Thera and the Aegean World III. Proceedings of the Third International Congress, Santorini, Greece, 3–9 September 1989*. Vol. 1, *Archaeology*, edited by D.A. Hardy, C.G. Doumas, J.A. Sakellarakis and P.M. Warren, 128–61. London: The Thera Foundation.

———. 1991. "The Nature and Control of Minoan Foreign Trade." In *Bronze Age Trade in the Mediterranean. Papers Presented at the Conference Held at Rewley House, Oxford, in December 1989*, edited by N.H. Gale, 325–50. *SIMA* 90. Jonsered: Paul Åströms.

———. 1994. "Cretan Connections: External Actors and Factors during the Bronze Age." Austrian-German Lecture Tour, December 1994.

———. 2003. "The Absolute Chronology of Late Helladic III A2 Revisited." *BSA* 98: 239–50.

———. Forthcoming. "Sailing the Wine Dark Sea."

Wilson, D.E. 1994. "Knossos Before the Palaces: An Overview of the Early Bronze Age (EM I—EM III)." In *Knossos: A Labyrinth of History. Papers Presented in Honour of Sinclair Hood,* edited by D. Evely, H. Hughes-Brock and N. Momigliano, 23–44. Athens: British School at Athens.

Wilson, D.E. and P.M. Day. 1994. "Ceramic Regionalism in Prepalatial Central Crete: The Mesara Imports at EM I to EM II A Knossos." *BSA* 89: 1–87.

Wilson, D.M. 1985. *The Bayeux Tapestry*. New York: Knopf.

Zoes, A. 1976. *Βασιλική*. Vol. 1, *Νέα Αρχαιολογική Ἔρευνα εἰς τό Κεφάλι πλησίον τοῦ χωρίου Βασιλική Ιεράπετρας.* Βιβλιοθήκη τῆς ἐν Ἀθήναις Ἀρχαιολογικῆς Ἑταιρείας 83. Athens: En Athenais Archaiologike Hetaireia.

POTTERY MAKING AND SOCIAL REPRODUCTION IN THE BRONZE AGE MESARA

PETER M. DAY, MARIA RELAKI & EDWARD W. FABER

It is a great pleasure to write in honor of Philip Betancourt's deserved award of the Gold Medal for Distinguished Archaeological Achievement from the AIA. On arrival for a first season of fieldwork in Crete, one of us (PD) was welcomed warmly at Kommos by Phil and presented with the newly published volume, *East Cretan White-on-Dark Ware*.[1] That important volume characterizes much of Betancourt's influential approach, of which we might highlight two aspects: a multi-disciplinary design, and an inclusive way of organizing research, particularly in his encouragement of younger scholars. With this in mind, our presentation in the Gold Medal Colloquium drew on a variety of analytical techniques and methodologies employed by our broad research team. The resulting paper integrates the efforts of our group and discusses whether Phil's vision of pottery illuminating a myriad of social and historical aspects of Minoan society is becoming a reality 20 years after the publication of *East Cretan White-on-Dark Ware*. We have departed from our normal emphasis on documenting all components of a given assemblage, to follow the example set in his studies of Vasiliki Ware[2] and East Cretan White-on-Dark Ware,[3] presenting some thoughts on pottery traditions in one key area of Crete, the Mesara Plain, from the Early Minoan period to the Middle Bronze Age. After a review of the thematic developments of Aegean pottery studies, we will examine the potential for

We are indebted to many colleagues who have been generous with their material, time, advice and patience. For access to material drawn upon in this paper, we thank Philip Betancourt, Gerald Cadogan, Filippo Carinci, Nicola Cucuzza, Sinclair Hood, Vincenzo La Rosa, Colin Macdonald, Sandy MacGillivray, Nicoletta Momigliano, Joseph Shaw and Simona Todaro. Professor Emanuele Greco and the Italian School of Archaeology at Athens kindly gave permission for the reproductions of figures 1, 2, 5 and 6. The Archaeological Institute of America and Institute for Aegean Prehistory made Day's attendance at the Gold Medal Colloquium possible. Funding for research was generously provided by INSTAP, the Arts and Humanities Research Board, the Natural Environment Research Council, NCSR "Demokritos," the National Scholarship Foundation of Greece (IKY), an educational grant from the Charles Henry Foyle Trust, a Wingate Scholarship from the Harold Hyam Wingate Foundation and by the "TMR" Network "GEOPRO—Integrating Geochemical and Mineralogical Techniques: a new approach to raw materials and archaeological ceramic provenance," funded by the European Commission (ERB FMRX CT 98-0165).

1. Betancourt 1984.
2. Betancourt et al. 1979.
3. Betancourt 1984.

linking a detailed study of pottery technology with an understanding of social reproduction in the Cretan Bronze Age, illustrated by a case study of the technology and historical context of Kamares Ware in the Mesara.

ACADEMIC TRADITIONS AND CERAMIC TRADITIONS

> Potsherds are asked to be heat-resistant or water-proof, matrilocal or patrilocal, relics of traumatic invasion or benign diffusion, insignia of domestic or market economies —in short, sensitive measures of virtually all cultural phenomena.[4]

THE STUDY OF POTTERY has always held a prominent position in archaeological investigations. The ubiquity, abundance and good preservation of ceramics have made them one of the most reliable types of archaeological evidence. Their use in archaeology has varied widely from indicating human presence in surface surveys, through constructing typologies and chronological sequences, to revealing complex social processes of production and exchange. Such is the reliance on pottery in interpretation that skeptics have suggested that this ceramic infatuation is less a feature of ancient society and more a reflection of the shortcomings of the archaeological record. Although there may be some truth in this criticism, one of the main aims of this paper is to examine one way in which the study of ceramic technology bears upon wider questions of social organization and sociopolitical transformation. We examine how the production and consumption of pottery may have had an important role in the articulation and reproduction of social identities in the area of the Mesara in south-central Crete during the Bronze Age. By studying specific aspects of the pottery system in a given area over time, we hope to demonstrate that the role of ceramics in the investigation of past cultural phenomena has not been overestimated; on the contrary, that ceramic technology can only be understood through the integrated study of both its material and social parameters.

Trajectories of Interpretation

Several authors have argued that the development of pottery studies can be organized into broad phases of a three-stage system: art historical, typological and contextual.[5] These classifications coincide broadly with the trajectory of the discipline of archaeology, with the duration and impact of the stages varying according to local archaeological traditions.

The same broad, historical development can be recognized in the study of Aegean ceramics. Early archaeological inquiry sprang out of antiquarianism, which placed primary value on the aesthetic evaluation of ancient objects. In this respect ceramic vessels were examined as art objects, the fine, decorated wares inevitably attracting most of the attention.

4. De Boer 1984, 529.
5. Orton et al. 1993, 3–22; see also Shepard 1956, 3; Matson 1984, 30; van der Leeuw 1984, 710–8; Arnold 1985, 4–12.

Such approaches emphasized vessel decoration: theme, composition, style and the recognition of individual artists. Although this might have been fruitful for Classical examples, where historical records and decorative scenes on the vessels aided identification and comment,[6] such approaches were not particularly suited to prehistoric ceramics. Nevertheless, prehistoric pottery studies followed the same route, with aesthetics prevailing over issues of production and technology, while exchange was thought possible only for high-quality, decorated examples. In addition, the appreciation of the significance of stratigraphy for archaeological studies meant that pottery was recognized as the most valuable tool for dating, with classifications constructed through a combination of stylistic and stratigraphic evidence.[7] However, its utility in constructing chronological sequences led to an underestimation of pottery in other areas of archaeological interpretation. In general, explanations of ceramics were restricted to their practical function as containers and, for the finest wares, as display items.

Aegean ceramics were also categorized according to regions of provenance. Hence chronological and stylistic categorizations were combined with findspots to generate cultural regions; for example, Minoan pottery, originating in Crete during the Bronze Age and having a particular style of vessel shape and decoration, was contrasted to Mycenaean, Helladic and Cycladic pottery, representing the products of other areas in the Aegean. Such classificatory schemes were extended to encompass particular types within cultural areas, such as Hagios Onouphrios Ware or Kamares Ware, named after their find location and their characteristic surface decoration. In this way the distribution of ceramic categories was correlated to cultural groups. Areas with similar pottery were considered a cultural unity and any changes in these patterns were ascribed to diffusion or invasion.[8]

Although the diffusionist accounts were largely discredited after the 1960s, certain associated assumptions persisted, notably that findspots represented production locations. This erroneous assumption of provenance has had serious repercussions in studies of Minoan pottery, and is very relevant to the case of Kamares Ware considered here. Pottery studies used an explanatory framework that viewed the vessels as a rather mundane craft item that was easy to manufacture, and when it came to coarse, unpainted vessels,[9] there seemed to be little doubt about the dominance of an unspecialized mode of production.

6. But see Morris 1994, for a critique of such one-dimensional approaches to the material culture of the Classical periods.

7. A prime early example of this method would be the ceramic sequence of Knossos as illustrated in Evans 1921; 1928; 1930; 1935.

8. A characteristic example exists in attitudes toward the transition from Neolithic to the Early Bronze Age. Changes in morphology and surface decoration appeared so pronounced that invasion of foreign tribes was considered a likely explanation. See, e.g., Hood 1990; for more detailed discussion, see Manteli 1993, 181–7.

9. Riley 1983, 284.

These assumptions remained unchallenged in the main, as pottery classification largely ignored technological parameters, relying instead on surface treatment or vessel shape, which provided meager grounds for highlighting technological information.[10]

Hence we were left with pottery as a chronological and cultural signpost. Read as an indicator of the nature of social groups, pottery existed as a material reflection of human presence within geographical space, with little recognition of value, exchange, reputation or its role as a social technology. Against this background, perhaps the most important contribution toward changing such views came with the application of scientific analysis to ceramics, initially from a reconsideration of pottery provenance.

The Contribution of Scientific Methods: Ceramic Analysis

From the 1960s onward, pottery studies witnessed a strong change of direction. Some of the earliest analytical work in the Aegean concentrated on establishing the long-distance trade in fine wares,[11] and further developments came in conjunction with the new concerns of archaeological theory, which sought to place more attention on issues of social organization.[12] In this respect, pottery was understood not simply as an object with aesthetic value, but rather as an ancient technology and, as a technological artifact, it acquired new significance for the exploration of economic and political issues.

The organization of production was placed at the center of inquiry with craft activity viewed as the best way to understand patterns of ancient production. It offered insights into the division of labor and relations of production, patterns of exchange and trade, the accumulation of wealth and the emergence of elites, all of which were central concerns of archaeological inquiry at the time. The application of scientific methods of analysis to illuminate aspects of ceramic manufacture and technology would prove highly beneficial to such research questions.

The first attempts in this direction focused mainly on decorated fine wares, in order to trace the provenance of specific vessels of the Late Bronze Age.[13] It was generally expected that most of the main sites of the Bronze Age Aegean would have manufactured their own pottery. However, the presence in Crete of vessels of obviously Mycenaean character meant that some movement of ceramics was possible, and consequently it was necessary to verify such observations with chemical analysis.[14] In this work, the legacy of an art-historical approach was evident in a preoccupation with individual vases and fine wares, and the explanatory focus was firmly on the palaces. Therefore it should not come as a surprise that the arti-

10. Wilson and Day 1994, 2.
11. Catling et al. 1961; 1963.
12. E.g., Renfrew 1972.
13. R.E. Jones 1986, 10.
14. Catling et al. 1961; 1963.

facts most evidently connected with the palaces were to come under scientific scrutiny first.

The next stage of analytical work emphasized economic aspects of the pottery system, particularly exchange and specialization. Initially, two types of ceramic exchange were considered: 1) individual vases exchanged as gifts between elites (favored by the art-historical approach); and 2) ceramic containers circulated through trade, being exchanged mainly for their contents (generally favored by the systemic approach). It was thought, moreover, that coarse, undecorated containers could be exchanged within the territory of a redistributive state centered around the palace, as well as between different states trading commodities such as wine and oil in ceramic vessels.[15] The abundance of pottery artifacts and the easy availability of raw materials for pottery manufacture implied to researchers that ceramics were so mundane they had to be produced by nearly everyone, and thus that pottery did not lend itself to the investigation of competitive acquisition and the symbolic. Therefore, the evidence of ceramic exchange served only to highlight functional aspects of pottery in the local economies.

When it came to craft specialization, however, pottery took on a more prominent role. A new emphasis on technology meant that the development of pottery manufacture could be traced through time, from the initial crude attempts to mold clay to high-quality vessels utilizing sophisticated firing technology and methods of forming and decoration. Thus pottery was examined from an evolutionary perspective, progressing from simple to complex with technical innovations, such as the introduction of the fast wheel, seen as effecting major transformations in the process of production.[16] The patterns of ceramic development, therefore, became closely connected with the emergence of social complexity. Concepts such as craft specialization and standardization of production were introduced in the archaeological literature largely on evidence deriving from the study of ceramics. Craft specialization in particular has been closely connected to the emergence of political elites and state societies in almost every part of the world[17] and until recently held a central position in the investigation of the emergence of elites and the rise of palatial society in Minoan Crete.[18]

The issue of specialization had initially been approached without the aid of scientific analysis. The evident elaboration of shape and decoration of Palatial pottery in comparison to Prepalatial examples was used to argue that craft specialization was characteristic of a more complex social system, such as that represented by Minoan Palatial societies, whereas Prepalatial settlements were thought to present no evidence for institutionalized

15. Riley 1983, 288–90; Day 1988a; 1997.

16. Betancourt 1985; Cherry 1986; cf. Day and Wilson 1998; Knappett 1999.

17. Rice 1981; 1991; Brumfiel and Earle 1987.

18. Renfrew 1972; Branigan 1983; 1987; Cherry 1983; 1986; Manning 1994.

divisions of labor and production beyond the needs of the household.[19] However, several researchers recognized elements of specialized craft production in the EM period,[20] but tended to consider such specialists as producing for their own community and on a small scale.[21] Moreover, evidence for specialization generally was not established through technological observations, but instead was based largely on evaluation of style and the identification of a putative potter's workshop in EM IIB Myrtos Phournou Koriphi.[22] Such approaches did not steer away from an evolutionary perspective of ceramic development inasmuch as they reproduced the picture of Early Minoan society as a simple precursor of the more advanced technological (and social) developments that were to follow.

Scientific analysis of distinctive ceramics, such as Vasiliki Ware[23] and East Cretan White-on-Dark Ware,[24] demonstrated that the production of some pottery required a substantial amount of specialized knowledge. It underemphasized, however, the identification of production centers. The distribution and relative frequency of certain ceramic wares in particular areas continued to represent the most influential way of recognizing production centers across the island.[25] The full potential of ceramic analysis was, however, realized in later studies. These demonstrated that, on the one hand, ceramics could move in large quantities despite the existence of local production in the areas participating in the exchanges,[26] and on the other, that the pottery system of the EM period was far more complex than previously assumed.[27] Integrated studies of EM ceramics demonstrated the clearly specialized nature of the production of certain wares in terms of raw material selection, clay paste recipes and ware/area specialization, indicating that advanced traditions of pottery making could be identified in different parts of Crete from the EM I period.[28] Studies of the Early Neolithic assemblage of Knossos further emphasized these points and highlighted a pattern of intra- and possibly inter-island exchanges of ceramics from this early period.[29] Although these studies cast doubt on the validity of specialization as a way to conceptualize and study ancient technology, the significance of such approaches for evaluating the link between technology and society has not yet been fully appreciated in Minoan studies.

19. Cherry 1983; 1984; Whitelaw 1983.
20. Branigan 1988, 74; Renfrew 1972, 342; Betancourt 1985, 35.
21. Day et al. 1997, 276.
22. Warren 1972.
23. Betancourt et al. 1979.
24. Betancourt 1984.
25. Betancourt et al. 1979, 27.
26. Riley 1983; 1984; Day 1988b; 1991; 1997; Knappett 1999.
27. Wilson and Day 1994; Day et al. 1997; 1998; Whitelaw et al. 1997.
28. Day et al. 1997.
29. Tomkins 2001; Tomkins and Day 2001; Tomkins et al. 2004.

Contemporary Perspectives

There has been a clear preoccupation, instead, with economic aspects of ancient ceramic technologies, which lend themselves easily to a comparative approach. Alternative perspectives often used ethnography to illuminate a symbolic dimension of ceramics,[30] but in many cases were undermined by an extreme specificity, which left no room for generalization regarding social aspects of pottery technology. Hence the exploration of symbolic aspects of technology was often restricted to studies of style while the more functional dimensions of technology were thought to be deprived of social implications. Any consideration of the relationship between technology and society remained largely characterized by a dichotomy that illustrates either the effects of technology on social organization (e.g., innovation enabling an increase in productivity, generating the need for centralized administrative control) or the opposite, sociopolitical changes triggering transformations in the technological cycle.[31]

Recently, a series of studies has focused on these problems, attempting to bridge this gap between economic and social aspects of technological production.[32] It has become clear that ceramic studies have the ability to transcend the false dichotomy between purely functional or exclusively symbolic dimensions and examine ceramic technology in its own right, as an activity that is embedded in society, and is bound equally by practical/physical and social constraints. One might argue that in Crete this has been covered by studies that draw attention to traditions in pottery making.[33] It would be true to say, however, that the precise nature and dynamics of such technological phenomena have yet to be explored fully.

It is argued here that the survival of stylistic elements from period to period is not a sufficient criterion by which to understand ceramic traditions, but that a range of factors needs to be explored and the dialectic between innovation and stability needs to be revealed. The investigation of long-lasting ceramic traditions in a specific area and within a specific historical context may allow us to demonstrate how pottery studies can move beyond such dichotomies, how observations on a micro-level (sherds, pots) can give us insights into macro-level inquiries (organization of production, long-term patterns, innovation, sociopolitical change). We must keep in mind that production processes and consumption patterns are interrelated domains, which cannot be understood separately, despite archaeological approaches that have treated them as separate aspects of the ceramic system. In this paper, we suggest that such an approach proves particularly advantageous because it examines a tradi-

30. E.g., Hodder 1982.
31. Lemonnier 1992, 13; van der Leeuw 1993, 240.
32. Lemonnier 1992; 1993; Mahias 1993; Dietler and Herbich 1998; Hegmon 1995; 1998; A. Jones 2002.
33. E.g., Betancourt 1984; Whitelaw et al. 1997.

tion of pottery manufacture in its historical context—how "ways of doing" were allowed or encouraged to persist through time by virtue of specific historical conditions that may have accentuated the role of pottery in social negotiation.

We use this case study as a summary, an illustrative example to indicate a profitable approach to the full-scale delineation of ceramic histories.[34] The study of Kamares Ware is a suitable way to explore the issues introduced above, since this particular type of pottery has been considered the epitome of palatial sophistication and the most obvious example of social transformation bringing about technological change. The Mesara offers a particularly advantageous setting for such an investigation because of the extensive documentation of ceramic activity in the area and its compatibility with the "state emergence-craft specialization" hypothesis.

Our study will examine the technology of Middle Minoan polychrome pottery in comparison with Prepalatial ware groups in the area, such as Fine Painted Ware. By the careful investigation of aspects of pottery manufacture, from raw material selection through decoration and firing, and the combined consideration of the patterns and contexts of the consumption of these vessels, we aim to demonstrate how the ways of producing pottery developed in a powerful tradition that became embedded in the everyday life of the inhabitants of the Mesara. We shall examine the implications of our observations:

1) for understanding the place of craft activity during the Palatial period, which has been distinguished from the Prepalatial on the basis of discontinuities in architectural and political organization;

2) for exploring the ways in which traditions of pottery making have operated as a means of negotiating and reproducing social identities in the Mesara during the Bronze Age; and finally,

3) for appreciating the potential of integrated technological approaches of ceramics for building an understanding of social production and reproduction in Minoan society.

KAMARES WARE

KAMARES WARE is the hallmark pottery of the Middle Minoan period. It was named after the Kamares Cave on the southern flank of the Ida mountain range, where it was first discovered.[35] Although the use of the term Kamares Ware can be problematic,[36] there are

34. We concentrate here on selected observations on pottery technology in the Mesara of the EM IIA and Protopalatial periods. Pottery of the EM IIB–MM IA period at Phaistos and Hagia Triada is currently under study by Simona Todaro and the extension of analysis to these later Prepalatial phases will cover vital lacunae in our illustrative case study.

35. Mariani 1895; Myres 1893–1895; Dawkins and Laistner 1912–1913.

36. MacGillivray 1986.

some generally accepted features that characterize this type of pottery. In stylistic terms it can be described as a type of polychrome pottery that has a black-slipped surface with an almost metallic sheen, on top of which abstract and naturalistic painted motifs are applied in white, red, orange and occasionally purple. It is encountered in both fine and coarse varieties. The former are usually wheel thrown, and there exist rare vessels with very thin walls that are referred to as Eggshell Ware. The larger vessels continue to be handmade for the most part.[37] Polychrome ware is attested in a range of shapes, with the most frequent examples in pouring and serving vessels (cups, bridge-spouted jars, beak-spouted jugs), but amphorae for liquid storage, large pedestaled bowls, low tripod stands or tables and storage pithoi also are decorated in polychrome.[38]

The first stage of the study of Kamares Ware focused mainly on chronological issues, as it was soon realized that this type of ware was common in the Middle Minoan assemblages from Knossos and Phaistos. Moreover, Kamares appeared to be found almost exclusively at these two palatial centers. The material from Knossos was the first to be subjected to a systematic study by Mackenzie.[39] As Walberg notes,[40] this, and the studies that followed,[41] examined Kamares vessels as archaeological finds, with stylistic considerations of form and decoration being treated separately. Stylistic analysis of Kamares was conducted later by Zoes[42] followed by Walberg[43] who focused exclusively on issues of surface decoration and vessel form, while a general study of the pottery groups of the Old Palace period by Andreou[44] clarified chronological issues and correlations between different sites. By the time Walberg's thorough study was published, a greater amount of Kamares pottery had been unearthed at both Knossos and Phaistos, but also at a number of other sites, prompting her to publish a second survey of polychrome ceramics under the title *Provincial Middle Minoan Pottery*.[45]

Our knowledge of Kamares pottery was also greatly enriched after the publication of Levi's excavations at Phaistos,[46] which included detailed illustration of a wide range of shapes and motifs. Although initial work on workshops and artisans of Kamares Ware[47] was criticized,[48] the subsequent years of research at Phaistos and Hagia Triada by the Ital-

37. Day and Wilson 1998, 352; Knappett 1999, 121–5.
38. Betancourt 1985, 97–100.
39. Mackenzie 1906.
40. Walberg 1976, 11.
41. Evans 1921; 1928; 1930; 1935; Pendlebury 1939.
42. Zoes 1968.
43. Walberg 1976.
44. Andreou 1978.
45. Walberg 1983.
46. Levi 1976; Levi and Carinci 1988.
47. Pelagatti 1961–1962.
48. Walberg 1981.

ian School of Archaeology at Athens[49] not only shed more light on the abundance and complexity of Kamares material from the Mesara, but also paved the way for exploration of the possibility that there was more than one production workshop for Kamares in the area.[50] Moreover, recent excavations have revealed late Prepalatial levels at Phaistos, with a rich ceramic sequence from EM IIB on, through to a series of MM IA floors.[51]

Although Kamares pottery had always been considered an exclusive feature of the palaces (with the exception of ritual sites such as the Kamares Cave), Walberg was the first to make a distinction between Kamares proper (i.e., of palatial origin) and provincial pottery (presumably manufactured by rural production centers in imitation of Kamares) and to correlate this difference to the existence of distinct ceramic workshops.[52] Most recently, our knowledge of Kamares has benefited from the publication of the Knossos Old Palace pottery groups by MacGillivray[53] and the examination of other Middle Minoan polychrome traditions in the east of the island.[54]

Although the benefits of Walberg's studies were substantial, such work also introduced a number of problematic assumptions about Kamares Ware that were reflected in the archaeological literature until very recently. Most influential among such approaches has been that put forward by Cherry[55] in his study of the Peer Polity Interaction model, which correlated Kamares Ware explicitly with the emergence of complex societies in Minoan Crete. The main factors affecting the understanding of Kamares pottery were its distribution (initially appearing to be restricted to palatial sites) and its remarkable stylistic and technological sophistication, which made it clear to researchers that it must be viewed as an elite product. Moreover, since the emergence of the palaces and the first appearance of Kamares vessels coincided, both in time and space, this particular pottery has been seen as a technological innovation brought about by the new social regime of the palaces. The general assumption is that palatial administration took over production by establishing craft workshops in the palaces, introducing wheel-thrown vessels and sponsoring exchange of the finished items with the aim of establishing and promoting elite alliances in neighboring polities.[56]

However, although there may be aspects of Kamares Ware that lend themselves to elite manipulation and power negotiation, reliance solely on stylistic features and find locations

49. Carinci 1997; 1999.

50. Carinci 1995.

51. Whitley 2002–2003, 82–3.

52. Walberg 1983; 1987.

53. MacGillivray 1998.

54. Poursat 1997; Knappett 1997; Floyd 1997.

55. Cherry 1986, 35–8.

56. Renfrew 1972; Cherry 1986; Betancourt 1985, 104; Branigan 1983.

in considering the organization of production and its social implications is unnecessarily limiting and potentially misleading. Recent analytic work, moreover, provides important hints as to the misconceptions of such approaches.[57] Let us examine these assumptions in more detail.

The belief that Kamares Ware has only a very restricted distribution has been challenged, since the polychrome style has been recognized at a substantial number of different sites. In the specific case of the Mesara, Kamares Ware has been retrieved not only from the palace of Phaistos but also from Hagia Triada,[58] Kommos[59] and in almost all the tholos cemeteries that continue to be used in this period, as well as at partially excavated sites like Kalamaki[60] and sites identified by surface surveys.[61] However, although the presence of Kamares material at Hagia Triada and Kommos is often considered natural by virtue of the privileged position of these sites in a political hierarchy, the rest of the material is dubbed "provincial" even though it is difficult to distinguish from the products of palatial workshops.[62] Before rushing to attribute all the Kamares material to the output of palatial workshops, however, it is desirable to examine in more detail the technological development and the historical context of Kamares production and consumption in the Mesara.

Apart from the misconceptions over distribution, Kamares Ware's spectacular, sophisticated nature has also affected its interpretation. The main argument behind Walberg's distinction of provincial and palatial varieties is based upon the refinement of the Kamares products: "The Kamares style is a sophisticated palatial style and could only have been produced in the social surroundings of the palaces."[63] Such views are also echoed in Cherry's treatment of the issue: "Although few scientific provenance analyses have been carried out and other ceramic production centres of 'palatial' character may have existed, it seems quite clear on present evidence that true Kamares pottery was an exclusive product of workshops at Knossos and Phaistos."[64] Clearly we must put these comments into context, for they were written before several recent analytical studies, and in any case contain some valid suggestions. However, it is still striking that despite the lack of clear evidence for the existence of pottery workshops in the palatial centers, the assertion seemed inevitable: Kamares is an elite artifact, therefore it must have been produced by the palaces. Thus it

57. Day and Wilson 1998; Faber et al. 2002.

58. Carinci 1997; 1999.

59. Betancourt 1990; Van de Moortel 1997; 2002.

60. Karetsou 1978; Vallianou 1979.

61. Blackman and Branigan 1977, 41–3, 58; Vasilakis 1989–1990, 56–8; Watrous et al. 1993, 224; Hope Simpson et al. 1995, 395–6.

62. Walberg 1983.

63. Walberg 1976, 126.

64. Cherry 1986, 37.

seems clear that apart from the artifacts themselves, our preconceptions about the economic role of the palaces as centers of production and distribution has also promoted the assumption that Kamares was manufactured in the palaces.[65]

The presumed economic role of the palaces had further repercussions for the study of Kamares. The elaboration of the decoration and the apparent technical achievements of this ware were thought to be clear indications of specialized production, which was seen as an unequivocal outcome of the emergence of social complexity, an emergence embodied in the palaces. Moreover, since the majority of Kamares vessels had been wheel thrown, the introduction of the fast wheel was interpreted as a palatial step toward standardization and mass production, which furthermore allowed the manufacture of more sophisticated shapes.[66] However, all these attributes must be reconsidered in the light of new analysis of Minoan ceramics.

Studies of Prepalatial ceramics[67] have demonstrated that Early Minoan pottery exhibited many of the technical features used to indicate specialization of production. Moreover, petrographic analysis of Prepalatial wares also hinted at large scale movement of ceramics between different regions of the island, an observation that ran contrary to the standard view of Prepalatial ceramics being consumed only in the communities producing them.[68] Therefore the assumption that the emergence of the palaces introduced specialization in the ceramic process would seem unfounded. Clearly, there were major changes in the ceramic system of the Middle Minoan period, but these should normally be viewed within a continuum of technological and other transformations and not only as the direct result of an institutionalization of ceramic production.

The reevaluation of specialization, and indeed the introduction of specific techniques, also has important repercussions for ideas of standardization and mass production. Although Cherry[69] maintains that the introduction of the fast wheel "allowed the creation of sophisticated shapes, standardization and mass production," such features do not characterize the products of Kamares Ware. There is so much variation in shape and decoration within the repertoire of Kamares that Walberg[70] remarked that it proves difficult to find two identical Kamares vessels, a view that seems widely shared.[71] Moreover, the timing and the implications of the wide introduction and adoption of the potter's wheel in the Protopalatial period have been recently reevaluated, placing greater emphasis on the

65. Day and Wilson 1998, 352.

66. Cherry 1986, 37.

67. Day et al. 1997; Whitelaw et al. 1997; Kiriatzi et al. 2000.

68. Wilson and Day 1994; Day et al. 1997; Whitelaw et al. 1997; Day et al. 1998; Kiriatzi et al. 2000.

69. Cherry 1986, 37.

70. Walberg 1976, 21.

71. Betancourt 1990, 3–37; Carinci 1997, 321; Van de Moortel 1997, 221.

intensified use of such a technology.[72] Indeed, Knappett's incisive paper on forming techniques[73] shows that the introduction of specific vessel types that exploit "rotative kinetic energy" was selective and not a natural technological progression. He suggests that, ultimately, the technological innovation may have been adopted by a palatial elite from its area of origin in the Near East. However, even in this case it is made clear that the new techniques were the exception, within a strong continuity of forming traditions.

Within such frameworks of consideration, Day and Wilson's[74] petrographic analysis of Kamares pottery from the palace of Knossos aimed to shed more light on the problem of the location of production of the ware. In contrast to what was believed before, their study indicated that a significant portion of the Middle Minoan polychrome pottery of Knossos had not been produced there, but instead was imported from south-central Crete and notably from locations in the western part of the Mesara Plain.[75] Such a pattern was strongly reminiscent of the situation in EM IIA, when fine drinking and serving vessels were imported to Knossos from the Mesara.[76] However, the most remarkable discovery was that certain fabrics identified in the EM ceramics continued almost unchanged in the imported Middle Minoan pottery. In a first consideration, such continuity led to the suggestion that "Kamares Ware may be viewed within the context of pottery production in centres which existed already in the Prepalatial period, and perhaps not as the product of workshops established with the First Palaces."[77] The implications of this observation may be significant not only for the way we understand the production of Kamares Ware, but also for our understanding of the organization of the palaces and their role in Minoan society. In the next section we offer a first elaboration of such an inquiry, by exploring in greater detail aspects of ceramic production in the Mesara from the EM to the MM period, along with the patterns of consumption. We attempt to define and evaluate the role of such ceramic traditions in the development of social life in the Mesara.

MESARA POLYCHROME POTTERY IN HISTORICAL CONTEXT: A CASE STUDY

In the present consideration of Middle Minoan polychrome pottery from the Mesara, we discuss a variety of evidence relating to the production of the vessels. The discussion is not intended to be exhaustive, but will highlight points of technology promi-

72. Day and Wilson 1998, 353; Knappett 1999.
73. Knappett 1999.
74. Day and Wilson 1998.
75. Day and Wilson 1998, 356.
76. Wilson and Day 1994.
77. Day and Wilson 1998, 355.

nent in the work of Betancourt and his coworkers. After brief comment on shapes and motifs, the more traditional aspects of the consideration of Kamares Ware, we move to three areas of technology: the choice and manipulation of raw materials, some specific evidence for forming techniques, and the technology of the surface decoration for which Kamares Ware is so well known.

Form and Function

Kamares Ware appears in a variety of shapes, sizes and coarseness of body: from fine cups through jugs and stands, to amphorae and pithoid jars. The most obvious factor that unites this broad spectrum of pottery vessels is, by definition, the distinctive, high quality of their decoration. But there are other features that bring them together as a class: their tendency to imitate vessels of metal and other precious materials[78] and their frequent connection with the drinking, pouring and storage of liquids.[79] MacGillivray[80] has noted that many of the vessels belong to drinking sets, with the bridge-spouted jar probably acting as a mixing and pouring vessel, perhaps for wine or another special drink. While the leap from form to function is not without danger, the basic shapes of many Kamares Ware vessels are those familiar in the Mesara from EM IIA onward with some shape features, such as the neck moldings on jugs,[81] appearing to continue into the Middle Minoan period. Late Prepalatial deposits in the Mesara, such as the teapots from Patrikies,[82] may have served a similar function, as did some of the long-spouted jars of the late EM II period and the even earlier side-spouted bowl of Fine Painted Ware from the Mesara.[83]

It could be argued that after the introduction of drinking sets by EM IIB,[84] drinking ceremonies formed the primary focus for the use of pottery vessels. Perhaps this continuity in form is so general as to carry little meaning? While practices clearly must have changed over time and it has been suggested that activity at the palaces entailed a deliberate appropriation of preexisting ritual practices,[85] the drinking vessels are certainly not the only distinctive vessels to show links between the Prepalatial and Protopalatial repertoire. Some shapes that are perhaps less generic also feature prominently in both EM IIA Dark-on-Light Painted and Middle Minoan Kamares Ware. One example is the pedestaled bowl or large fruitstand, which was found frequently in EM IIA contexts at Hagia Kyriaki and

78. Walberg 1976, 34–42.
79. Walberg 1976, 14–21.
80. MacGillivray 1998.
81. Walberg 1976, 36.
82. Bonacasa 1967–1968.
83. Wilson and Day 1994; Day and Wilson 2004.
84. Day and Wilson 2004.
85. Day and Wilson 2002.

elsewhere.[86] These vessels seem to be a continuing component of ritual life in south-central Crete, with the focus of their use moving perhaps from the funerary arena to that of the palatial central buildings.

One specific aspect of the forms of Kamares also has a long tradition in the area: skeuomorphism, or the imitation in pottery of other materials (metal, stone, leather bags, ostrich eggs). Walberg[87] details the ways in which Kamares pots imitate metal vessels, by means of details such as crinkle rims, laid-on handles, rivets and raised bases. She demonstrates that these vessels become increasingly "metallizing" over the period of Kamares Ware and that they are altered versions of originally metal types. Walberg is right to note the roots of this skeuomorphic trend in EM II.[88] Not only can it be argued that the earlier Prepalatial Fine Painted and Fine Gray Wares deliberately imitate metals vessels,[89] but it also can be suggested of the even earlier vessels of EM I.[90] This tendency becomes almost extreme in the Middle Minoan period when details of relief of the polychrome vessels make clear their imitation of metal prototypes.

While these properties are in no way exclusive to this region of production, drinking vessels that imitate metal seem to be one of the main features of prehistoric Cretan ceramics; the combination of continuity of form and imitation is one aspect of diachronic ceramic tradition in the Mesara.

Motifs and Color Combination

Walberg's thorough scholarship offers detailed analysis of the decorative motifs of Kamares Ware, putting these motifs in perspective in the consideration of tradition and innovation in the prehistoric art of Crete.[91] She has pointed out the ways in which the decorative schemes used are far from standardized in their combination, but employ repeated motifs. While it seems clear that the representational motifs on pottery find their origin in the EM III period, and especially in the White-on-Dark style in eastern Crete,[92] other aspects of Kamares decoration Walberg traces to earlier times. She argues convincingly that EM I Hagios Onouphrios vessels from the Mesara have a unity of decoration similar to that of Kamares Ware, as well as sharing many aspects of syntax, from torsion to experimentation with disintegration products of designs. One of the most striking links between the Prepalatial and Protopalatial Mesara is the use of reversible decoration.[93] Specific motifs

86. Wilson and Day 1994, 44–7; Blackman and Branigan 1982, fig. 13.170–2.
87. Walberg 1976, 36–42.
88. Walberg 1976, 39.
89. Wilson and Day 1994.
90. Wilson and Day 2000, 57–8.
91. Walberg 1986.
92. Walberg 1986, 6–38.
93. Walberg 1976, 80–1, 126.

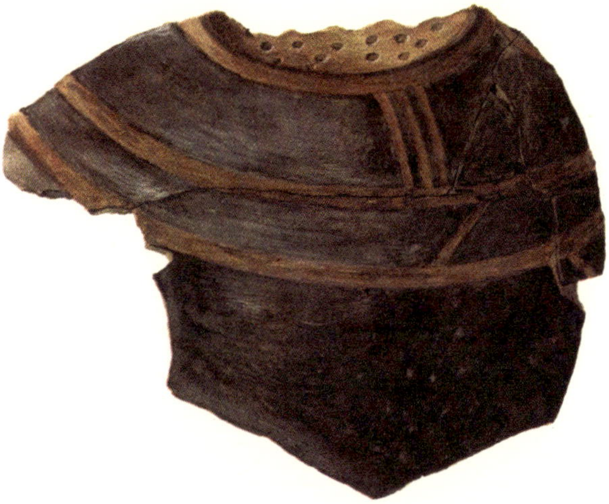

FIG. 1. Final Neolithic vessel 1871 (Levi 1976, pl. IIb, courtesy of the Italian School of Archaeology at Athens).

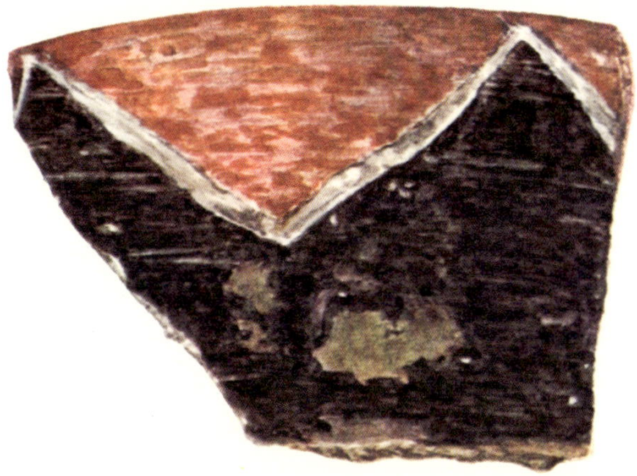

FIG. 2. Final Neolithic vessel (Levi 1976, pl. IIIa, courtesy of the Italian School of Archaeology at Athens).

popular in products of the Mesara in EM II, such as the checkerboard pattern[94] and small "slashed handles" that appear in Fine Gray Ware pyxides,[95] can be seen in some Classical Kamares products from the same region, with painted, slashed handles being very common and the checkerboard pattern occurring in some key Kamares examples.[96]

A vessel from the new excavations at Phaistos (fig. 4) sheds further light on the continuity of motifs. Dating to MM IA, its shoulder has groups of three crossing diagonal lines in black paint on a reserved buff area, with polychrome decoration around the neck. The motif on the reserved ground is very familiar from EM IIA in the Mesara.[97]

Similarly, the combination of colors in Mesara pottery has a long history. Kamares itself uses combinations of black, white, red, orange and in some instances a purple color (figs. 5, 6). Walberg[98] points to a pre-Kamares phase as heralding a number of elements in decoration that signal the start of the specific Kamares style. These vessels belong to the MM IA phase and therefore predate the construction of the palace of Phaistos. But this inventive use of a combination of colors goes back much earlier in the Mesara. Levi's observation[99] that Final Neolithic pottery at Phaistos used combinations of white and red paint on a black background[100] prompted him to consider the EM period to be only a short interlude before the palaces (figs. 1, 2). But we do not have to accept his chronology to see

94. Blackman and Branigan 1982, fig. 12; Wilson and Day 1994, figs. 3–4, 6.
95. Wilson and Day 1994, 10, fig. 40.
96. Walberg 1976, fig. 13; Schiering 1998, table 50.1.
97. Blackman and Branigan 1982, fig. 11.117, 119.
98. Walberg 1976, 76–7.
99. Levi 1957–1958, 159–66.
100. For discussion and illustrations, see Vagnetti 1972–1973, 73–4, 80–2, table II, esp. II.1; Vagnetti and Belli 1978, 127.

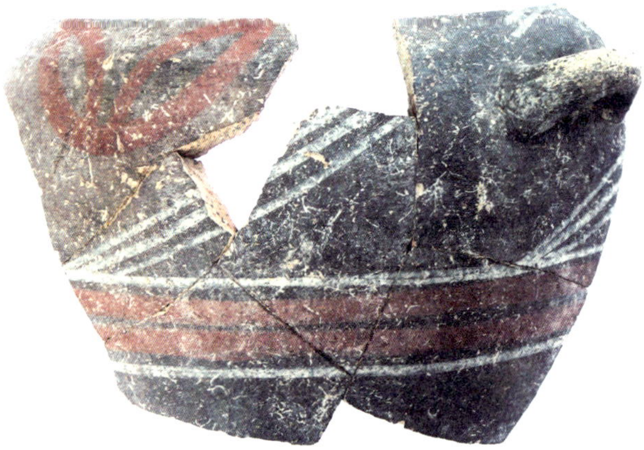

Fig. 3. Late Prepalatial polychrome vessel from recent excavations at Phaistos (La Rosa 2002, fig. 460, courtesy of V. La Rosa and S. Todaro).

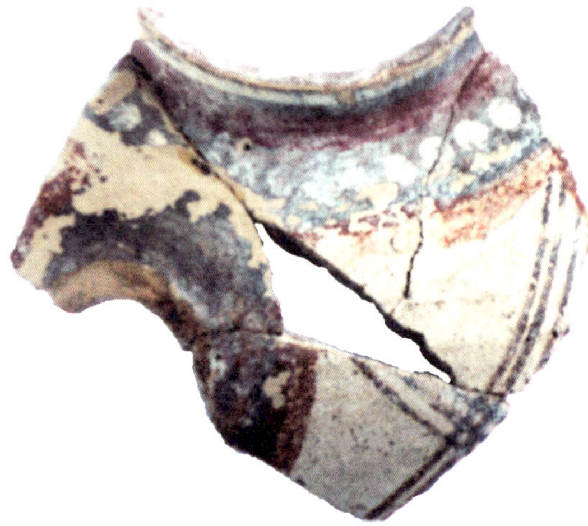

Fig. 4. Late Prepalatial polychrome vessel from recent excavations at Phaistos (La Rosa 2002, fig. 455, courtesy of V. La Rosa and S. Todaro).

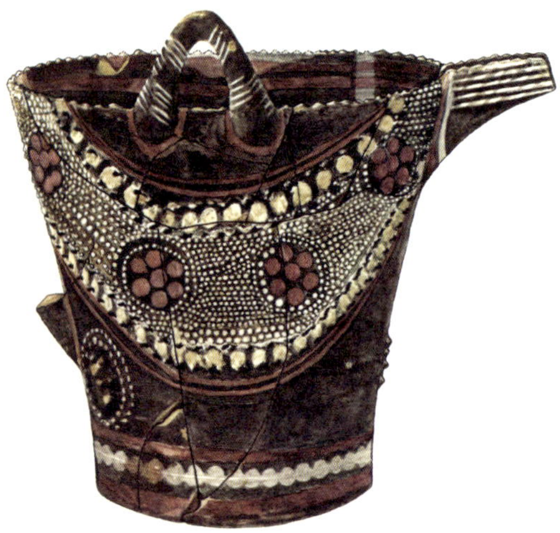

Fig. 5. Middle Minoan polychrome vessel F5482 (Levi 1976, pl. XVa, courtesy of the Italian School of Archaeology at Athens).

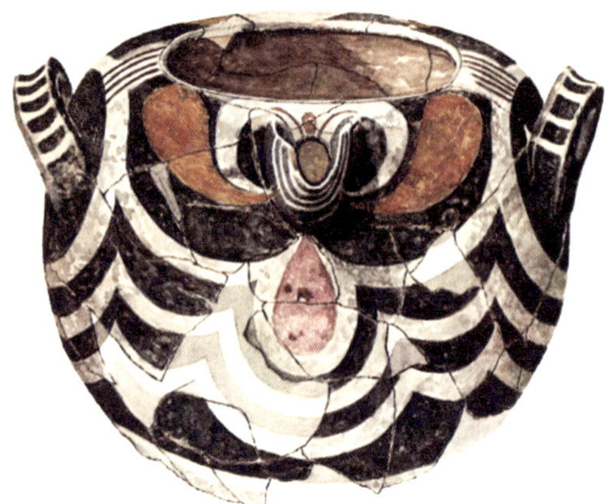

Fig. 6. Middle Minoan polychrome vessel F6160 (Levi 1976, pl. XXXVIIa, courtesy of the Italian School of Archaeology at Athens).

why such continuity might be posited, as there existed both light-on-dark and dark-on-light decoration from the EM I period, in the forms of Lebena Ware and Hagios Onouphrios Ware. Late Prepalatial pottery from recent excavations at Phaistos shows the purple paint present in some Mesara Kamares products, in one example in combination with dark-on-light crosshatching familiar from EM IIA (figs. 3, 4).[101]

101. The black-slipped pot is in La Rosa 2002, fig. 460.

Analytical Approaches: An Introduction

With the exception of a summary petrographic report[102] and some restricted investigations by chemical analysis of its provenance,[103] most previous analyses of Kamares Ware have concentrated on an appreciation and reconstruction of the techniques of its decoration. It is not our intention to discuss broad issues of provenance in this paper, but the technological observations of previous investigations will be discussed together with our own. We will demonstrate that analytical work suggests some strong lines of continuity in details of the pottery production process in the Mesara region. Clear changes in technological practice emerge, mainly involving firing competence, but these improvements, whether gradual or sudden, can be shown to have a firm basis in previous production within the same area. Regardless of the arguments over the longevity of traditions, this study offers important new evidence on the technology of white pigments and their ability to distinguish palatial production.

Raw Materials and Recipes

In seeking diachronic patterns in pottery technology, raw materials might seem to be the most likely to produce a picture of stability. After all, if clays and other ingredients were obtained near the production location, surely geological factors would lead to a homogeneity of composition. This, of course, is the underlying assumption of pottery provenance research: that within a given study area intra-source variability will be less than that on an inter-source level—the provenance postulate.[104] Yet clearly, archaeological ceramics are much more than clay altered by firing through human action.[105] Raw materials are chosen, they are added to or refined; they are levigated, mixed, tempered. Undoubtedly, the raw materials of a specific area may have properties that would benefit from specific alteration. The dominant clay source in an area might be too plastic for efficient forming and require the addition of coarser material; a silty deposit might require levigation. But such choices and actions of the potter have much more than a mechanical basis. They do not rely simply on choices made on the spur of the moment.

Rather, the ingredients of a clay recipe are something that is learned by craftspeople from their teachers, and is part of their technological *habitus*.[106] Most pottery producing environments present the potter with a myriad of possible raw material combinations, only some of which are perceived to be possible by the potter.[107] The potter, thus, navigates a chosen course in a culturally informed manner. This is important, as the potter's repeated ac-

102. Day and Wilson 1998.

103. Kilikoglou et al. 1990; Fitton et al. 1998.

104. Weigand et al. 1977; Hein, Day, Cau Ontiveros and Kilikoglou 2004; Hein, Day, Quinn and Kilikoglou 2004.

105. Contra Peacock 1977; Whitbread 1989; Burton and Simon 1996.

106. Dietler and Herbich 1998; Livingstone Smith 2000.

107. van der Leeuw 1993.

tions form part of the broader sphere of social reproduction. As much as the consumption of food, the structure of marriage celebrations and the nature of gift giving, pottery production is a technology of life and, therefore, a rich source of information for the archaeologist.

While change over time in shape and decoration of pottery forms the very basis of our ceramic chronologies, times of stability and change in ceramic fabric are also common. More recently this has been exploited in the dating by fabric of pottery from surface surveys.[108] What, perhaps, has not been given equal prominence in the literature are the strong traditions that persist over time and space in the clay recipes used in Crete. Perhaps the best known of these characteristic fabrics is that produced around the Isthmus of Ierapetra from the Early Neolithic onward, commonly referred to as the Mirabello fabric.[109] Although coming in a variety of forms (the most obvious split being between calcareous and non-calcareous versions, as well as the more traditional coarse/fine division), the Mirabello family of fabrics reflects a clear trajectory of a history of raw material choice within what was clearly an important ceramic production area. The continuities in choices made are the result of knowledge and practice, reproduced and passed down by craftspeople over long swaths of time.

The choice and manipulation of raw materials in the Mesara Plain might not, as yet, have the recorded antiquity of the Mirabello fabrics, but their consistency from late in the Neolithic, at least throughout the entire Bronze Age, is clear. One specific, broad fabric type is characterized by frequent sand inclusions in a relatively fine matrix, whose specific origin, lithological derivation and clay matrix has been discussed at some length.[110] The issue here is to examine some of the fabrics used in the production of Mesara polychrome pottery, to determine what they represent in terms of potters' behavior and to assess the degree of continuity in such practices.

The nature of the ceramic paste in some of the Mesara polychrome pottery is often very distinctive. The Middle Minoan examples discussed here come primarily from Phaistos, but are also present as imports at Knossos. Although there exists a variety of fabrics, we will concentrate on two: one fine and one coarse. Characteristic of Mesara products is the combination of the two distinct fabrics in the same vessel (see Layering discussion below), a practice that highlights the fabrics' existence as independent, operationalized craft concepts, rather than simply the products of a specific resource environment.

There is, of course, an almost unlimited range of factors that we could discuss in an account of Mesara fabrics. Here we will emphasize the following in consideration of the coarser fabrics: the texture of the clay matrix or micromass, the petrological and textural nature of the aplastic inclusions, and the voids present in the fabrics.

108. Moody 1985; Haggis and Mook 1993.

109. Day 1991; Day 1997, 225; Myer et al. 1995, 143–5.

110. Myer and Betancourt 1990, 9–10; Wilson and Day 1994.

CLAY MATRIX. Some of the finest fabrics present in Kamares Ware appear to be comprised of a very fine clay matrix derived from a fine, calcareous Neogene clay. These are widely available across central Crete and in petrographic analysis offer few clues to discriminate origin. Such very fine clays first appeared in EM IIA in this area of Crete and are employed in Fine Painted Ware (fig. 7a–f).[111]

Myer and Betancourt were the first to point out the frequency of evidence for clay mixing of the finer fractions of Mesara fabrics.[112] They suggested that the most likely combination was of calcareous Neogene clays with low-calcareous, red *terra rossa* deposits, a recipe familiar from modern potters on Crete. While textural concentration features are often difficult to interpret, let alone describe,[113] the evidence for clay mixing is clear, for example, in the case of the Neopalatial kiln at Kommos.[114]

The coarse polychrome fabrics often contain textural concentration features in their micromass. While some of them may indicate merely an inconsistency within the unmixed clay, others clearly represent the incomplete mixing of two raw material components. Clearly, the optical activity of a specific micromass, even its color, is affected primarily by the specific temperature and atmosphere of firing. However, if we move beyond individual samples, the consistency in the clay matrix of these coarse polychrome vessels is striking. It seems to represent the choice of a fine Neogene clay, which might then be levigated and fired at a relatively high temperature.

SAND INCLUSIONS. The petrology of the sand inclusions in Mesara fabrics has caused many problems for ceramic analysts due to their wide variability.[115] Although there may well have been different locations of production in the plain, the likely origin of the aplastics in the beds of water courses may account for the different lithologies represented. On the other hand, in the Neopalatial period, the products of the kilns at Hagia Triada and Kommos have very similar compositions,[116] even though their distance from each other makes it unlikely that their raw materials were obtained from the same locations.

Within the Middle Minoan material, there is a common fabric whose sand-sized aplastics most frequently contain quartz-biotite schists, phyllites, fine-grained volcanic rocks, sandstones and hornblende (fig. 8d–f). These inclusions reflect the schist and ophiolitic deposits of the broader area, but in technological terms represent simply the choice of a suitable temper that does not contain limestone (that would lead to lime spalling).

111. Wilson and Day 1994, pl. 8c, d, f.
112. Myer and Betancourt 1990.
113. Whitbread 1995, 386.
114. Shaw et al. 2001, 118.
115. Shaw et al. 2001, 118, 141–4.
116. Shaw et al. 2001; Belfiore et al. 2003.

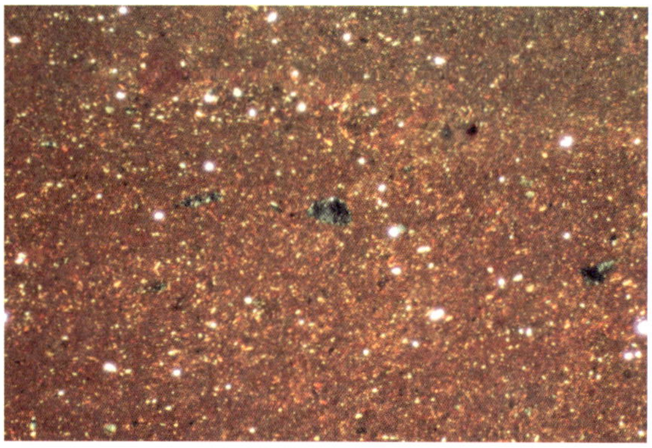

Fig. 7 a

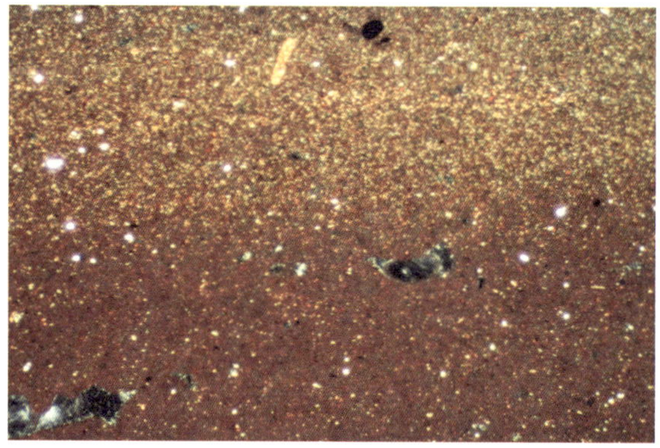

Fig. 7 b

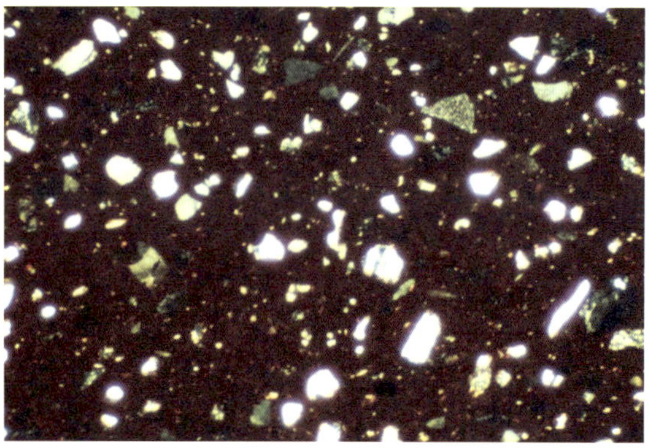

Fig. 7 c

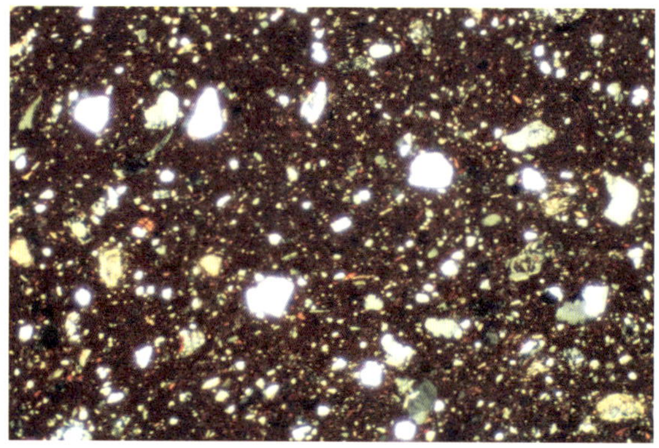

Fig. 7 d

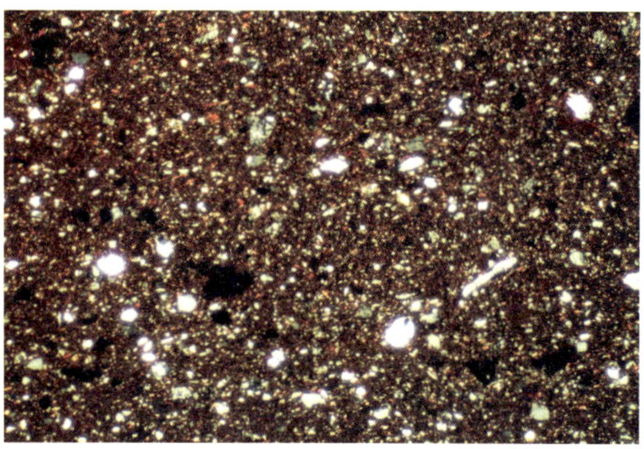

Fig. 7 e

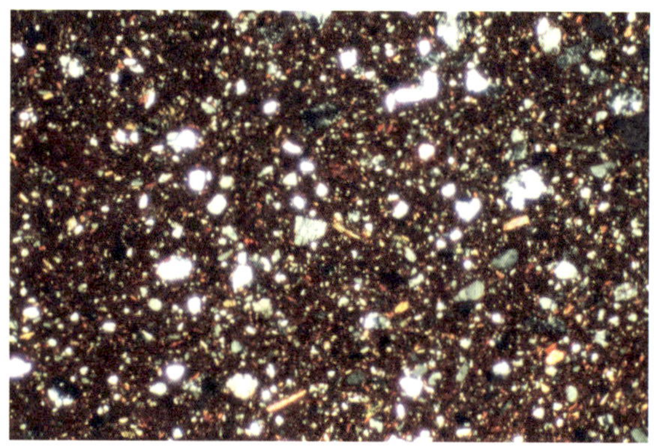

Fig. 7 f

Fig. 7. Fine textured fabrics of the Mesara, crossed polars, 4 mm horizontal dimension.
a. EM IIA Dark-on-Light jug, very fine fabric, Phaistos 95/41.
b. MM IB–IIA jar with very fine fabric, Phaistos 95/61.
c. EM IIA Light-on-Dark jug, to illustrate quartz-rich fabric, Phaistos 95/63.
d. MM IB polychrome large shallow bowl/fruitstand, cf. quartz-rich fabric, Phaistos 98/17.
e. EM IIB red-black mottled bowl/cup, Phaistos 95/97.
f. MM IB black-slipped bowl, Phaistos 98/50.

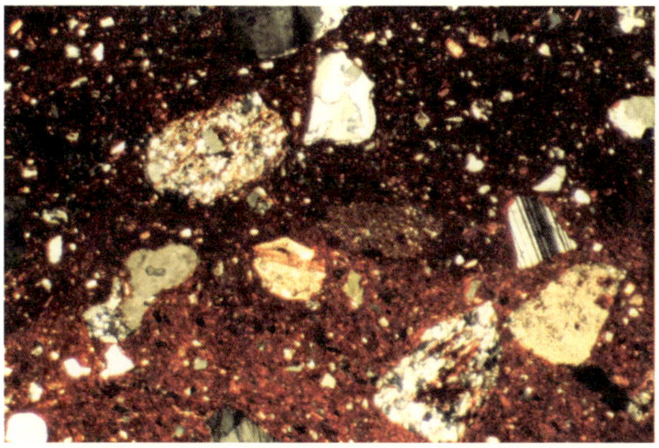

Fig. 8 a

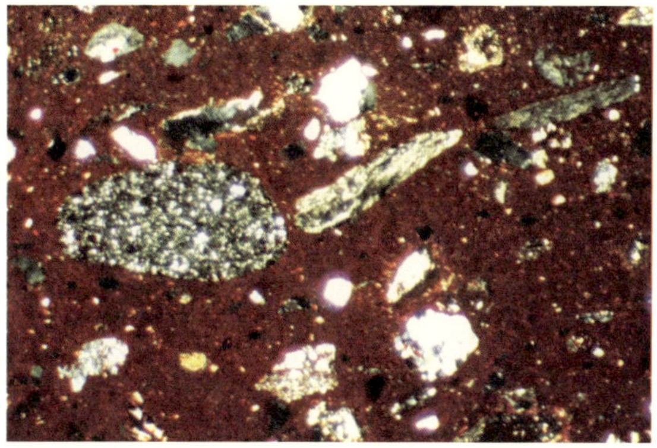

Fig. 8 b

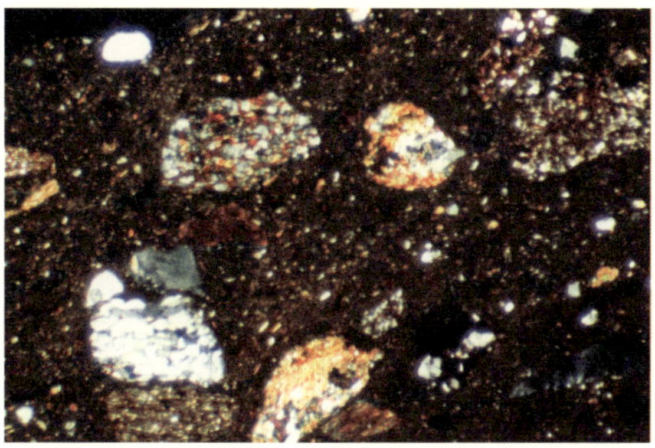

Fig. 8 c

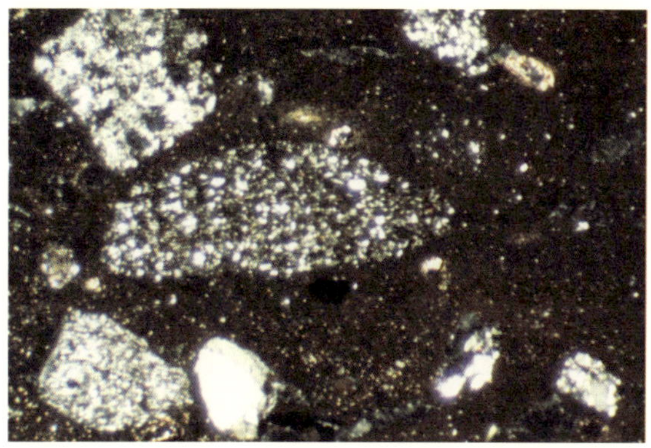

Fig. 8 d

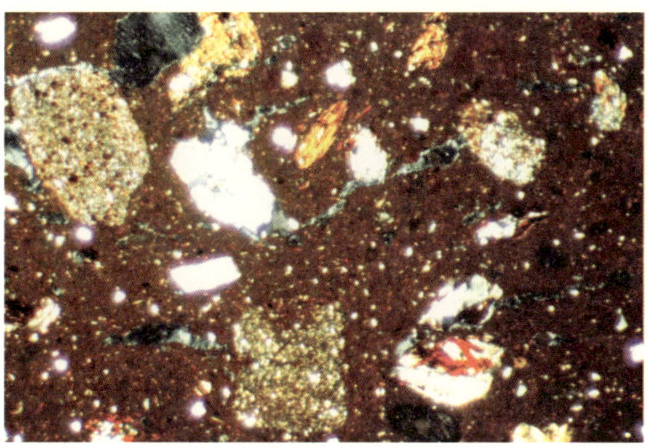

Fig. 8 e

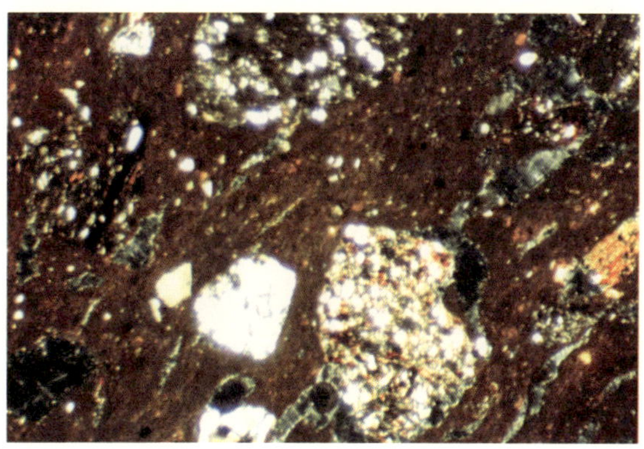

Fig. 8 f

Fig. 8. Sand-tempered fabrics of the Mesara over time, crossed polars, 4mm horizontal dimension.
a. Final Neolithic Encrusted Ware, Phaistos 92/6.
b. EM I Dark-on-Light jar, Hagia Triada 95/28.
c. EM IIA Dark-on-Light jug, Phaistos 95/57.
d. MM IB polychrome bowl, Phaistos 98/11.
e. MM IB–IIA jug/jar, Phaistos 98/26.
f. MM IB–IIA polychrome jar, Phaistos 98/24.

As with all temper, the addition of sand may have mitigated the effect of an overplastic, or sticky Neogene clay that might have been caused by a high calcareous content. The sand would also have counteracted the deleterious effects of shrinkage and perhaps have aided the vessel during firing. As we are mainly considering decorative tablewares, it seems unlikely that the sand's ability to increase vessel toughness would have been a high priority in this case.

VOIDS. The voids are the final property of the fabric highlighted here. These are frequent, usually channel voids, and have a distinct orientation that is often parallel to the pot wall (fig. 9a–f). These characteristic voids may have their origins either in the way that the well-sorted, rounded sand temper acts when wedged into the matrix, or may be due to a specific method of wedging or preparing the clay prior to forming the vessel.

DIACHRONIC COMPARISON OF SAND-TEMPERED FABRICS. The petrological and textural features of these coarser polychrome vessels form the basis of a very distinctive fabric, one that is instantly recognizable when found at other locations on the island.[117] However, as figure 8a–c shows, the same fabrics are found in Prepalatial vessels of the Mesara Plain. Those illustrated here are mainly taken from the sites of Phaistos and Hagia Triada, but there exist many Prepalatial examples at sites such as Hagia Kyriaki, Moni Odigitria and even Knossos.[118] Although mainly of the EM IIA period, some 500 years earlier, the fabrics show the same types of clay matrix, added inclusions and, in some cases, the characteristic voids. This type of fabric is not generic, produced with widely available materials for a specific function, nor is it the inevitable result of a restricted range of local raw materials. Instead, the strong similarity and sometimes identical nature of these fabrics separated by several hundred years is due to the fact that they are the products of the same raw material choices and the same sets of actions in the processing of those raw materials. In the case of the voids, we might suggest that they represent the same gestures of the craftsperson, the same repeated, learned bodily movements in wedging or vessel forming.

It is worth noting that these fabrics continue in use throughout the Bronze Age, being present in coarse vessels at least until the LM III period at Kommos, as shown by recent analyses of stirrup jars from the site.

FINE FABRICS. Only some of the vessels have sand-tempered bodies. Most common in the finest EM and MM pottery is a fine calcareous clay, fired at a high temperature, a process that produces a fabric that generates an almost metallic ring. These are high-quality clays indeed and are perhaps less easy to characterize. Fine, calcareous clays are widely available

117. Day and Wilson 1998.
118. Wilson and Day 1994.

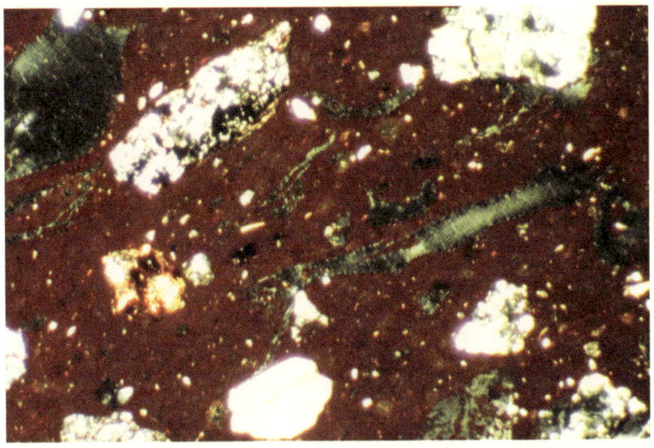

FIG. 9 a

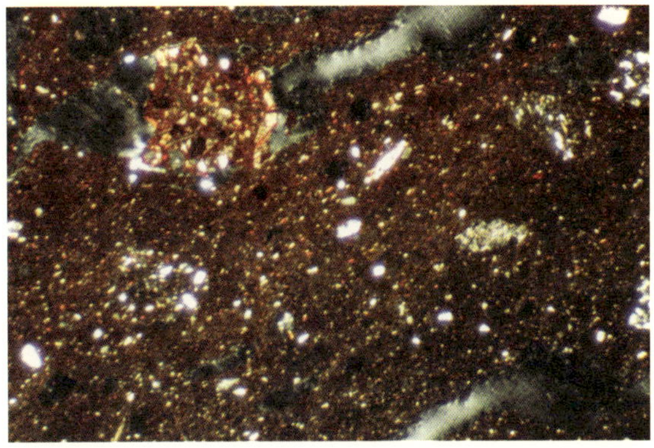

FIG. 9 b

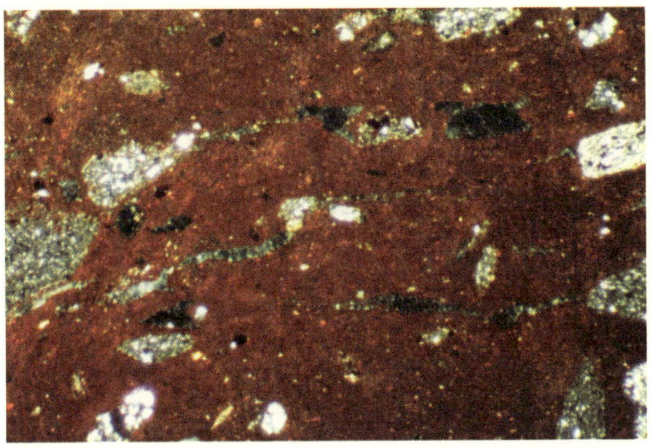

FIG. 9 c

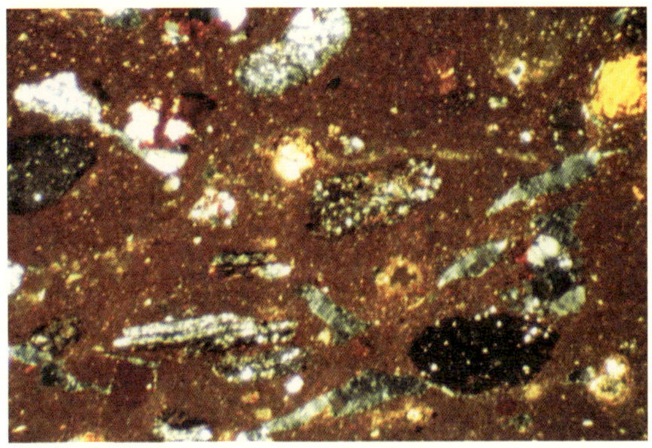

FIG. 9 d

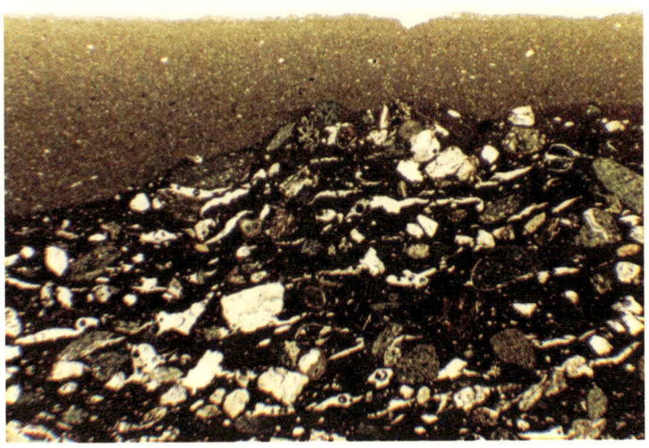

FIG. 9 e

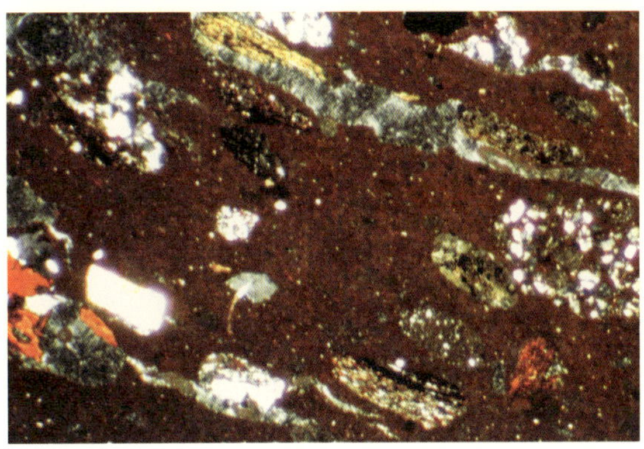

FIG. 9 f

FIG. 9. Distinctive void patterns in ceramic fabrics.
a. EM I wiped and washed storage jar, crossed polars, horizontal dimension 4 mm, Hagia Triada 95/21.
b. EM IIA Dark-on-Light storage jar, crossed polars, horizontal dimension 4 mm, Hagia Triada 95/59.
c. EM IIB bowl with brown slip, crossed polars, horizontal dimension 4 mm, Phaistos 95/77.
d. MM IB polychrome jar, crossed polars, horizontal dimension 4 mm, Phaistos 98/26 MM00.
e. MM IB polychrome bowl, plane polarized light, horizontal dimension 8 mm, Phaistos 98/15.
f. MM IIB black-slipped jug/jar, crossed polars, horizontal dimension 4 mm, Monastiraki 98/26.

in Crete from Neogene deposits[119] and were often used in the production of ceramics.[120] Not only does such clay form a suitable, vitrified structure over a relatively broad range of temperatures,[121] it also produces a relatively smooth and pale background, suitable for decoration, and is easily worked. As many of the Neogene clays were deposited in marine conditions, clays of a very similar nature can be found over the island and compositional differences, both chemical and mineralogical, are sometimes minimal. Nevertheless, there are features of color and appearance that may be characteristic of specific production locations. As such, we can observe that there exist similarities between Prepalatial fabrics from the Mesara and those that are found in Middle Minoan polychrome within the same area. In most cases, it would be problematic to relate the coarse and fine fabrics of the polychrome tradition, except perhaps through a comparison of their decorative motifs and techniques.[122] In the case under consideration, however, both petrographic and chemical analysis link the two strongly,[123] showing that the chemical differences can be explained by the presence of mafic minerals in the coarse fraction of the tempered fabric. In any case, the two different fabrics are related to each other without question, as they are used in combination on the same vessels, employing a method of joining and layering that is characteristic of the Mesara.

Layering

A characteristic property of the Mesara polychrome vessels is the use of different clay bodies in the same vessel (figs. 10–13). On a small scale, this is familiar throughout the Early and Middle Bronze Age of Crete in the attachment of feet and handles, which are often more heavily tempered than the body to which they are attached. In the Mesara polychrome tradition, however, this use of different clays is taken much further. In some cases, sand-tempered clay is used to join slabs of finer clay, but more commonly, very fine clay is used to provide a fine surface for decoration, for the addition of molded appliqué, for trailed and punctuated Barbotine patterning, for the molding of fine ridges and the production of rims (figs. 12–13), especially those that imitate metal vessels. The technique is used on a variety of vessels ranging from small bowls to large pithoid jars, whose rim areas are often finished with a gray-buff firing clay which is at times impressed and is molded to form the overhanging thickened rim and other fine surface features. The elements added in clay layers are very substantial and are not to be confused with the application of slip (fig. 10f).

119. Hein, Day, Quinn and Kilikoglou 2004.
120. Day et al. 1999.
121. Kilikoglou 1994.
122. Day and Wilson 1998.
123. Faber et al. 2002, 132.

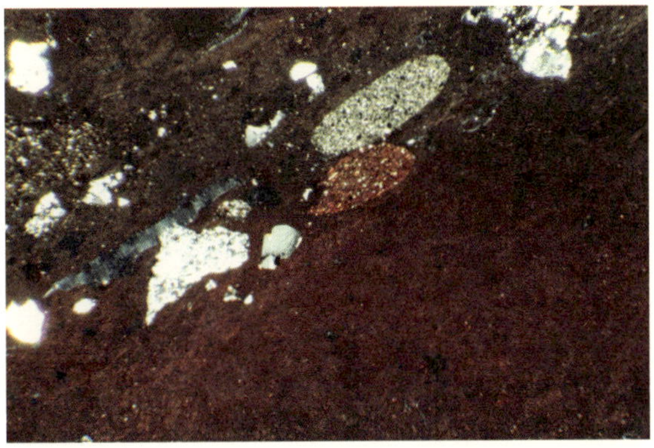

FIG. 10 a

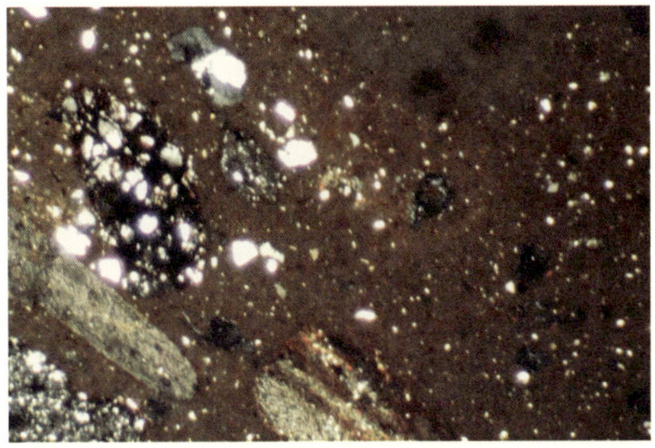

FIG. 10 b

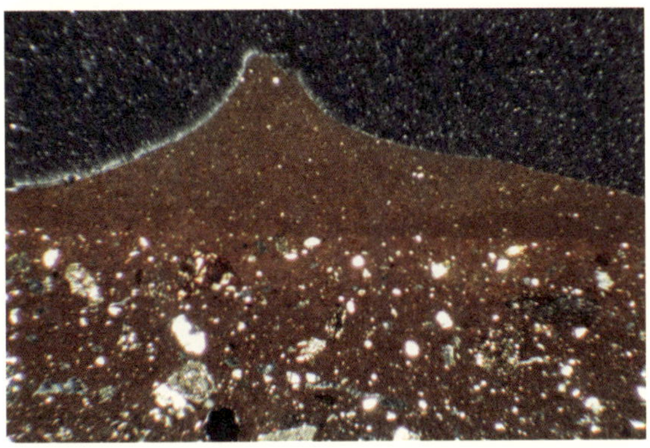

FIG. 10 c

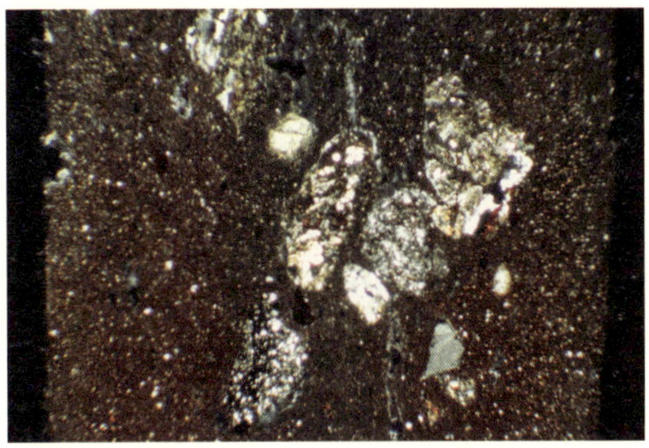

FIG. 10 d

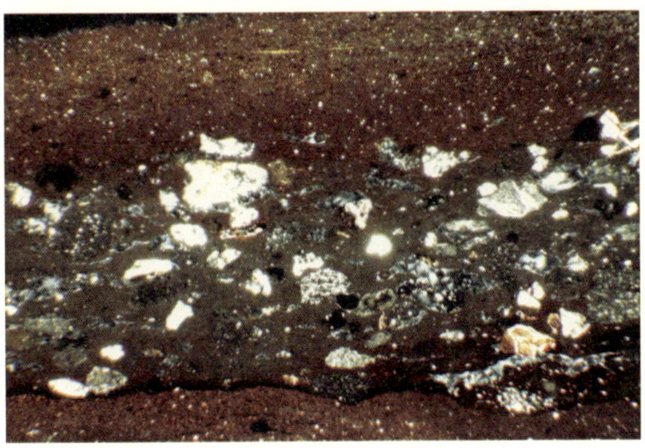

FIG. 10 e

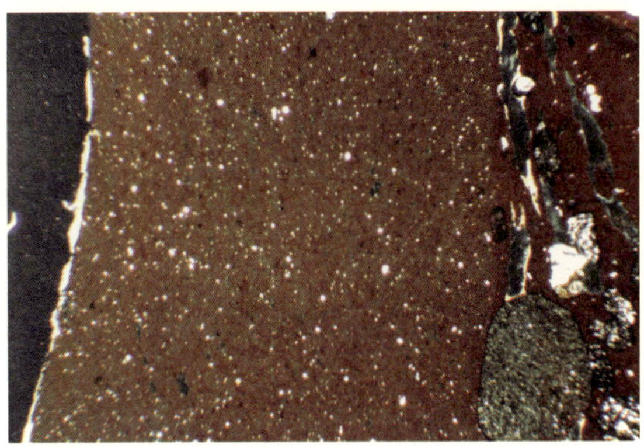

FIG. 10 f

FIG. 10. Layers of different fabrics in the same vessel, in thin section.
a. EM I Dark-on-Light small closed vessel, crossed polars, horizontal dimension 8 mm, Hagia Kyriaki 94/88.
b. EM IIA Fine Painted Ware spouted bowl, crossed polars, horizontal dimension 4 mm, Knossos 92/288.
c. MM IB Dark-on-Light jar, crossed polars, horizontal dimension 8 mm, Phaistos 98/21.
d. MM IB-IIA polychrome jar, crossed polars, horizontal dimension 5 mm, Phaistos 98/30.
e. MM IIA polychrome bowl, crossed polars, horizontal dimension 8 mm, Mesara, Knossos 95/286.
f. MM IIB Light-on-Dark jug, crossed polars, horizontal dimension 8 mm, Mesara, Knossos 95/335.

Two points regarding this layering technique are worthy of our attention: 1) it represents a long-lived technique; and 2) it has major implications for understanding the way in which the vessels were formed, at least in a general way.

DIACHRONIC PATTERNS IN DIFFERENT CLAY BODIES ON ONE VESSEL. The technique of using both fine and coarse clays on the same vessel is characteristic of Fine Painted Ware in EM IIA (fig. 10b),[124] and indeed is present in EM I pottery from Hagia Kyriaki (fig. 10a). During EM IIA fine clay was used for handles on coarser vessel bodies, for details of bowl rims and sometimes for necks on jugs. Additionally, the layering technique was also practiced in the same way that it is used in the Palatial period, to provide complex detail and a high-quality, smooth surface (fig. 10c). Late Prepalatial ceramics from the Mesara likewise show many of the same techniques. The spouted jars often have relief-decorated surfaces, using the finer clay on a coarser clay body.

This unusual practice has not been encountered in Prepalatial ceramics in other parts of the island, but instead appears to be a very strong local tradition. The production of a fine surface layer over a coarser body or core continues in the Mesara after the First Palace period, is often related to a careful relief or appliqué decoration of the surface and is clearly visible in the production of a range of vessels.

IMPLICATIONS FOR FORMING METHOD. The onset of the Palatial period is normally taken to represent a revolution in ceramic forming technology, as well as in the scale and intensity of production. However, Knappett's work has eloquently demonstrated that even when we have undisputed evidence for knowledge and use of the potter's wheel, it was by no means an innovation that was universally adopted.[125] Indeed much of Protopalatial production seems to continue the practice of hand-fashioning vessels. It is clear that change does not occur across all types or in an abrupt fashion. However, the layering processes used in the production of some Kamares and other vessels in the Mesara still appear surprisingly labor intensive.

The layering technique documented seems to preclude the possibility that these vessels were simply wheel-made. Instead, the vessel's main shape must have been formed, next perhaps smoothed or scraped and then the required clay layer attached to the surface, perhaps by being smoothed on, or by the addition of coils. Although the advantages are clear in terms of the addition of decorative relief on the vessels and providing a surface suitable for fine decoration, this would have been a rather labor-intensive technique. While the addition of a relatively small amount of fine clay to add detail to a large, coarse jar is perhaps understandable, it is more difficult to understand why smaller bowls might

124. Wilson and Day 1994, 61 sample 92/288.
125. Knappett 1999.

be manufactured from a coarse core, sandwiched between an exterior and interior layer of fine clay (fig. 10d–e). This is indeed a very particular way of forming a pot and one that stretches back in the Mesara to at least the EM IIA period.

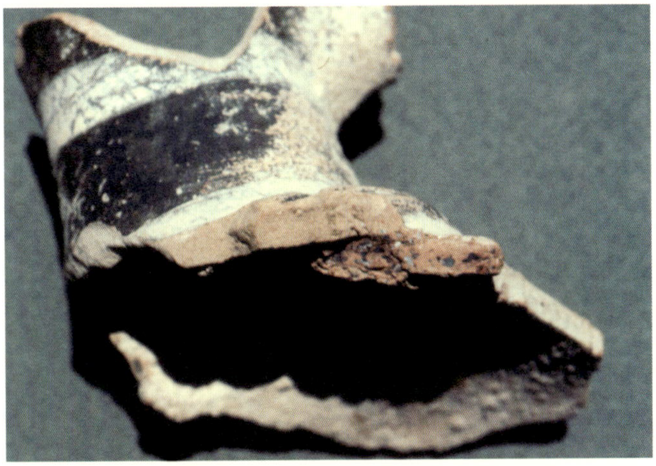

FIG. 11. Jug neck constructed using fine fabric joined to coarse body, with a combination of distinct layers.

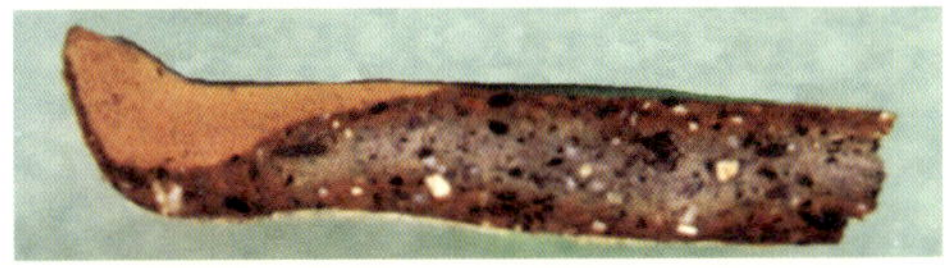

FIG. 12. Middle Minoan polychrome jar, with a combination of distinct layers, Phaistos 98/15.

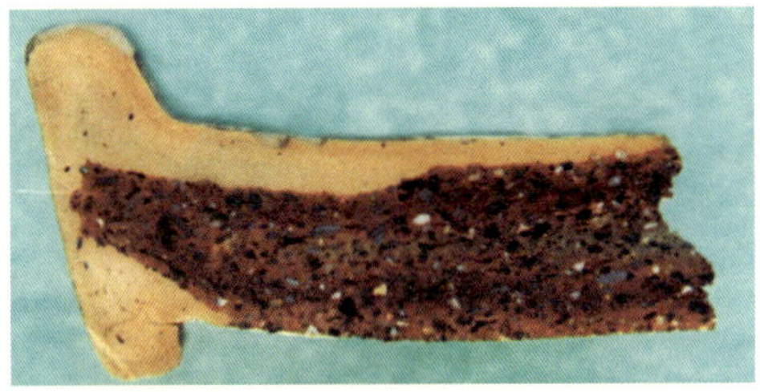

FIG. 13. Middle Minoan polychrome shallow bowl, with a combination of distinct layers, Phaistos 98/11.

Surface Decoration

Our consideration of decorative motifs, specific forms, raw material recipes and the use of different clay bodies on the same vessel all represent the results of very specific processes and actions used by the potters of the Mesara. In turning to pigments, slips and paints of the polychrome vessels, we might be considered to be venturing into the detail of technology that is so generic as to have little regional meaning, i.e., that these techniques are so open to transmission and imitation that they tell us little about the potters that practiced them. Yet increasingly we are aware of the sophistication of these decorative techniques and the fact that their execution does not rely exclusively on the simple application of the correct material to the pot surface, but rather is dependant also on a great amount of skill in the matching of materials, the application of decoration and the sequence and nature of firing.

Such an approach has been used elsewhere on Crete in the examination of Dark-on-Light Painted and black-slipped pottery from the EM IIB settlement of Myrtos Phournou Koriphi, where a contrast was observed regarding the quality and nature of the iron-reduction black slip used to decorate pots in the Mirabello production area and in the workshops closer to Myrtos.[126] In studying pottery production and consumption in detail, such consideration of practice and of skill can be valuable in reconstructing regional traditions.

It is well known that the surface finishes produced on Kamares Ware are often, but not

126. Whitelaw et al. 1997.

exclusively, of excellent quality and that they betray a sophistication of technical execution. Their examination allows us to look at these exceptional ceramic products in detail and to trace patterns of development over time and space. Middle Minoan polychrome relies on repeated, basic colors to form the decorative patterns: black, white, red, orange/yellow and, in some cases, purple. Of these, it has been the technology of the black slip and the white pigments that have attracted the most attention. Here we consider each of the main colors in polychrome pottery from the Mesara, discussing the specific actions and processes that contributed to their production.

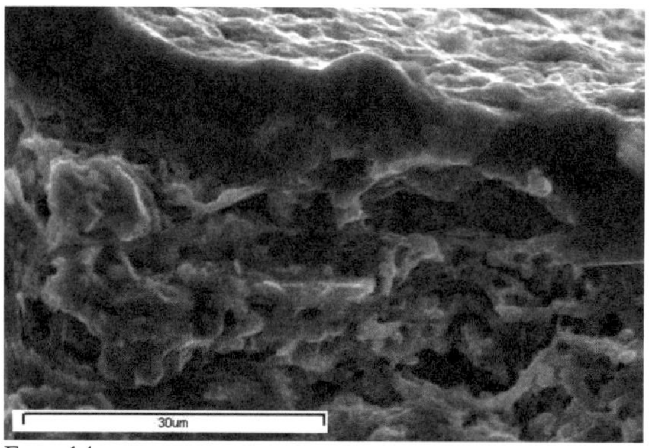

Fig. 14 a

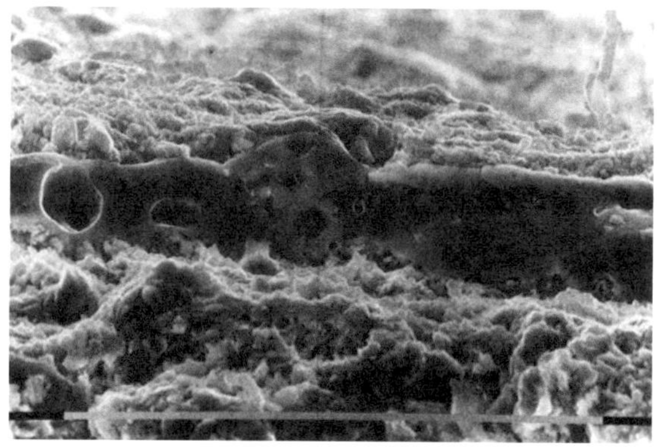

Fig. 14 b

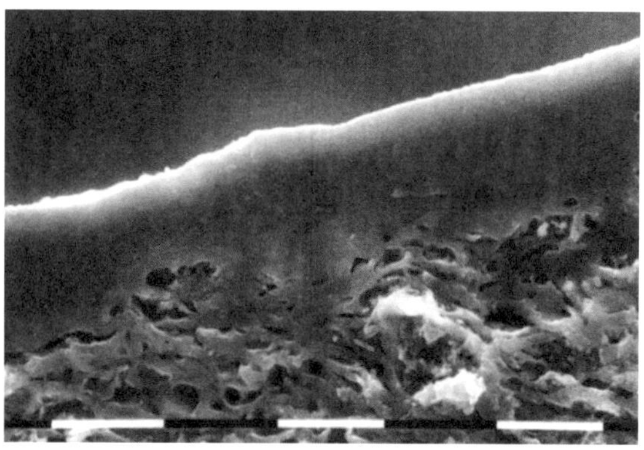

Fig. 14 c

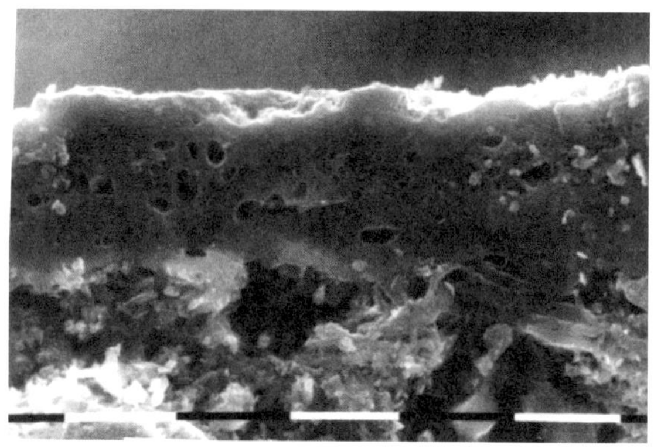

Fig. 14 d

Fig. 14. SEM secondary electron images of black slips on Mesara pottery.
a. EM IIA Dark-on-Light jug, exhibiting vitrified microstructure. Equivalent firing temperature = 850–950°C. Scale bar = 30µm.
b. EM II Dark-on-Light jug, exhibiting vitrified microstructure with few coarse bloating pores. Equivalent firing temperature = 850–950°C. Scale bar = 100µm.
c. MM IIA polychrome bridge-spouted jar, exhibiting vitrified microstructure with few, fine bloating pores. Equivalent firing temperature = 1000–1080°C. Scale bar = 10µm. Mesara. Knossos 95/293.
d. MM IB/IIA polychrome jug/jar, exhibiting vitrified microstructure with very frequent, fine bloating pores. Equivalent firing temperature = 950–1050°C. Scale bar = 10µm. Phaistos 98/28.

BLACK SLIP. Noll performed the first detailed analyses of the paints and pigments used on Kamares Ware. He demonstrated that the black was formed from a fine-grained, iron-rich slip that had undergone an oxidation-reduction-oxidation sequence in a firing that must have reached above 1000°C.[127] Further chemical analysis and microstructural examination of the black slip provides additional information. A direct comparison between the composition of the slip and the clay body is perhaps most informative. Most slip samples examined show a higher relative amount of aluminum (Al), potassium (K), and iron (Fe), and in many cases of magnesium (Mg) and titanium (Ti), combined with a relatively lower value for silicon (Si), as compared to the body clay. This, along with their low- or non-calcareous nature suggests that the slip was produced by using a fine suspension of an illitic clay.

The production of a high-quality black slip is a complex technique requiring good control of firing conditions, i.e., a body of knowledge of resources and techniques. The refinement of suitable clay, its application and the correct firing are not trivial matters. In Crete we first see the accomplished application of this technique during the Early Minoan period, notably in the Mesara, during EM IIA (fig. 14a–b). There a high-quality iron black is first produced in precisely the same manner as that of the polychrome (fig. 14c–d).[128]

While a similar technology is used for black decoration throughout Crete, there are regional differences in quality from the Early Minoan onward, due not only to variability in raw materials, but also to the level of competence in different production centers (cf. fig. 14c–d).[129]

RED PAINT. Several shades of orange and red decoration are often present on Middle Minoan polychrome pottery. The red pigment usually is comprised of a coarse-grained, non-vitrified, low- to medium-calcareous iron-rich earth, which usually contains little or no clay (fig. 15a–b). However, in some cases this red also contains Mg-rich inclusions, which have been identified as talc. Unlike the black, this red layer did not vitrify during firing because the differences in composition and texture ensured that it remained porous and permeable to oxygen during the reoxidation stage of firing. The iron compounds contained in the paint would have been reduced to a black-colored magnetite during the reduction stage, their porosity would have allowed the magnetite to reoxidize during the final oxidization stage resulting in the final red-colored hematite. The red, based on an iron-rich material, is prepared employing the same technology used from the beginning of the Early Minoan period in central Crete. While the use of talc in the preparation of red paint in the MM period represents a change from the EM, the practice never becomes predominant.

127. Noll et al. 1971, 618; 1975, 611–2; Noll 1982, 151.
128. Kilikoglou 1994, 73.
129. E.g., Whitelaw et al. 1997.

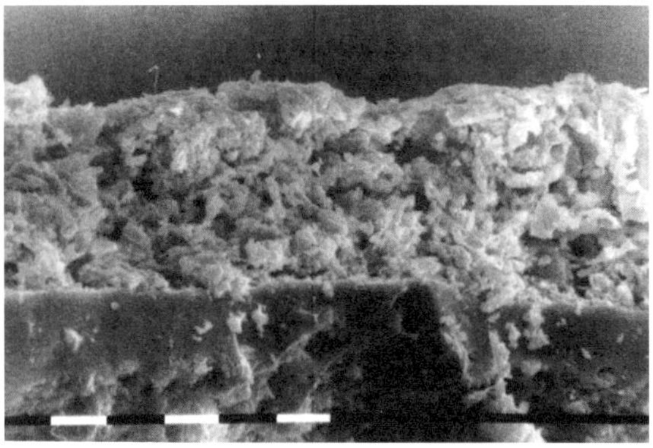

FIG. 15 a

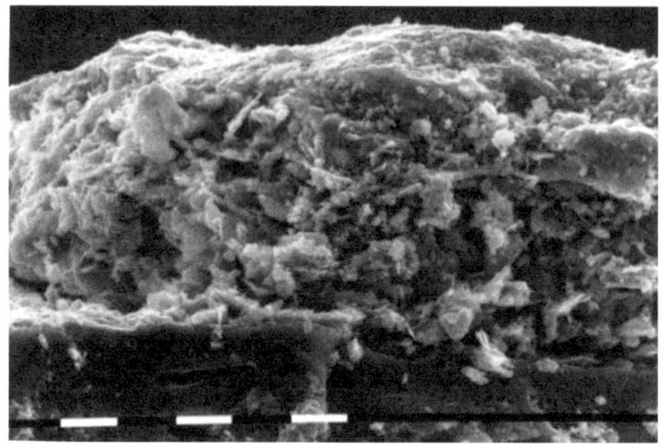

FIG. 15 b

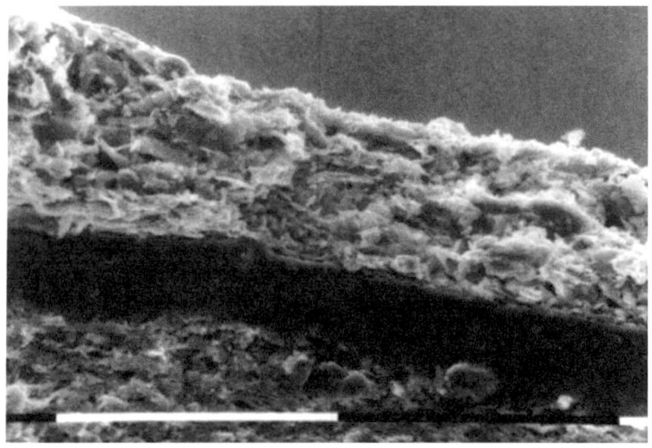

FIG. 15 c

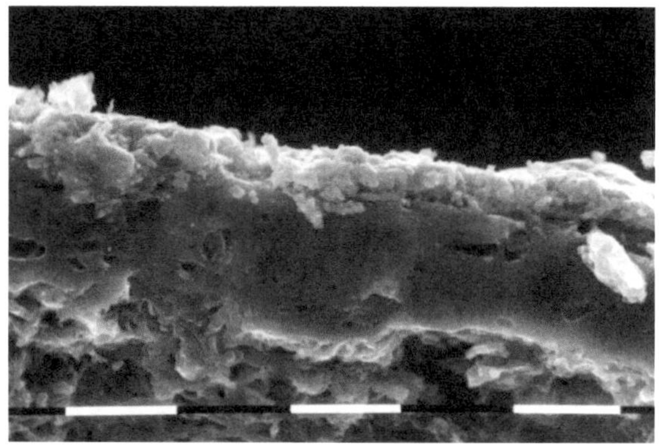

FIG. 15 d

FIG. 15. SEM secondary electron images of red and orange paints.
a. Red pigment on MM IB/IIA polychrome jar, with coarse, non-vitrified microstructure above black slip. Equivalent firing temperature = 1000–1080°C. Scale bar = 10μm. Phaistos 98/10.
b. Red pigment on MM IB/IIA polychrome jug/jar, with coarse, non-vitrified microstructure above the black slip. Equivalent firing temperature = 950–1050°C. Scale bar = 10μm. Phaistos 98/28.
c. Orange pigment on MM IIB polychrome bowl, with coarse, non-vitrified microstructure containing both irregularly rounded and platy grains, above the black slip. Equivalent firing temperature = 1000–1080°C. Scale bar = 100μm. Phaistos 98/42.
d. Orange pigment on MM IA/IB polychrome cup, with coarse, non-vitrified microstructure, above black slip. Equivalent firing temperature = 1000–1080°C. Scale bar = 10μm. Myrtos-Pyrgos 99/13.

ORANGE PAINT. The orange decoration generally consists of a coarse-grained, non-vitrified layer (fig. 15c–d). Chemical analysis suggests that the orange layer is a mixture of areas of a low- to medium-calcareous, iron-rich material and areas or platelets of a material rich in magnesium and silicon. The latter signify the most noticeable difference from the red slip and paint technology of the Early Minoan period. While the orange color may have a basis in an iron-rich earth similar to that used for red decoration, the magnesium seems to indicate the more consistent use of talc/steatite to produce a lighter color in some cases.[130] Certainly, analysis reveals that the brighter orange color contained a higher pro-

130. Faber et al. 2002, 133.

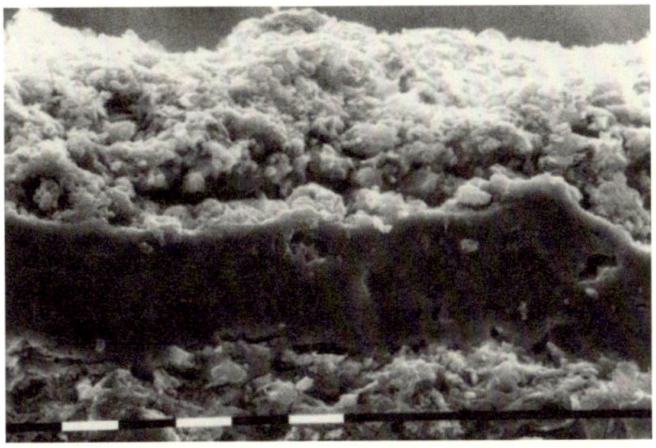

FIG. 16 a

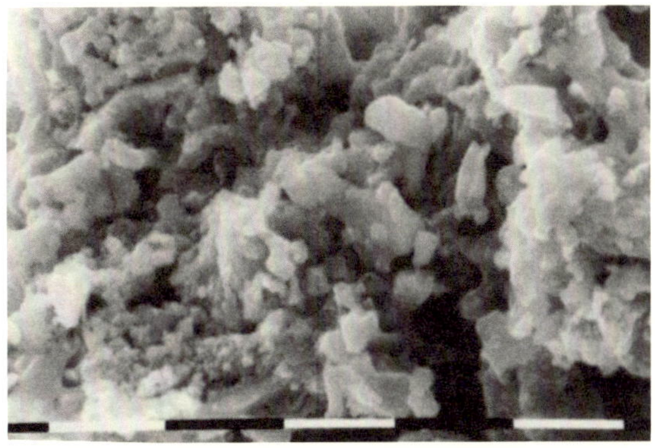

FIG. 16 b

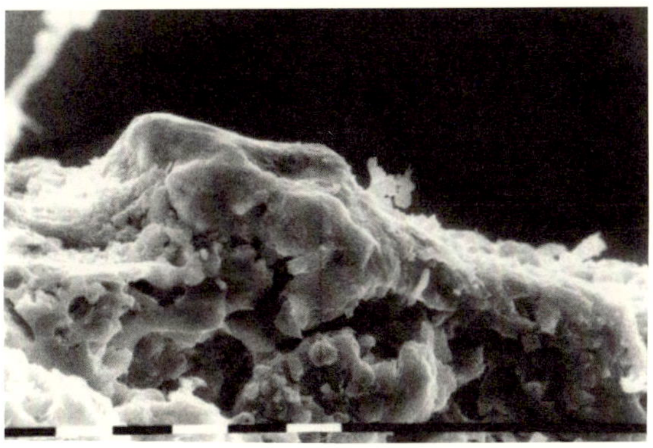

FIG. 16 c

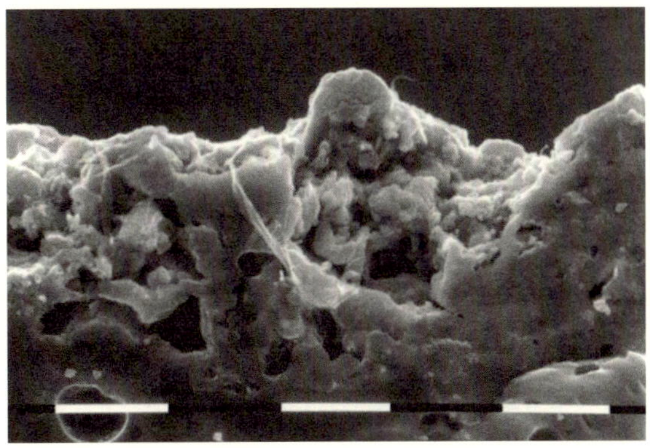

FIG. 16 d

FIG. 16. SEM secondary electron images of purple pigments.
a. MM IIB polychrome jug, with coarse, non-nvitrified microstructure, above black slip. Equivalent firing temperature = 1000–1080°C. Scale bar = 10μm. Knossos 95/332.
b. MM IB/IIA polychrome jug, with coarse, non-vitrified microstructure consisting of irregularly rounded grains. Equivalent firing temperature = 1000–1080°C. Scale bar = 10μm. Phaistos 98/13.
c. MM IB polychrome jug, with coarse microstructure that varies from non-vitrified to initial vitrification, almost fused to the underlying black slip. Equivalent firing temperature = 1050–1080°C. Scale bar = 10μm. Phaistos 98/14.
d. MM IB/IIA polychrome bridge-spouted jar, with coarse microstructure varying from non-vitrified to incompletely vitrified, above black slip. Paint layer appears partly destroyed during firing. Equivalent firing temperature = 1000–1080°C. Scale bar = 10μm. Phaistos 98/4.

portion of talc/steatite than the darker red/orange, which probably accounts for the difference in color.[131] Nevertheless, there are cases where the orange color is present and is not accompanied by chemical indications of the presence of talc. Therefore both red and orange pigments display a variability in composition. When, however, they are present on the same vessels, the orange tends to contain a greater amount of talc.

PURPLE PAINT. Although this color has been previously classified as a deep red, there is a distinctly purple paint that appears on some vessels, all of which appear to be Mesara prod-

131. Noll 1982, 151.

ucts, regardless of their findspot. The paint color can be seen in pottery of the late Prepalatial period (figs. 3–4). When examined analytically, most examples of the purple paint appear to be comprised of an iron-rich earth, but some examples may have been the result of a mixture between an iron-rich earth and talc (fig. 16a–d). In this respect, the purple pigments are very similar to those of the red and orange layers. There are, however, some differences in micromorphology. While some examples of purple also have non-vitrified microstructures (fig. 16a–b), there is a higher incidence of vitrification in this color (fig. 16c) and it may be that the purple's more consistent small grain size promoted a differential, partial vitrification that created the darker color. While the purple pigments examined are more likely to have a higher Fe content than the other colors, there are nevertheless only a few differences in their chemical composition, and even those are inconsistent.

WHITE PAINT. The white pigments of Kamares Ware have received much attention and been the subject of complex archaeological interpretation. Noll identified two main types: talc white and lime silicate white.[132] The differences between the two were discussed by Walberg, who suggested that talc white was a product of the palaces and that lime silicate white originated from provincial workshops, as a continuation of a lower-quality preexisting technology.[133] This theory was flawed by the assumption that the findspots of the polychrome pottery were in most cases also the places of their production, an often unsupportable claim.[134]

Although two Mg-rich pigments have been mineralogically identified in studies of MM polychrome pottery, namely talc[135] and huntite,[136] Betancourt et al.[137] have suggested that these may represent the misidentification of the same Mg-rich mineral. However, they do not specify what would be the correct interpretation. Betancourt and Swann[138] use proton induced X-ray emission (PIXE) spectrometry to identify the pigments on polychrome samples from the Minoan port of Kommos. While in general agreement with Noll, their work documents the use of two white pigments occurring on different vessels found at this one site: a Mg-rich pigment and a Mg-poor pigment (calcium silicate).[139] The most recent analyses of Betancourt and co-workers[140] suggest that the talc white was restricted in its production to the Mesara, not only in "palatial" contexts of production, but also at the harbor town of Kommos.

132. Noll 1982, 151.
133. Walberg 1983, 70.
134. E.g., Day and Wilson 1998.
135. Noll 1982, 151.
136. Stos-Fertner et al. 1979, 193.
137. Betancourt et al. 1984, 72.
138. Betancourt and Swann 1989.
139. Betancourt and Swann 1989, 180.
140. Ferrence et al. 2001.

Our own analyses of white pigments show that there were two main types of white pigment in use in the Mesara. The first is a pigment rich in calcium, which is likely to be based on a white firing clay, but may have several variants (fig. 17a–b). One version of this calcium silicate white with raised levels of Mg, also discussed by Ferrence et al.,[141] may in fact derive from a dolomitic source, although further mineralogical analysis is needed.

Perhaps of most interest is the talc white pigment, which occurs in many examples of Mesara polychrome. In energy dispersive X-ray (EDAX) microanalysis, Mg and Si are predominant and the ratio of the two elements is similar to that obtained from the analysis of

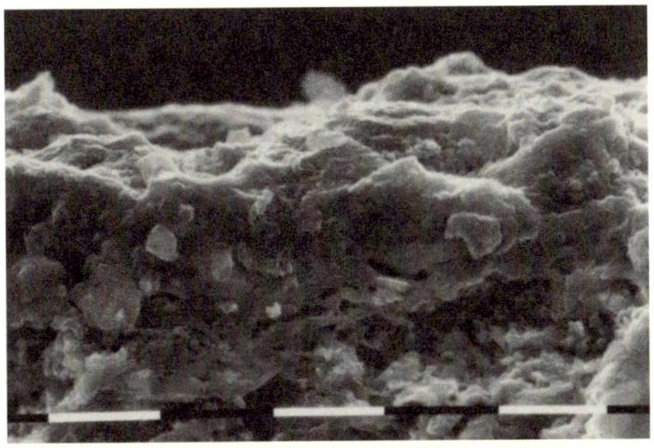

Fig. 17 a

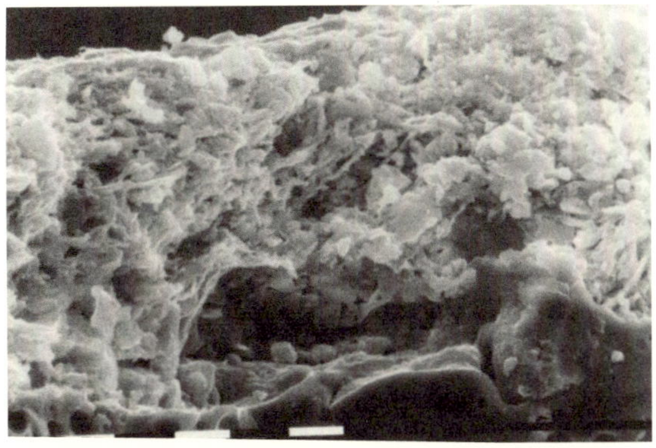

Fig. 17 b

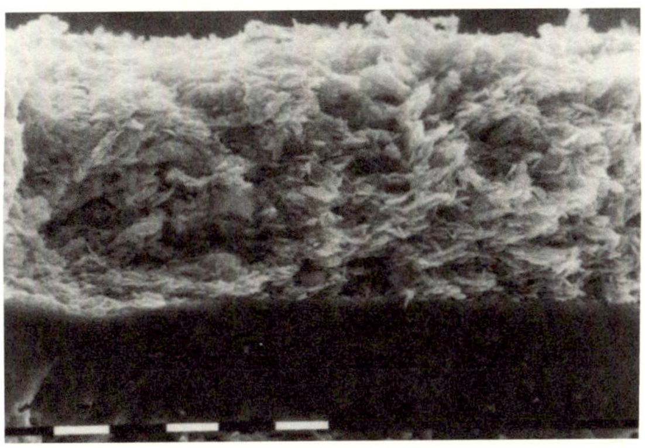

Fig. 17 c

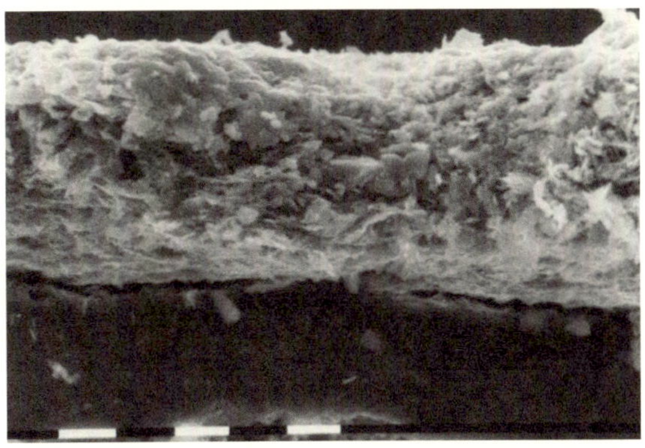

Fig. 17 d

Fig. 17. SEM secondary electron images of white paints.
a. Calcium silicate white on MM IB polychrome bowl, with coarse, non-vitrified microstructure that may show signs of compaction, above black slip. Equivalent firing temperature = 950–1050°C. Scale bar = 10µm. Phaistos 98/25.
b. Calcium silicate white on MM IB/IIA polychrome bridge-spouted jar, with coarse, non-vitrified microstructure that consists of both regular crystalline and irregularly rounded grains, above black slip. Equivalent firing temperature = 1000–1080°C. Scale bar = 10µm. Phaistos 98/4.
c. Talc white on MM IB jar, with coarse, non-vitrified microstructure that consists almost entirely of platy grains, above the black slip. Equivalent firing temperature = 1000–1080°C. Scale bar = 10µm. Phaistos 98/9.
d. Talc white on MM IIB polychrome bowl, with coarse, non-vitrified microstructure, above black slip. A thin layer of the talc white pigment left adhered to the underlying black slip supports the suggestion that the white decoration was applied before firing. Equivalent firing temperature = 1000–1080°C. Scale bar = 10µm. Phaistos 98/42.

141. Ferrence et al. 2001.

geological samples of talc. The talc-rich layers are comprised of a non-vitrified microstructure, with platy grains (fig. 17c–d). They have a unimodal grain size and none of the incongruously large grains often found in red and orange paints. This may suggest that the talc used for white was prepared in a slightly different fashion than that mixed to produce orange.

When the evidence for the technology of the white pigments is combined with that of the fabrics of the vessels on which they occur, an interesting pattern emerges. In polychrome wares, talc white appears to have been an exclusive product of the Mesara. Certainly Middle Minoan polychrome pottery produced near Malia, Palaikastro and Myrtos-Pyrgos all use calcium white pigments. However this would seem to have been an innovation that occurred at the onset of the Middle Bronze Age, as so far all white pigments analyzed from Early Bronze Age contexts are of calcium silicate white. To confirm this diachronic pattern, further sampling of white pigments from south-central Crete would be needed, notably from EM I Lebena Ware.

Of great interest is the fact that both calcium silicate and talc white pigments appear on vessels that petrographic and chemical analyses suggest are the products of the same workshop.[142] Therefore, although the technology of talc white may well be closely associated with the Mesara region, the production centers in that area producing the finest Kamares Ware do not seem to use only one technology of white pigment.

SLIP, PAINT AND PIGMENT APPLICATION. Noll's work provided strong evidence that the painted decoration (white, red and orange) was applied prior to firing. Both types of white pigment were shown to contain high temperature phase minerals that were interpreted as having been produced during firing; the talc white pigment was found to contain protoenstatite and the lime silicate white contained diopside.[143] The presence of protoenstatite was of particular use for technological interpretations since it forms at temperatures over 1100°C or slightly lower in the presence of Fe ions,[144] which were also present in the talc white,[145] while diopside forms at 950°C. Thus the firing temperature of the vessel must have been in the range of 950°C to 1100°C.[146]

It is clear that the red and orange pigments were applied in a similar manner before firing. In the mixtures of iron-rich earth and talc, the hematite and protoenstatite were accompanied by olivine, which is a high temperature phase mineral formed by the reaction of the hematite and protoenstatite.[147] It is possible that the olivine could have occurred

142. Faber et al. 2002, 134.
143. Noll 1982, 151 and table 9.
144. Noll et al. 1971, 617; 1975, 611.
145. Noll 1982, table 9.
146. Noll et al. 1971, 617; 1975, 611.
147. Noll et al. 1975, 611; Noll 1982, table 8.

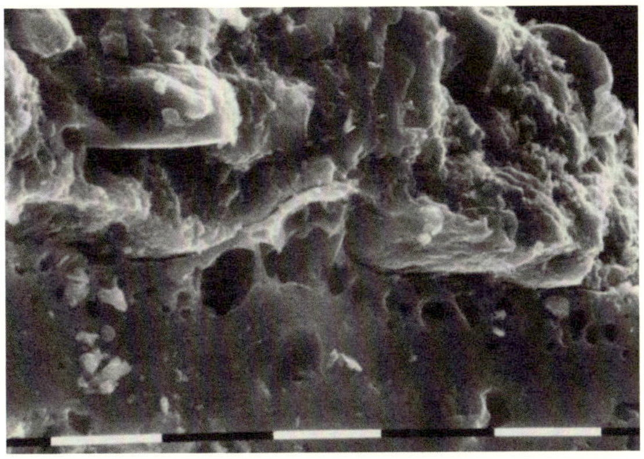

FIG. 18. SEM secondary electron image of interdigitating joint between the calcium silicate white pigment and a black slip on a MM IB/IIA polychrome jug/jar, exhibiting a coarse, non-vitrified microstructure. The interlocking nature and good adhesion between the layers suggests the white decoration was applied before firing. Scale bar = 10μm. Phaistos 98/28.

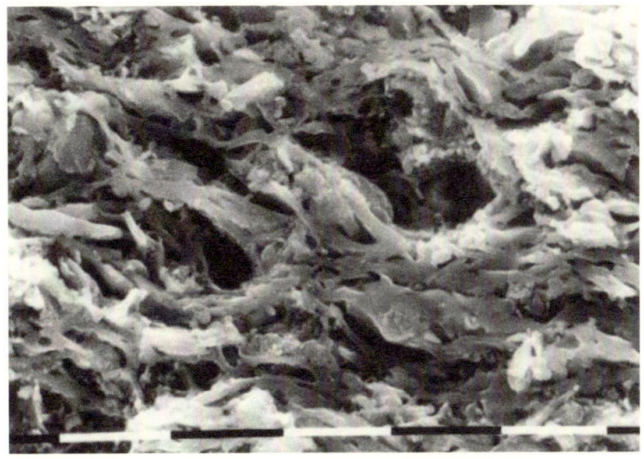

FIG. 19. SEM secondary electron image of well vitrified, calcareous body from Middle Minoan polychrome vessel. Scale bar = 10μm. Phaistos 98/27.

naturally in the iron-rich earth since it was not a pure deposit of hematite, but the evidence of the white pigments alone seems to suggest the prefiring application of the slips.

Scanning electron microscope (SEM) imaging confirms this by demonstrating the good adherence and interdigitating effect at the junction of these colors placed over the black slip (fig. 18). Hence these different colors on Kamares pottery were all applied prior to firing, relying for their different effects on composition, firing temperature and atmosphere. While some colors applied on Kamares Ware, such as talc white, iron-earth/talc white mixture and orange, are new formulations, others are based on a known material applied in a fashion already established in the Early Bronze Age.

Firing Temperatures and Atmospheres

While the mineralogical changes in the pigments were shown by Noll to have implications for our understanding of firing temperatures (see above), further evidence of firing temperature and atmosphere have been obtained by examination of vitrification microstructures with a scanning electron microscope.[148] The majority of the fine-bodied Mesara Kamares Ware examples exhibit a well-developed cellular structure of glass filaments, indicating a clay with well-distributed, very fine-grained calcite and a high firing temperature (fig. 19). The coarser fabrics also exhibit a similar microstructure and seem to be produced from a very similar clay base.

These clay bodies are similar to those used in Early Minoan Fine Painted Ware, as was suggested in the petrographic analysis above. However, the EM examples appear in the

148. Maniatis and Tite 1981.

main to have been fired to lower temperatures. The quality of the iron-reduction black slip relies, in part, on the control of firing temperature and atmosphere and here there are distinct similarities in the practice in Prepalatial and Palatial contexts. Nevertheless, there appears to be a change in the competence of controlling the firing atmosphere, with the Middle Minoan examples showing impressive control of all conditions.

Although we know little or nothing of kiln design until the end of the First Palace period,[149] we can still suggest that the designs of these structures may have changed and indeed the competence with which they were utilized.

Mesara Painted Pottery: Continuity of Technology?

To summarize, technological characterization of polychrome pottery from the Mesara Plain reveals some key points in its production, from the choice of raw materials, their alteration and manipulation to the vessel forming, to surface decoration and firing. In all these areas, much of the production of polychrome in the Mesara has links with the skills and practices already present in the Early Minoan period of the same area. Some features, such as the presence of exactly the same ceramic fabrics in both the Palatial and Prepalatial periods, and the same, rather idiosyncratic, methods of forming with layers of very different clay bodies, would seem to indicate a strong continuity of tradition in pottery manufacture between the two periods. Indeed some fabric parallels are so strong as to indicate production in the same location and utilization of the technique of layering in use from at least EM I.

This is not to say that nothing changed in the world of pottery manufacture. While we have chosen to highlight the continuity in the method of forming in layers, clearly change did take place in construction methods, but there does not seem to be evidence for a radical, immediate shift at the beginning of the Palatial period.

In terms of surface decoration and firing, patterns are more difficult to recognize. What is clear, however, is that in the Middle Bronze Age south-central Crete was prominent in the production of high-quality, fine pottery, with decoration that stood out in terms of technological sophistication. From the first production in the Mesara of a high-quality iron-reduction black in EM IIA, the decorative techniques seem to have had a strong continuity. Even in EM I Crete, the Mesara and Asterousia areas stand out in their production of high-quality pottery, with different coloring effects. It may be argued that Middle Minoan polychrome pottery in the same area developed out of that Prepalatial expertise.

While there are undeniable developments in pottery manufacture with the emergence of Kamares Ware, most changes had their roots in the earlier local sequence, perhaps in much the same way as EM IIA pottery in the Mesara shows a change from EM I.

149. Tomasello 1996; Shaw et al. 2001; Belfiore et al. 2003.

POTS, PALACES, HISTORY AND BELONGING: A DISCUSSION

> ...certain tastes and needs common to his founding grandfather's contemporaries vis-à-vis ceramics would remain unchanged *per omnia saecula saeculorum* or, at least, for the rest of his life, which, when you think about it comes to the same thing. We have seen the very traditional way in which the clay is kneaded, we have seen the rustic, almost primitive wheels they use, we have seen that the kiln outside shows traces of an antiquity unforgivable in the modern age, which, for all its scandalous defects and prejudices, has had the goodness to allow a potter like this to coexist with a Center like that, at least until now.[150]

THE DETAILED COMPARISON of technological attributes between Early Minoan and Middle Minoan pottery from the Mesara demonstrates that there existed a notable continuity in the way pottery was produced in the area, although with some clear developments in technology. What are the implications of such observations for the aims we set ourselves at the beginning of this study?

Key to the issue is the relationship between technology and society. Kamares Ware, the most common fine ceramic ware of the Protopalatial period, can be examined using two traditional approaches. First, it can be assumed that this sophisticated technology occurred through the institutionalization of craft production by the palace. In other words, the palace, by investing in craft production, favored technological innovation such as the adoption of the potter's wheel, which in turn enabled the standardization of products and the increase of production output.[151] In this argument, social structure determined the technological trajectory. In the second scenario, production slowly became specialized during the Prepalatial period, aided by the use of new technologies (e.g., plow agriculture, the introduction of "polyculture" and metal tools). This encouraged the emergence of managerial elites, who redistributed surplus agriculture produce and institutionalized craft production in order to ensure the procurement of specialized craft goods for elite exchanges.[152] In this argument, technological innovations are primarily responsible for changes in social organization.

However, arguments suggesting such straightforward links between social changes and the technological process have been strongly criticized, as often they examine limited aspects of material culture in order to produce broad generalizations about human society.[153] Moreover, in light of the above discussion, as far as the pottery system in the Mesara is concerned, both arguments would prove seriously flawed. First, the remarkable continuity in pottery manufacture in the Mesara would run contrary to the first approach inso-

150. Saramago 2002, 124.
151. E.g., Cherry 1986.
152. E.g., Renfrew 1972; Branigan 1988; Manning 1994.
153. Lemonnier 1992, 13–4.

far as the ceramic technological processes employed during the Protopalatial period long predate the establishment of the palace. Such continuity cannot be dismissed as simply the result of conservatism, since the pottery itself undergoes dramatic changes in appearance, which, however, leave many technological attributes largely unaffected. Secondly, regarding the opposite model of institutionalization of production, there are several factors that render it inapplicable. On the one hand, it has been demonstrated that ceramic production had been specialized at least since the beginning of the EM I period, without resulting in major social transformations. On the other hand, the emergence of the palace and the presumed centralization of production activities that accompanied it, appear to leave the process of ceramic manufacture generally unaltered. It has to be stressed that changes in the *scale* of ceramic production during the Palatial period are beyond doubt. However, such changes occurred simultaneously with an increase in the scale of consumption. They do not seem to have been informed by purely economic concerns, such as increase in productivity, because the basic operational sequence of manufacturing a ceramic vessel appears to have remained intact in many cases (as demonstrated by the consistency in the use of specific forming techniques, the application of decoration and firing). Moreover, the reevaluation of the introduction and widespread adoption of the potter's wheel technology[154] would cast doubt on the critical importance of economic factors spurring technological innovation in the ceramic system.

How, then, can we explain the development of ceramic technology and its relation to other social phenomena characterizing life during the Bronze Age in the Mesara? The answer to this question would seem to lie with the second aim of this study, namely to demonstrate that the production and consumption of ceramics played an important role in the articulation of social identities in the Mesara.

First, let us examine the implications of our analytical observations for the understanding of the process of ceramic production in the Mesara. Lemonnier in his study of the anthropology of technology has proposed five basic components that define a technique: matter, energy, objects (tools, etc.), gestures and knowledge.[155] Three out of these five components can be shown to continue unaltered for centuries in the ceramic system of the Mesara and it might be surmised that another remained largely unchanged as well: 1) Matter. The use not only of specific clay sources but also the same recipes of mixing and tempering clays are documented from the Prepalatial to the Protopalatial period while the same fabrics continue in the Neopalatial and even the modern period in the area.[156] 2) Energy. The energy used in the specific technique would be difficult to assess in archaeological con-

154. Day and Wilson 1998, 352; Knappett 1999.

155. Lemonnier 1992, 5–6.

156. Day 1988b, 505; 1997, 227 n. 46; Shaw et al. 2001, 118–9.

texts. However, to the degree that the quality of the finished products is indicative at least of the investment on the part of the potter, then the consistent high quality of Mesara ceramics can be demonstrated through the centuries.[157] 3) Objects. It is possible (and perhaps expected) that the tools used by the potters may have changed over long periods of time, but such changes, if they happened at the transition from the Prepalatial to the Protopalatial period, do not seem to have an obvious effect on the ceramic technological process. 4) Gestures. Some gestures on the other hand, can be proven to continue fairly unaltered from one period to the next. Petrographic analysis demonstrates such continuity in the most eloquent manner: the use of the same forming procedures can be clearly inferred from the common practice of forming the vessel from a sand-tempered clay, scraping the surface and smearing it with finer clay in order to create a smooth surface effect, while the existence of frequent, rather wavy voids in the pottery of both periods may indicate a consistency in the way the clay was mixed and wedged, hinting at the repetition of specific bodily movements of the potters. 5) Knowledge. Finally, all the technological attributes that continue from the Prepalatial to the Protopalatial period demonstrate that a body of knowledge was transmitted from one generation of potters to the next, through face-to-face interaction and the active demonstration of skills by the instructor to the apprentice.

It would seem therefore that some basic components of the ceramic technique not only continue without changes after the emergence of the palace, but also that such continuity appears to be a matter of face-to-face transmission of knowledge between potters, perhaps even working in the same locations. This would indicate that a very strong tradition of pottery making had already become crystallized in the Prepalatial Mesara and was continued through the major sociopolitical transformation effected by the emergence of the palace of Phaistos.

A few points on the nature and the significance of tradition need to be clarified before we continue. Tradition is embodied in the learning of every technique insofar as every kind of knowledge relating to this technique presupposes and relies on preexisting knowledge. Moreover, innovation must be seen in a dialectic relationship to tradition, since the invention and implementation of new ways of doing utilize knowledge of already existing practices and know-how. The most crucial point in this discussion, though, is that the elements that are perpetuated as part of a technological tradition are the result of an arduous process of understanding all the relevant possibilities for technological action and choosing specific paths.[158] It seems then that the particular knowledge of manufacturing ceramics in the Mesara, shaped through choices over several centuries, has been crystallized into a distinct technological tradition that was passed on through the generations.

157. See Van de Moortel 2002.

158. Lemonnier 1992, 6; Mahias 1993.

However, innovation penetrates the ceramic system in quite obvious manners: for instance, the dramatic change of vessel decoration from the Prepalatial to the Protopalatial, the use of the potter's wheel, the technique for making such exceptional products as Eggshell Ware, and the introduction of talc white. These are undeniable changes, as are the intensified scales of production and consumption of ceramics in the Protopalatial period. Nevertheless, the clear persistence of specific ways of manufacturing pots should be seen as intentional. Although there may exist "functional" reasons behind such choices, the very long-term reproduction of these particular ways of doing within a ceramic system that does not remain static, as well as within a sociopolitical milieu that is drastically transformed, must have more than practical significance. In order to understand the social dimensions of such choices we need to explore in more detail the particular historical context within which ceramic technology unfolded in the Mesara.

The standard view of the Prepalatial Mesara is one of a culturally and socially integrated region. Such an understanding has been influenced equally by the distinct topography of the area as well as by the distribution of homogeneous items of material culture such as tholos tombs and their contents. New research examining the patterns of interaction between the various Mesara communities during the Prepalatial period hints at a more dynamic pattern with several setbacks and disturbances in the integrative process.[159] It is argued that the more unified regional pattern, which can be observed during the Final Neolithic period in the area, breaks down progressively during the Early Minoan period, and that relationships between the Mesara communities become characterized by more competitive strategies toward the later stages of the Prepalatial period.[160] Such competition is manifested not only in the spatial circumscription of territories by the architectural enhancement of settlements and cemeteries, but also in the more symbolic demarcation of the boundaries of communities by participation in distinct consumption practices utilizing mainly ceramics and seal iconography.

With regard to ceramic production, the study of Mesara imports in north-central Crete has demonstrated the existence of several production groups in the Mesara whose products were exchanged with other sites, including Knossos.[161] However, such groups use similar raw materials and techniques of forming and decoration that place them firmly within the realm of a common technological tradition.[162] In other words, it seems that several production groups in the Prepalatial Mesara manufactured the same ceramic wares using similar production techniques and processes. How can such a situation be explained? In light of the new observations concerning the relationships between the different

159. Relaki 2003.

160. Relaki 2004.

161. Wilson and Day 1994.

162. Wilson and Day 1994, 82; Shaw et al. 2001, 131–3.

Mesara communities toward the end of the Prepalatial period, it may be argued that pottery production was used to implement strategies of competition among them. The manufacture of high-quality pottery had been an established practice in the region since Final Neolithic times, and Mesara ceramics had traveled to Knossos and farther across the island beginning early in the EM period. It is quite possible, therefore, that ceramics conferred substantial prestige on their producers as well as on their consumers in other areas of the island. Moreover, it is no coincidence that the greatest number of Mesara imports to Knossos is noted during EM IIA, the period when more localized strategies of communal identification start to become obvious within the Mesara. More importantly, fine ceramic wares had been at the center of communal consumption practices that placed considerable emphasis on the visibility and display of the ceramics. Can we suggest that by producing the same wares in similar manners, potters may have encouraged the comparison of their finished products that would ultimately reveal the most skilled artisan among them?

It is important to note that within the same wares there were differences in the shapes exchanged with other areas of Crete and the ones consumed locally in the Mesara. For example, it has been suggested that Fine Gray Ware in the Mesara is attested generally in globular pyxides that are consumed exclusively in funerary contexts, whereas exports of this ware to the rest of the island include a wider range of shapes found largely in domestic contexts.[163] If this picture is accurate, it would indicate that there was a degree of consciousness on the part of the potters regarding the esteem conferred by their products. Moreover the differences in the consumption patterns of this ware within the Mesara imply that the pottery system was also subjected to the same rules that defined and influenced other social practices during this period in the Mesara. Therefore, irrespective of what could have been produced by the craftspeople, the patterns of consumption within the region largely dictated what was actually produced and in what precise ways.

Although among the Mesara communities pottery appears to have served more competitive strategies, when exchanged outside the region, it operated as a unifying factor representing a more collective "Mesara identity." Internally, different production groups might have used similar technological processes in order to compete. Outside the area, such strategies were no longer relevant and Mesara ceramics would have been consumed as craft goods representing the common technological style of an entire region (particularly since different provenances could not have been inferred by the appearance of the vessels). In this sense, and perhaps rather unintentionally, pottery may have begun to function as a unifying element promoting a distinct regional identity within the Mesara.

The effects of such attitudes would have become more obvious to the Mesara communities in the long run. Although the contexts of ceramic consumption prove particularly

163. Wilson and Day 1994, 78–9.

significant in shaping the patterns of ceramic production, we should not underestimate the bonding potential of the consistent use of similar methods of ceramic manufacture among these communities for several centuries. As their technological style became crystallized into a tradition embraced across the entire region (and perhaps despite sociopolitical frictions), the unifying effect of sharing a common tradition would have become even more pronounced.

The trail of ceramic exchanges between the Mesara and other areas is lost during the EM III and MM IA periods, but this could be attributed to some extent to our poor knowledge at present of local Mesara styles in the late Prepalatial. However, such exchanges are rejuvenated in the Protopalatial period and Kamares Ware is the ceramic artifact that has the lead part in such transactions. Our knowledge of production groups in the Protopalatial period is still insufficient. However, the analytical part of our study demonstrates that, while there are also some indications of different production groups at each of the three main sites of the area,[164] Kamares Ware was developed within preexisting production groups. In view of its very extensive distribution in the Mesara region, in comparison with other areas of Crete, it could be suggested that several production groups continued to manufacture pottery as they had done in the Prepalatial period.

It is interesting to note that such a diachronic consistency in the patterns of pottery production is not restricted to the perpetuation of specific technological features, but also extends to the sharing by potters of the innovations of the ceramic system (e.g., the new shapes introduced with Kamares Ware, as well as developments in decoration and perhaps firing technology). Such common ground is on the one hand due to the longevity of these traditions in the Mesara, but on the other it is the result of common consumption strategies. As noted above, both the Fine Painted and Fine Gray Wares in the Prepalatial and Kamares Ware in the Protopalatial represent the finest drinking and serving sets of their respective periods. A review of the history of the Mesara from Final Neolithic to Middle Minoan shows that drinking practices held a very prominent role in the processes of social negotiation in the area and received consistent investment from the majority of the Mesara communities.[165] Moreover the argument for the palaces fulfilling, among others, the role of sophisticated venues for drinking and feasting consumption has been proposed by a number of recent studies.[166] Accordingly, it would seem that the persistent investment in the ceramic system in the Mesara had been shaped by long traditions of social life that the palace at Phaistos did not take over and institutionalize, but rather appropriated and manipulated within specific power strategies. These traditions shaped both the old and the new.

164. Carinci 1995; 1997; 1999; Betancourt 1990; cf. Van de Moortel 1997, 224–5.

165. Relaki 2003.

166. Hamilakis 1999; 2002; Day and Wilson 2002; Driessen 2002; Schoep 2002.

PETER M. DAY, MARIA RELAKI & EDWARD W. FABER

THE POWER OF POTTERY—PAST AND PRESENT

We hope in this paper to have demonstrated the longevity of a pottery tradition, the deliberate continuation of a way of doing, and of practice stemming from a specific body of knowledge. Contextualizing the continuity and changes in the Mesara pottery system has been shown to be a powerful tool in forging an understanding of the radical social and political transformations at the onset of the Palatial period. In this case the power of the pottery lies both in the past and the present.

In the past, ceramics formed part of the strategies of social reproduction for the Mesara potters, the inseparable domain of production and consumption forming an everyday arena of action at a time of profound change. Such observations bring us closer to a human scale of analysis, in which we consider how individuals and groups made sense of changes in the political landscape. There was no overnight transformation of society or craft. It seems unlikely that potters leapt from one clear-cut status to another, in a way that mirrored our categories of independent and attached. Not only is it clear that some aspects of life continued unchanged, but also this did not happen simply through inertia. The production of pottery may simply be similar to continuity in other aspects of Minoan life, but it may also be that the world of pottery was more than neutral. In the Mesara the creation of pottery and the use to which it was put lived through the many changes and it is clear that these were appropriated and manipulated by palatial authorities.

Likewise, for us in the present, the power of pottery holds great potential. Our observations and actions on the micro-level have the ability to illuminate our macro-level questions, the big picture of long-term patterns and histories. It is the integrated, multi-technique analytical approach to the material world of pottery, developed in part upon Philip Betancourt's pioneering work, which holds the promise to make possible such detailed insights into the human past on Crete.

WORKS CITED

Andreou, S. 1978. "Pottery Groups of the Old Palace Period in Crete." Ph.D. diss., University of Cincinnati.

Arnold, D.E. 1985. *Ceramic Theory and Cultural Process*. New Studies in Archaeology. Cambridge: Cambridge University Press.

Belfiore, C., P.M. Day, V. Kilikoglou, V. La Rosa, P. Mazzoleni and A. Pezzino. 2003. "Mineralogical, Petrographical and Geochemical Characterisation of Pottery Production of the Late Minoan I Kiln at Haghia Triada (Crete): Preliminary Data." *Creta Antica* 4: 419–36.

Betancourt, P.P., ed. 1984. *East Cretan White-on-Dark Ware: Studies on a Handmade Pottery of the Early to Middle Minoan Periods*. University Museum Monograph 51. Philadelphia: The University Museum.

———. 1985. *The History of Minoan Pottery*. Princeton, NJ: Princeton University Press.

———. 1990. *Kommos*. Vol. 2, *The Final Neolithic through Middle Minoan III Pottery*. Princeton, NJ: Princeton University Press.

Betancourt, P.P., T.K. Gaisser, E. Koss, R. Lyon, F.R. Matson, S. Montgomery, G.H. Myer and C.P. Swann. 1979. *Vasiliki Ware: An Early Bronze Age Pottery Style in Crete. SIMA* 56. Göteborg: Paul Åströms.

Betancourt, P.P., T.K. Gaisser, F.R. Matson, G.H. Myer, C.P. Swann and R.G. White. 1984. "Studies on the Gournian White Slip." In *East Cretan White-on-Dark Ware*, edited by P.P. Betancourt, 71–4. University Museum Monograph 51. Philadelphia: The University Museum.

Betancourt, P.P. and C.P. Swann. 1989. "PIXE Analysis of Middle Minoan Pigments from Kommos." In *Archaeometry. Proceedings of the 25th International Symposium*, edited by Y. Maniatis, 177–81. Amsterdam: Elsevier.

Blackman, D. and K. Branigan. 1977. "An Archaeological Survey of the Lower Catchment of the Ayiofarango Valley." *BSA* 72: 13–84.

———. 1982. "The Excavation of an Early Minoan Tholos Tomb at Ayia Kyriaki, Ayiofarango, Southern Crete." *BSA* 77: 1–57.

Bonacasa, N. 1967–1968. "Patrikiès. Una stazione medio-minoica fra Haghia Triada e Festòs." *ASAtene* 45–46 (n.s. 29–30): 7–54.

Branigan, K. 1983. "Craft Specialization in Minoan Crete." In *Minoan Society. Proceedings of the Cambridge Colloquium 1981*, edited by O. Krzyszkowska and L. Nixon, 23–32. Bristol: Bristol Classical Press.

———. 1987. "The Economic Role of the First Palaces." In *The Function of the Minoan Palaces. Proceedings of the Fourth International Symposium at the Swedish Institute in Athens, 10–16 June 1984*, edited by R. Hägg and N. Marinatos, 245–9. *SkrAth* 4, 35. Stockholm: Svenska Institutet i Athen.

———. 1988. *Prepalatial: The Foundations of Palatial Crete. A Survey of Crete in the Early Bronze Age,* 2nd updated edition. Amsterdam: A.M. Hakker.

Brumfiel, E.M. and T.K. Earle. 1987. "Specialization, Exchange and Complex Societies: An Introduction." In *Specialization, Exchange and Complex Societies*, edited by E.M. Brumfiel and T.K. Earle, 1–9. New Directions in Archaeology. Cambridge: Cambridge University Press.

Burton, J.H. and A.W. Simon. 1996. "A Pot Is Not a Rock: A Reply to Neff, Glascock, Bishop and Blackman." *American Antiquity* 61: 405–13.

Carinci, F. 1995. "Ceramiche con decorazioni a rilievo da Festòs e Haghia Triada." In *Πεπραγμένα του Ζ' Διεθνούς Κρητολογικού Συνεδρίου*. Vol. A1, *Τμήμα Αρχαιολογικό*, 105–109. Rethymnon: Iera Mitropolis Rethymnis & Aulopotamou.

———. 1997. "Pottery Workshops at Phaistos and Haghia Triada in the Protopalatial Period." In *TEXNH: Craftsmen, Craftswomen and Craftsmanship in the Aegean Bronze Age. Proceedings of the 6th International Aegean Conference, Philadelphia, Temple University, 18–21 April 1996*, edited by R. Laffineur and P.P. Betancourt, 317–22. *Aegaeum* 16. Liège: Université de Liège.

———. 1999. "Haghia Triada nel periodo dei Primi Palazzi: i nuovi dati sulle produzioni ceramiche." In *Επὶ Πόντον Πλαζόμενοι. Simposio italiano di Studi Egei dedicato a Luigi Bernabò Brea e Giovanni Pugliese Carratelli*, edited by V. La

Rosa, D. Palermo and L. Vagnetti, 115–32. Rome: Scuola Archeologica Italiana di Atene.

Catling, H.W., A.E. Blin-Stoyle and E.E. Richards. 1961. "Spectrographic Analysis of Mycenaean and Minoan Pottery." *Archaeometry* 4: 31–8.

Catling, H.W., E.E. Richards and A.E. Blin-Stoyle. 1963. "Correlations between Composition and Provenance of Mycenaean and Minoan Pottery." *BSA* 58: 94–115.

Cherry, J.F. 1983. "Evolution, Revolution, and the Origins of Complex Society in Minoan Crete." In *Minoan Society. Proceedings of the Cambridge Colloquium 1981*, edited by O. Krzyszkowska and L. Nixon, 33–45. Bristol: Bristol Classical Press.

———. 1984. "The Emergence of the State in the Prehistoric Aegean." *PCPS* 210, n.s. 30: 18–48.

———. 1986. "Polities and Palaces: Some Problems in Minoan State Formation." In *Peer Polity Interaction and Socio-Political Change*, edited by C. Renfrew and J.F. Cherry, 19–45. New Directions in Archaeology. Cambridge: Cambridge University Press.

Dawkins, R.M. and M.L.W. Laistner. 1912–1913. "The Excavation of the Kamares Cave in Crete." *BSA* 19: 1–34.

Day, P.M. 1988a. "Ceramic Analysis and Pottery Systems: The Case of Minoan Crete." In *New Aspects of Archaeological Science in Greece. Proceedings of a Meeting Held at the British School at Athens, January, 1987*, edited by R.E. Jones and H.W. Catling, 39–45. Fitch Laboratory Occasional Paper 3. Athens: British School at Athens.

———. 1988b. "The Production and Distribution of Storage Jars in Neopalatial Crete." In *Problems in Greek Prehistory. Papers Presented at the Centenary Conference of the British School of Archaeology at Athens, Manchester, April 1986*, edited by E.B. French and K.A. Wardle, 499–508. Bristol: Bristol Classical Press.

———. 1991. "A Petrographic Approach to the Study of Pottery in Neopalatial East Crete." Ph.D. diss., University of Cambridge.

———. 1997. "Ceramic Exchange between Towns and Outlying Settlements in Neopalatial East Crete." In *The Function of the "Minoan Villa." Proceedings of the Eighth International Symposium at the Swedish Institute at Athens, 6–8 June 1992*, edited by R. Hägg, 219–28. *SkrAth* 4, 46. Stockholm: Svenska Institutet i Athen.

Day, P.M., E. Kiriatzi, A. Tsolakidou and V. Kilikoglou. 1999. "Group Therapy in Crete: A Comparison between Analyses by NAA and Thin Section Petrography of Early Minoan Pottery." *JAS* 26: 1025–36.

Day, P.M. and D.E. Wilson. 1998. "Consuming Power: Kamares Ware in Protopalatial Knossos." *Antiquity* 72: 350–8.

———. 2002. "Landscapes of Memory, Craft and Power in Prepalatial and Protopalatial Knossos." In *Labyrinth Revisited: Rethinking 'Minoan' Archaeology*, edited by Y. Hamilakis, 143–66. Oxford: Oxbow.

———. 2004. "Ceramic Change and the Practice of Eating and Drinking in Early Bronze Age Crete." In *Food, Cuisine and Society in Prehistoric Greece*, edited by P. Halstead and J.C. Barrett, 45–62. Sheffield Studies in Aegean Archaeology 5. Oxford: Oxbow.

Day P.M., D.E. Wilson and E. Kiriatzi. 1997. "Reassessing Specialization in Prepalatial Cretan Ceramic Production." In *TEXNH: Craftsmen, Craftswomen and Craftsmanship in the Aegean Bronze Age. Proceedings of the 6th International Aegean Conference, Philadelphia, Temple University, 18–21 April 1996*, edited by R. Laffineur and P.P. Betancourt, 275–89. *Aegaeum* 16. Liège: Université de Liège.

———. 1998. "Pots, Labels and People: Burying Ethnicity in the Cemetery of Aghia Photia, Siteias." In *Cemetery and Society in the Aegean Bronze Age*, edited by K. Branigan, 133–49. Sheffield Studies in Aegean Archaeology 1. Sheffield: Sheffield Academic Press.

De Boer, W.R. 1984. "The Last Pottery Show: System and Sense in Ceramic Studies." In *The Many Dimensions of Pottery: Ceramics in Archaeology and Anthropology*, edited by S.E. van der Leeuw and A.C. Pritchard, 527–71. Amsterdam: Universiteit van Amsterdam.

Dietler, M. and I. Herbich. 1998. "*Habitus*, Techniques, Style: An Integrated Approach to the Social Understanding of Material Culture and Boundaries." In *The Archaeology of Social Boundaries*, edited by M. Stark, 232–63. Smithsonian Series in Archaeological Inquiry. Washington, DC: Smithsonian Institution.

Driessen, J. 2002. "'The King Must Die.' Some Observations on the Use of Minoan Court Compounds." In *Monu-*

ments of Minos: Rethinking the Minoan Palaces. Proceedings of the International Workshop "Crete of the Hundred Palaces?" Held at the Université Catholique de Louvain, Louvain-la-Neuve, 14–15 December 2001, edited by J. Driessen, I. Schoep and R. Laffineur, 1–14. *Aegaeum* 23. Liège: Université de Liège.

Evans, A. 1921. *The Palace of Minos at Knossos*. Vol. 1. London: Macmillan.

———. 1928. *The Palace of Minos at Knossos*. Vol. 2. London: Macmillan.

———. 1930. *The Palace of Minos at Knossos*. Vol. 3. London: Macmillan.

———. 1935. *The Palace of Minos at Knossos*. Vol. 4. London: Macmillan.

Faber, E.W., V. Kilikoglou, P.M. Day and D.E. Wilson. 2002. "A Technological Study of Middle Minoan Polychrome Pottery from Knossos, Crete." In *Modern Trends in Scientific Studies on Ancient Ceramics. Papers Presented at the 5th European Meeting on Ancient Ceramics, Athens, 1999*, edited by V. Kilikoglou, A. Hein and Y. Maniatis, 129–41. *BAR-IS* 1011. Oxford: Archaeopress.

Ferrence, S., C.P. Swann and P.P. Betancourt. 2001. "PIXE Analysis of White Pigments on Pottery from Five Bronze Age Minoan Archaeological Sites." *Aegean Archaeology* 5: 47–54.

Fitton, L., M. Hughes and S. Quirke. 1998. "Northerners at Lahun: Neutron Activation Analysis of Minoan and Related Pottery in the British Museum." In *Lahun Studies*, edited by S. Quirke, 112–40. Reigate: SIA.

Floyd, C. 1997. "The Alternating Floral Style as Evidence for Pottery Workshops in East Crete during the Protopalatial Period." In *TEXNH: Craftsmen, Craftswomen and Craftsmanship in the Aegean Bronze Age. Proceedings of the 6th International Aegean Conference, Philadelphia, Temple University, 18–21 April 1996*, edited by R. Laffineur and P.P. Betancourt, 313–6. *Aegaeum* 16. Liège: Université de Liège.

Haggis, D.C. and M.S. Mook. 1993. "The Kavousi Coarse Wares: A Bronze Age Chronology for Survey in the Mirabello Area, East Crete." *AJA* 97: 265–93.

Hamilakis, Y. 1999. "Food Technologies/Technologies of the Body: The Social Context of Wine and Oil Production and Consumption in Bronze Age Crete." *World Archaeology* 31: 38–54.

———. 2002. "Too Many Chiefs? Factional Competition in Neopalatial Crete." In *Monuments of Minos: Rethinking the Minoan Palaces. Proceedings of the International Workshop "Crete of the Hundred Palaces?" Held at the Université Catholique de Louvain, Louvain-la-Neuve, 14–15 December 2001*, edited by J. Driessen, I. Schoep and R. Laffineur, 179–99. *Aegaeum* 23. Liège: Université de Liège.

Hegmon, M. 1995. *The Social Dynamics of Pottery Style in the Early Puebloan Southwest*. Occasional Papers of the Crown Canyon Archaeological Center 5. Cortez, CO: Crow Canyon Archaeological Center.

———. 1998. "Technology, Style and Social Practices: Archaeological Approaches." In *The Archaeology of Social Boundaries*, edited by M. Stark, 264–79. Washington, DC: Smithsonian Institution.

Hein, A., P.M. Day, M.A. Cau Ontiveros and V. Kilikoglou. 2004. "Red Clays from Central and Eastern Crete: Geochemical and Mineralogical Properties in View of Provenance Studies on Ancient Ceramics." *Applied Clay Science* 24: 245–55.

Hein, A., P.M. Day, P.S. Quinn and V. Kilikoglou. 2004. "The Geochemical Diversity of Neogene Clay Deposits in Crete and Its Implications for Provenance Studies of Minoan Pottery." *Archaeometry* 46, 3: 357–84.

Hodder, I. 1982. *Symbols in Action: Ethnoarchaeological Studies of Material Culture*. Cambridge: Cambridge University Press.

Hood, S. 1990. "Settlers in Crete c. 3000 B.C." *Cretan Studies* 2: 151–8.

Hope Simpson, R. with P.P. Betancourt, P.J. Callaghan, D.K. Harlan, J.W. Hayes, J.W. Shaw, M.C. Shaw and L.V. Watrous. 1995. "The Archaeological Survey of the Kommos Area." In *Kommos*. Vol. 1, *The Kommos Region and Houses of the Minoan Town*. Part 1, *The Kommos Region, Ecology and Minoan Industries*, edited by J.W. Shaw and M.C. Shaw, 325–402. Princeton, NJ: Princeton University Press.

Jones, A. 2002. *Archaeological Theory and Scientific Practice*. Cambridge: Cambridge University Press.

Jones, R.E. 1986. *Greek and Cypriot Pottery*. Fitch Laboratory Occasional Paper 1. Athens: British School at Athens.

Karetsou, A. 1978. "Εφορεία Προϊστορικών και Κλασικών Αρχαιοτήτων Ηρακλείου: Καλαμάκι." *ArchDelt* 33, B2: 357–8.

Kilikoglou, V. 1994. "Scanning Electron Microscopy." In "Ceramic Regionalism in Prepalatial Central Crete: The Mesara Imports at EM I to EM II A Knossos," by D.E. Wilson and P.M. Day, 70–5. *BSA* 89: 1–87.

Kilikoglou V., M.I. Karayannis and A.P. Grimanis. 1990. "Neutron Activation and Statistical Analysis of Pottery from Thera, Greece." *Journal of Radioanalytical and Nuclear Chemistry, Articles*, 141: 347–55.

Kiriatzi, E., P.M. Day and D.E. Wilson. 2000. "Διακίνηση της Κεραμεικής και Κοινωνικοπολιτική Οργάνωση: Η Γραπτή Κεραμεική της ΠΜ II και I Περιόδου στην Ανατολική Κρήτη." In *Πεπραγμένα Η′ Διεθνούς Κρητολογικού Συνεδρίου. Προϊστορική και Αρχαία Ελληνική Περίοδος*, Vol. A2, edited by A. Karetsou, 99–115. Heraklion: Etairia Kretikon Istorikon Meleton.

Knappett, C. 1997. "Ceramic Production in the Protopalatial Mallia 'State': Evidence from Quartier Mu and Myrtos Pyrgos." In *TEXNH: Craftsmen, Craftswomen and Craftsmanship in the Aegean Bronze Age. Proceedings of the 6th International Aegean Conference, Philadelphia, Temple University, 18–21 April 1996*, edited by R. Laffineur and P.P. Betancourt, 305–11. *Aegaeum* 16. Liège: Université de Liège.

———. 1999. "Tradition and Innovation in Pottery Forming Technology: Wheel-Throwing at Middle Minoan Knossos." *BSA* 94: 101–29.

La Rosa, V. 2002. "Le campagne di scavo 2000–2002 a Festòs." *ASAtene* 80 (3rd ser. 2): 635–869.

Lemonnier, P. 1992. *Elements for an Anthropology of Technology*. Anthropological Papers (University of Michigan, Museum of Anthropology) 88. Ann Arbor, MI: Museum of Anthropology, University of Michigan.

———, ed. 1993. *Technological Choices: Transformation in Material Cultures since the Neolithic*. Material Cultures. London: Routledge.

Levi, D. 1957–1958. "L'archivio di cretule a Festòs." *ASAtene* 35–36 (n.s. 19–20): 7-192.

———. 1976. *Festòs e la civiltà minoica*. Vol. 1. Incunabula Graeca 60. Rome: Edizioni dell'Ateneo.

Levi, D. and F. Carinci 1988. *Festòs e la civiltà minoica*. Vol. 2. Incunabula Graeca 77. Roma: Edizioni dell'Ateneo.

Livingstone Smith, A. 2000. "Processing Clay for Pottery in Northern Cameroon: Social and Technical Requirements. *Archaeometry* 42: 21–42.

MacGillivray, J.A. 1986. Review of *Provincial Middle Minoan Pottery*, by G. Walberg. *JHS* 106: 249–50.

———. 1998. *Knossos: Pottery Groups of the Old Palace Period. BSA* Studies 5. London: British School at Athens.

Mackenzie, D.E. 1906. "The Middle Minoan Pottery of Knossos." *JHS* 26: 243–67.

Mahias, M.-C. 1993. "Pottery Techniques in India: Technical Variants and Social Choice." In *Technological Choices: Transformation in Material Cultures since the Neolithic*, edited by P. Lemonnier, 157–80. Material Cultures. London: Routledge.

Maniatis, Y. and M.S. Tite. 1981. "Technological Examination of Neolithic–Bronze Age Pottery from Central and Southeast Europe and from the Near East." *JAS* 8: 59–76.

Manning, S.W. 1994. "The Emergence of Divergence: Development and Decline on Bronze Age Crete and the Cyclades." In *Development and Decline in the Mediterranean Bronze Age*, edited by C. Mathers and S. Stoddart, 221–70. Sheffield Archaeological Monographs 8. Sheffield: J.R. Collis.

Manteli, K. 1993. "The Transition from the Neolithic to the Early Bronze Age in Crete, with Special Reference to Pottery." Ph.D. diss., University College London.

Mariani, L. 1895. "Antichità cretesi: Note sulla ceramica cretese, 1. Vasi di Kamares." *MonAnt* 6: 333–48.

Matson, F.R. 1984. "Ceramics and Man Reconsidered with Some Thoughts for the Future." In *The Many Dimensions of Pottery: Ceramics in Archaeology and Anthropology*, edited by S.E. van der Leeuw and A.C. Pritchard, 25–54. Amsterdam: Universiteit van Amsterdam.

Moody, J.A. 1985. "The Development of a Bronze Age Coarse Ware Chronology for the Khania Region of West Crete." *TUAS* 10: 51–65.

Morris, I. 1994. "Archaeologies of Greece." In *Classical Greece: Ancient Histories and Modern Archaeologies*, edited by I. Morris, 8–47. New Directions in Archaeology. Cambridge: Cambridge University Press.

Myer, G.H. and P.P. Betancourt. 1990. "The Fabrics at Kommos." In *Kommos*. Vol. 2, *The Final Neolithic through Middle Minoan III Pottery*, edited by P.P. Betancourt, 1–13. Princeton, NJ: Princeton University Press.

Myer, G.H., K.G. McIntosh and P.P. Betancourt. 1995. "Definition of Pottery Fabrics by Ceramic Petrography." In *Pseira*. Vol. 1, *The Minoan Buildings on the West Side of Area A*, edited by P.P. Betancourt and C. Davaras, 143–53. University Museum Monograph 90. Philadelphia: The University Museum.

Myres, J.L. 1893–1895. "Prehistoric Polychrome Pottery from Kamárais in Crete." *Proceedings of the Society of Antiquaries of London* 15, 2nd series: 351–6.

Noll, W. 1982. "Mineralogie und Technik der Keramiken Altkretas." *Neues Jahrbuch für Mineralogie Abhandlungen* 143: 150–99.

Noll, W., R. Holm and L. Born. 1971. "Chemie und Technik altkretischer Vasenmalerei vom Kamares-Typ." *Die Naturwissenschaften* 58: 615–8.

———. 1975. "Painting of Ancient Ceramics." *Angewandte Chemie International Edition* 14, 9: 602–13.

Orton, C., P. Tyers and A.G. Vince. 1993. *Pottery in Archaeology*. Cambridge Manuals in Archaeology. Cambridge: Cambridge University Press.

Peacock, D.P.S. 1977. "Ceramics in Roman and Medieval Archaeology." In *Pottery and Early Commerce: Characterization and Trade in Roman and Later Ceramics*, edited by D.P.S. Peacock, 21–34. London: Academic Press.

Pelagatti, P. 1961–1962. "Osservazioni sui ceramisti del I palazzo di Festos." *Πεπραγμένα του Α' Διεθνοῦς Κρητολογικοῦ Συνεδρίου*. Vol. 1. *CretChron* 15–16: 99–111.

Pendlebury, J.D.S. 1939. *The Archaeology of Crete: An Introduction*. London: Methuen.

Poursat, J.-C. 1997. "Potiers et peintres à Malia (Quartier Mu), Crète: Le Camares provincial entre tradition et innovation." In *TEXNH: Craftsmen, Craftswomen and Craftsmanship in the Aegean Bronze Age. Proceedings of the 6th International Aegean Conference, Philadelphia, Temple University, 18–21 April 1996*, edited by R. Laffineur and P.P. Betancourt, 301–4. *Aegaeum* 16. Liège: Université de Liège.

Relaki, M. 2003. "Social Arenas in Minoan Crete: A Regional History of the Mesara in South-Central Crete from the Final Neolithic to the End of the Protopalatial Period." Ph.D. Diss., University of Sheffield.

———. 2004. "Constructing a *Region*: The Contested Landscapes of Prepalatial Mesara." In *The Emergence of Civilisation Revisited*, edited by J.C. Barrett and P. Halstead, 170–88. Sheffield Studies in Aegean Archaeology 6. Oxford: Oxbow Books.

Renfrew, C. 1972. *The Emergence of Civilisation: The Cyclades and the Aegean in the Third Millennium B.C.* Studies in Prehistory. London: Methuen.

Rice, P. 1981. "Evolution of Specialized Pottery Production: A Trial Model." *Current Anthropology* 22: 219–40.

———. 1991. "Specialization, Standardization and Diversity: A Retrospective." In *The Ceramic Legacy of Anna O. Shepard*, edited by R.L. Bishop and F.W. Lange, 257–79. Boulder: University Press of Colorado.

Riley, J.A. 1983. "The Contribution of Ceramic Petrology to our Understanding of Minoan Society." In *Minoan Society. Proceedings of the Cambridge Colloquium 1981*, edited by O. Krzyszkowska and L. Nixon, 283–92. Bristol: Bristol Classical Press.

———. 1984. "Pottery Analysis and the Reconstruction of Ancient Exchange Systems." In *The Many Dimensions of Pottery: Ceramics in Archaeology and Anthropology*, edited by S.E. van der Leeuw and A.C. Pritchard, 55–78. Amsterdam: Universiteit van Amsterdam.

Saramago, J. 2002. *The Cave*. Translated by M.J. Costa. London: Harcourt.

Schiering, W. 1998. *Minoische Töpferkunst: Die bemalten Tongefäße der Insel des Minos*. Mainz on Rhine: Philipp von Zabern.

Schoep, I. 2002. "The State of the Minoan Palaces or the Minoan Palace-State?" In *Monuments of Minos: Rethinking the Minoan Palaces. Proceedings of the International Workshop "Crete of the Hundred Palaces?" Held at the Université Catholique de Louvain, Louvain-la-Neuve, 14–15 December 2001*, edited by J. Driessen, I. Schoep and R. Laffineur, 15–33. *Aegaeum* 23. Liège: Université de Liège.

Shaw, J.W., A. Van de Moortel, P.M. Day and V. Kilikoglou. 2001. *A LM IA Ceramic Kiln in South-Central Crete: Function and Pottery Production*. *Hesperia* Suppl. 30. Princeton, NJ: American School of Classical Studies at Athens.

Shepard, A.O. 1956. *Ceramics for the Archaeologist*. Carnegie Institution of Washington Publication 609. Washington, D.C.: Carnegie Institution of Washington.

Stos-Fertner, Z., R.E.M. Hedges and R.D.G. Evely. 1979. "The Application of the XRF-XRD Method to the Analysis of the Pigments of Minoan Painted Pottery." *Archaeometry* 21: 187–94.

Tomasello, F. 1996. "Fornaci a Festòs ed Haghia Triada dall "età" mediominoica alla geometrica." In *Κεραμεικά Εργαστήρια στην Κρήτη απο την Αρχαιότητα ως Σήμερα. Πρακτικά Ημερίδας Μαργαρίτες, 30 Σεπτεμβρίου 1995*, edited by I. Gavrilaki, 27–37. Rethymnon: Istorike Laographike Etaireia Rethymnis.

Tomkins, P.D. 2001. "The Production, Circulation and Consumption of Ceramic Vessels at Early Neolithic Knossos, Crete." Ph.D. diss., University of Sheffield.

Tomkins, P.D. and P.M. Day. 2001. "Production and Exchange of the Earliest Ceramic Vessels in the Aegean: A View from the Early Neolithic Knossos, Crete." *Antiquity* 75: 259–60.

Tomkins, P.D., P.M. Day and V. Kilikoglou. 2004. "Knossos and the Earlier Neolithic Landscape of the Herakleion Basin." In *Knossos: Palace, City, State. Proceedings of the Conference in Herakleion Organised by the British School at Athens and the 23rd Ephoreia of Prehistoric and Classical Antiquities of Herakleion, in November 2000, for the Centenary of Sir Arthur Evans's Excavations at Knossos*, edited by G. Cadogan, E. Hatzaki and A. Vasilakis, 51–9. *BSA* Studies 12. London: British School at Athens.

Vagnetti, L. 1972–1973: "L'insediamento neolitico di Festòs." *ASAtene* 50–51 (n.s. 34–35): 7–138.

Vagnetti, L. and P. Belli. 1978. "Characters and Problems of the Final Neolithic in Crete." *SMEA* 19 (Incunabula Graeca 68): 125–63.

Vallianou, D. 1979. "Εφορεία Προϊστορικών και Κλασικών Αρχαιοτήτων Ηρακλείου: Μάρτσαλος-Καλαμάκι." *ArchDelt* 34, B2: 383–4.

Van de Moortel, A. 1997. "The Transition from the Protopalatial to the Neopalatial Society in South-Central Crete: A Ceramic Perspective." PhD. diss., Bryn Mawr College.

———. 2002. "Pottery as a Barometer of Economic Change: From the Protopalatial to the Neopalatial Society in Central Crete." In *Labyrinth Revisited: Rethinking 'Minoan' Archaeology*, edited by Y. Hamilakis, 189–211. Oxford: Oxbow.

van der Leeuw, S.E. 1984. "Dust to Dust: A Transformational View of the Ceramic Cycle." In *The Many Dimensions of Pottery: Ceramics in Archaeology and Anthropology*, edited by S.E. van der Leeuw and A.C. Pritchard, 707–78. Amsterdam: Universiteit van Amsterdam.

———. 1993. "Giving the Potter a Choice: Conceptual Aspects of Pottery Techniques." In *Technological Choices: Transformation in Material Culture since the Neolithic*, edited by P. Lemonnier, 238–88. Material Cultures. London: Routledge.

Vasilakis, A. 1989–1990. "Προϊστορικές Θέσεις στη Μονή Οδηγήτριας-Καλούς Λιμένες." *Κρητική Εστία* 3: 11–79.

Walberg, G. 1976. *Kamares: A Study of the Character of Palatial Middle Minoan Pottery*. Acta Universitatis Upsaliensis. Boreas 8. Uppsala: [Universitet]; Stockholm: Almqvist & Wikell.

———. 1981. "The Identification of Middle Minoan Painters and Workshops." *AJA* 85: 73–5.

———. 1983. *Provincial Middle Minoan Pottery*. Mainz on Rhine: Philipp von Zabern.

———. 1986. *Tradition and Innovation: Essay in Minoan Art*. Mainz on Rhine: Philipp von Zabern.

———. 1987. "Palatial and Provincial Workshops in the Middle Minoan Period." In *The Function of the Minoan Palaces. Proceedings of the Fourth International Symposium at the Swedish Institute in Athens, 10–16 June 1984*, edited by R. Hägg and N. Marinatos, 281–5. *SkrAth* 4, 35. Stockholm: Svenska Institutet i Athen.

Warren, P. 1972. *Myrtos: An Early Bronze Age Settlement in Crete*. *BSA* Suppl. 7. Oxford: British School of Archaeology at Athens and Thames and Hudson.

Watrous, L.V., D. Xatzi-Vallianou, K. Pope, N. Mourtzas, J. Shay, C.T. Shay, J. Bennet, D. Tsoungarakis, C. Vallianos and H. Blitzer. 1993. "A Survey of the Western Mesara Plain in Crete: Preliminary Report of the 1984, 1986, and 1987 Field Seasons." *Hesperia* 62: 191–248.

Weigand, P.C., G. Harbottle and E.V. Sayre. 1977. "Turquoise Sources and Source Analysis: Mesoamerica and the Southwestern U.S.A." In *Exchange Systems in Prehistory*, edited by T.K. Earle and J.E. Ericson, 15–34. Studies in Archaeology. New York: Academic Press.

Whitbread, I.K. 1989. "A Proposal for the Systematic Description of Thin Sections towards the Study of Ancient Ceramic Technology." In *Archaeometry. Proceedings of the 25th International Symposium*, edited by Y. Maniatis, 127–38. Amsterdam: Elsevier.

———. 1995. *Greek Transport Amphorae: A Petrological and Archaeological Study*. Fitch Laboratory Occasional Paper 4. London: British School at Athens.

Whitelaw, T.M. 1983. "The Settlement at Fournou Korifi Myrtos and Aspects of Early Minoan Social Organisation." In *Minoan Society. Proceedings of the Cambridge Colloquium 1981*, edited by O. Krzyszkowska and L. Nixon, 323–45. Bristol: Bristol Classical Press.

Whitelaw, T.M., P.M. Day, E. Kiriatzi, V. Kilikoglou and D.E. Wilson. 1997. "Ceramic Traditions at EM IIB Myrtos, Fournou Korifi." In *TEXNH: Craftsmen, Craftswomen and Craftsmanship in the Aegean Bronze Age. Proceedings of the 6th International Aegean Conference, Philadelphia, Temple University, 18–21 April 1996*, edited by R. Laffineur and P.P. Betancourt, 265–74. *Aegaeum* 16. Liège: Université de Liège.

Whitley, J. 2002–2003. "Archaeology in Greece 2002–2003." *AR* 49: 1–88.

Wilson, D.E. and P.M. Day. 1994. "Ceramic Regionalism in Prepalatial Central Crete: The Mesara Imports at EM I to EM II A Knossos." *BSA* 89: 1–87.

———. 2000. "EM I Chronology and Social Practice: Pottery from the Early Palace Tests at Knossos." *BSA* 95: 21–63.

Zoes, A. 1968. *Der Kamares-Stil: Werden und Wesen*. Tübingen: Fotodruck Präzis.

A REEXAMINATION OF THE POTTERY FROM THE KAMARES CAVE

ALEYDIS VAN DE MOORTEL

THE KAMARES CAVE, or *Mavrospelio* as it is locally called, is located high (el. 1524 m) on the southern flank of the Ida mountain range in central Crete (fig. 1). It is well-known among Aegeanists as the place where for the first time polychrome Minoan pottery of superb quality dating to the period of the First Palaces (c. 1900–1700 B.C.) was found. From its first archaeological investigation by Taramelli in 1894, the cave has been identified as an important Minoan sanctuary.[1] Whereas its discovery generated great interest around the turn of the century, the cave has received little attention in more recent times. Since its excavation and publication by British archaeologists Dawkins and Laistner in 1913, now ninety years ago, no examination of its material has been undertaken until the present study.

The following is a first report on the restudy of this pottery, conducted by the author in 2002 and 2003. This work forms part of a larger project reinvestigating the cave and all its finds, carried out in cooperation with Loeta Tyree under the auspices of the Canadian Archaeological Institute at Athens. Even though the pottery study is not complete, it is already possible to make a number of new observations which, the author hopes, may be of interest to Phil Betancourt, given his and James Muhly's current excavation of the Hagios Charalambos Cave on Crete. Together with Watrous' publication of the Psychro Cave and Kanta and Tyree's current work on the material from the Skoteino Cave, we are experiencing a true renaissance of interest in Minoan cave use.[2]

It is a pleasure to contribute a paper to a volume honoring Philip Betancourt. From the time when I was a graduate student embarking on a dissertation about Minoan pottery, Philip Betancourt has always been gracious to me, providing help and guidance. I would like to dedicate this article to him as a token of thanks.

Loeta Tyree and I would like to thank directors David Blackman and James Whitley of the British School at Athens and director Emanuele Greco of the Italian School at Athens for permission to study and publish the Kamares Cave material. We also are grateful to the Canadian Archaeological Institute at Athens, its directors Nigel and Stefanie Kennell, and assistant director Jonathan Tomlinson for their support of this project.

The present pottery study would not have been possible without the generous support of the Institute for Aegean Prehistory, as well the hard work and dedication of artists A. Glynnis Fawkes, Christina L. Kolb, and Mary Jane Schumacher, photographer Ioannis Papadakis-Plumidis, and conservator Tasos Karousos. My sincere thanks to all.

1. Taramelli 1901, 437, 443–4, 449–51.
2. Watrous 1996.

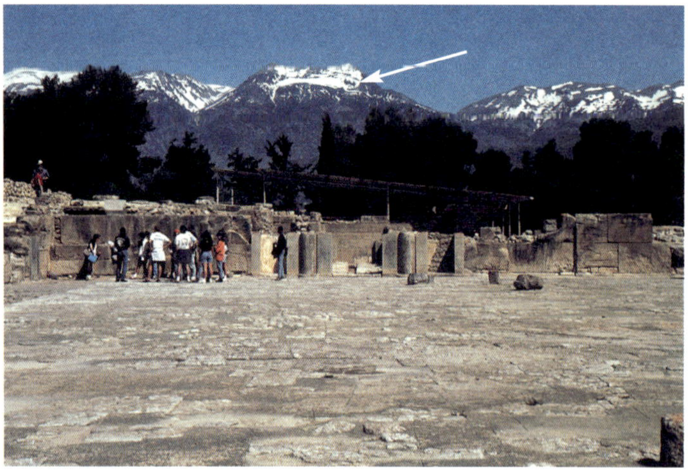

FIG. 1. The twin *Mavri* peaks of the Ida mountain range and the Kamares Cave seen from the Central Court of the palace at Phaistos. The cave is the black dot indicated by the white arrow. North-south Corridor 41 and its monumental doorway in the north facade of the Court are aligned with the cave (A. Van de Moortel).

KAMARES WARE VERSUS KAMARES CAVE POTTERY

THE HIGH-QUALITY POLYCHROME POTTERY found by the earliest explorers of the Kamares Cave in the late nineteenth century was immediately labeled Kamares Ware. This name has stuck as a designation of high-quality polychrome pottery of the Protopalatial period in spite of problems of definition.[3] It is important to point out that highly decorated pottery formed but a minority of the ceramic finds from the cave. Most vases were of utilitarian quality, their surfaces being unpainted, painted with a solid dark slip, or decorated with simple linear patterns. The present study encompasses all pottery from the cave, whatever its quality. To avoid confusion, the term "Kamares Ware" will not be employed. Instead, the term "Kamares Cave pottery" will be used to denote the entire pottery assemblage found at the cave, including vases of utilitarian as well as higher quality.[4]

EARLY INVESTIGATIONS

POTTERY FROM THE KAMARES CAVE first came to the attention of archaeologists in the early 1890s, when shepherds brought some 24 high-quality vases and sherds as well as a few figurines to Joseph Hazzidakis, then director of the Museum of the Archaeological *Syllogos* at Herakleion—the forerunner of the present Archaeological Museum.[5] These finds generated enormous interest among archaeologists, and in subsequent years unsuccessful attempts at reaching the cave were made by Myres, Mariani, and Evans.[6] In 1894, Taramelli was able to visit the cave and conduct the first scholarly exploration, even though he was restricted in his activities by a large mass of snow filling most of the cave.

3. MacGillivray 1986.
4. For detailed definitions of higher-quality and lower-quality pottery, see Van de Moortel 2002, 192–3.
5. Dawkins and Laistner 1912–1913, 1.
6. Myres 1893–1895, 351; Mariani 1895, 334 n. 1; Taramelli 1901, 438.

Working on behalf of the Archaeological Institute of America, he published his findings in the *American Journal of Archaeology* of 1901. In the intervening years, short illustrated reports by Myres and Mariani appeared about the pottery collected and deposited in the Herakleion Museum.[7] A systematic excavation of the Kamares Cave was finally carried out in 1913 by the British School of Archaeology at Athens under Dawkins, its director, and published by Dawkins and Laistner in a lengthy article.[8]

A SACRED CAVE

Dawkins and Laistner produced the first detailed plan and section of the cave.[9] The rough and steep terrain in front of the cave entrance makes it seem unlikely that any large-scale activities took place there in Minoan times. There is no trace of any leveling by human hands, nor have any archaeological remains been found by the early explorers at that location.

The cave itself is divided into two parts: a large, vaulted outer chamber with a steeply sloping floor strewn with enormous boulders and a much smaller sloping inner chamber at the bottom of the cave, which is entered through a narrow, contorted passage. Flimsy walls were seen in one of the deepest parts of the outer chamber. Taramelli reports finding the remains of a hearth there, but his observation could not be confirmed by Dawkins or Laistner, nor by Faure, who visited the cave in 1955. The interior cave is described by Taramelli as having stalactites and a pool of clear water.[10] Dawkins and Laistner found here parts of 1 m high terrace walls of uncertain date.[11]

The overwhelming majority of movable finds consists of pottery. In all, the present author estimates that some 17,000 ceramic fragments were recovered from the cave.[12] Nearly all this pottery comes from the outer chamber, and primarily from the deepest parts along the northern edge. It was found lying in powdery black earth, which probably represents the remains of one or more fires, since many pottery fragments show traces of burning. The excavators do not clarify whether this black earth formed a continuous layer or discrete pockets.[13] Particularly abundant in ceramic finds was a small area just in front of the passage to the inner cave. In contrast, the interior chamber yielded little pottery.

7. Myres 1893–1895; Mariani 1895.

8. Dawkins and Laistner 1912–1913.

9. Dawkins and Laistner 1912–1913, pls. II–III.

10. Taramelli 1901, 447. Taramelli visited the cave in June 1894. A few stalactites and a pool of water were seen also by Faure in 1955 (Faure 1964, 179). Due to an unusually mild winter with little snow there was no water in the pool in June 1913, when Dawkins and Laistner excavated the cave (Dawkins and Laistner 1912–1913, 10).

11. Dawkins and Laistner 1912–1913, 11. They were also observed by Faure in 1955 (1964, 179).

12. This estimate includes the vases and fragments stored in the Herakleion Museum as well as the pottery still lying in Dawkins and Laistner's camp near the cave.

13. Taramelli 1901, 448; Dawkins and Laistner 1912–1913, 9–10.

Taramelli found some lime-encrusted pottery fragments as well as a largely complete Early Minoan I Hagios Onouphrios jug there, and Dawkins and Laistner a few coarse sherds. Most vases from the cave are in very good condition but highly fragmentary. Only some 50 mendable vessels have been restored at present.

Non-pottery objects are fragments of three clay animal figurines (two solid bulls' heads and one hollow body fragment possibly belonging to a boar), a bone awl and two needles, other worked pieces of bone, a piece of pumice, a stone borer, a strip of bronze, and six iron spearheads of post-Minoan date.[14] Except for the metal objects most come from the small area just in front of the entrance to the inner cave. The flat piece of bronze was found farther to the northwest in the deepest reaches of the outer cave, whereas the spearheads were unearthed near the cave entrance.[15]

The inner cave was devoid of ancient non-pottery artifacts, but Taramelli reports finding an ox head and bones of goats and *agrimia*.[16] Dawkins and Laistner some twenty years later also encountered these faunal remains, but deemed them too well-preserved to be ancient.[17] It seems to the present author that the ox skull and other animal bones may well be ancient and very important for our understanding of ritual activities in the cave. Their fresh appearance could be a result of the stable climatic conditions and scarcity of human activity in the cave, which also preserved the Minoan pottery remarkably well. The presence of a modern ox skull would otherwise be difficult to explain in such a remote and high mountainous area unsuitable for cattle grazing. Unfortunately the present location of the bucranium is unknown, so it is unavailable for analysis. Some of the smaller bones were taken to the Herakleion Museum together with the pottery, but they have not been analyzed.

From its first exploration the Kamares Cave was considered to be a Minoan sacred place, even though it did not contain the prestigious votive gifts or large numbers of figurines commonly found in Minoan cave or mountaintop sanctuaries.[18] Taramelli first came to this conclusion based on the cave's setting high among the barren rocks near one of the peaks of Mt. Ida and its impressive size—its entrance being c. 18 to 20 m high and 42 m

14. Dawkins and Laistner 1912–1913, 30–1.

15. One was found in a trial pit dug just outside the cave, and five come from the shallow recess marked E on Dawkins and Laistner's plan (1912–1913, pl. II).

16. Taramelli 1901, 447.

17. Dawkins and Laistner 1912–1913, 10.

18. Peatfield 1990. It is of course likely, as Mariani (1895, 333) has pointed out, that the Kamares Cave has been thoroughly plundered in the course of time. Nevertheless, Dawkins and Laistner recovered even very small pottery fragments, and one would expect that they would have found parts of clay figurines or votive objects in other materials if they once had been deposited in the cave. Taramelli bought from a local villager a bronze double ax with curved edges, but he could not establish whether it came from the cave or from a Mycenaean cemetery near the village (1901, 442). The seller was a relative of the man who owned the land of the Mycenaean cemetery, which makes it somewhat more likely that the ax came from that cemetery.

wide, and its interior plunging 50 m into the mountain.[19] Dawkins and Laistner added to these arguments the prominence of its location, visible from the entire western Mesara Plain; its damp and cold micro-climate unsuited for human habitation; the very limited range of pottery shapes found; and the scarcity or apparent absence of normal household pottery such as cups, lamps, and cooking pots.[20]

To these one can add the obvious importance that the Kamares Cave had for the Phaistian ruling elite, since it was the focal point for the orientation of the Central Court of the palace, as Graham observed.[21] More specifically, north-south Corridor 41 and its monumental doorway in the north facade of the Central Court are aligned with the cave (fig. 1).[22]

A further peculiarity was observed by the present author in April 1992. At that time, most of the area around the cave was still full of snow, leaving a bare patch of steep rocks near the cave which was seen from Phaistos as a dark horned shape (fig. 2). If this shape was visible also to the Minoans, it may have contributed to their choice of the cave as a sanctuary. However, the value of this argument is uncertain since we do not know whether the cave area in Minoan times had the same configuration.

Even without the last argument, no one at present doubts that the Kamares Cave was a sanctuary at least during the Palatial periods. It was one of only three major Minoan sacred caves in central Crete, together with the Idaean Cave and the Psychro Cave at the foot of Mt. Dicte. Now that the Psychro Cave has been restudied and published, and Minoan peak sanctuaries have received much investigation, it is time to take a closer look at the

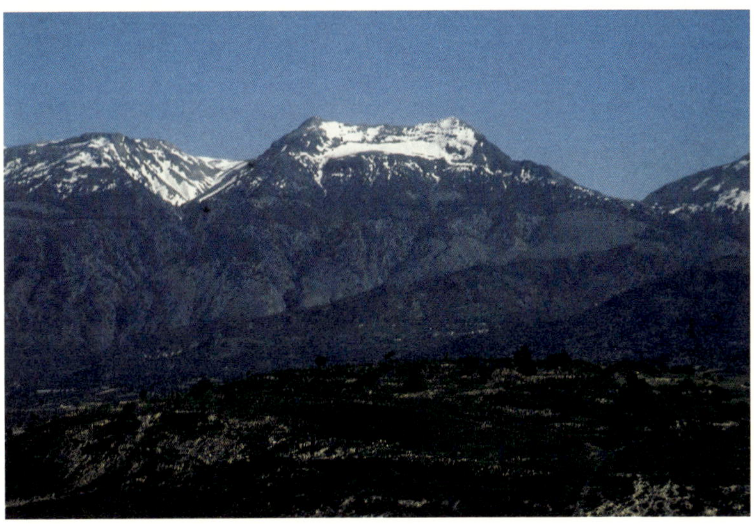

FIG. 2. The Kamares Cave area covered with snow, seen from the Central Court of the Phaistian palace in April 1992. The bare patch of steep rocks near the cave appears as a dark horned shape (A. Van de Moortel).

19. Taramelli 1901, 449–51.
20. Dawkins and Laistner 1912–1913, 3–4, 32.
21. Graham 1987, 80, fig. 51.
22. Faure 1964, 182. Faure's observation has been confirmed visually by the present author, but needs to be verified by measurements.

material from the Kamares Cave, so as to gain a better understanding of the cult activities that took place there and to reevaluate the role and importance of this sanctuary in the Minoan world.

GOALS OF THIS STUDY

THE FIRST OBJECTIVE of the present pottery study was to reexamine the chronology of cave use. Dawkins and Laistner dated the era of major cult activity in the cave to Middle Minoan I–II, roughly coinciding with the life span of the First Palace at Phaistos.[23] Earlier and later use of the cave was deemed sporadic. In view of the advances made in Minoan pottery chronology since Dawkins and Laistner's time, it was necessary to reinvestigate their dates. If confirmed, their chronological limits would be extremely important for the history of Minoan sacred caves and for our understanding of the relationship of the Kamares Cave to larger political developments that took place in central Crete at the transition from the Protopalatial to the Neopalatial period.

A second goal of this study was to check the excavators' conclusions about ceramic vessel shapes found in the cave and their relation to cult practices. For the Protopalatial period Dawkins and Laistner listed large numbers of pouring vessels—mostly open-spouted and bridge-spouted jars—but very few cups. This scarcity of drinking vessels provides a marked contrast with the large numbers of cups occurring in other sacred caves during the subsequent Neopalatial period.[24] If confirmed, such a difference could indicate a change in ritual. Also the purported absence of lamps and cooking pottery needed to be verified. In addition, it was decided to investigate the presence of wear patterns to see if these vases had been deposited unused as offerings, or if they had been worn by use.

The third objective was related to the author's earlier research into the organization of Minoan pottery production.[25] The high quality of the polychrome Protopalatial pottery from the cave, similar to that found at the palace of Phaistos, has led many scholars to believe that it was produced by a palatial workshop, and that the Kamares Cave was closely connected with the Phaistian ruling elite.[26] Having examined characteristics and distribution of the entire late Protopalatial and Neopalatial pottery assemblage of Kommos and compared it to that of the other two major settlements of the western Mesara Plain—Phaistos and Hagia Triada—the present author has come to the opposite conclusion: that high-quality vases were most likely produced not by palatial potters but by independent specialists, and that they were widely distributed in society rather than limited to the pala-

23. Dawkins and Laistner 1912–1913, 12, 32–3.
24. Tyree 2001, 45.
25. Van de Moortel 1997; 2002.
26. E.g., Walberg 1983, 96–7; 1987; Cherry 1986, 37.

tial elite. In this context, it was decided to investigate whether the high-quality Kamares Cave pottery belonged to the same production tradition as the pottery of the three western Mesara towns or whether it had been produced by a different tradition.

The fourth goal was to investigate more broadly the provenance of all of the cave's pottery and to test Dawkins and Laistner's assessment that it came from the western Mesara, i.e., the area visible from the cave.[27] If it could be demonstrated that a substantial proportion of pottery had come from other areas of Crete, it could be argued that cult activities at the Kamares Cave were important also to Minoans outside the western Mesara.

A final aim of this project was to republish the Kamares Cave pottery. Dawkins and Laistner's publication was excellent for the standards of that time, but it was highly selective—the catalog contained only some 40 vases and fragments—and its illustrations were limited to outline and watercolor drawings and rather murky black-and-white photographs. Modern standards require the publication of much larger numbers of vases with more detailed descriptions, pottery quantifications, accurate profile drawings, and high-quality photographs.

THE EVIDENCE

In addition to the 23 vases from the Kamares Cave currently on display, the Herakleion Museum houses over 120 registered and some 3,500 unregistered vases and fragments.[28] Moreover, some 13,000 pottery fragments, mostly of unpainted vases, were left by Dawkins and Laistner at their encampment on Mt. Ida, about a 20-minute walk southeast of the cave.[29] All this pottery has now been studied for the first time, and it is possible to answer with some confidence most of the research questions listed above.[30]

27. Dawkins and Laistner 1912–1913, 33–4.

28. A straight-sided cup [HM 509] decorated with white-painted ivy tendrils on a black ground, on display in Case 30 of the Herakleion Museum together with the Kamares Cave vases, is not from the cave but from the Zakros pits. Some pieces mentioned in the publications were missing from the study material. These include two Neolithic sherds found in the nineteenth century, the largely complete, lime-encrusted EM I Hagios Onouphrios jug discovered by Taramelli (1901, 447; Mariani 1895, pl. X.23), two Protopalatial open-spouted jars, several jugs, two vases described by Dawkins and Laistner as flowerpot shaped, a cup rim with a bull's head in relief, some collar-necked "stamnoid" jars and pithoi, possibly an LM IB teacup, and two LM III stirrup jars found by Dawkins and Laistner (1912–1913, 10, 12, 14, 15, 19, 20, 24, 27, 28, 30, 31, figs. 3d, 4d, f, 5a–b, 7b, pls. VIIa, VIIIa–b). The two stirrup jars are thought by Kanta to have come from the Mycenaean cemetery of Kamares, and not from the cave (see infra n. 58). It is expected that these missing pieces will be discovered in the course of the current reinventorying of the Herakleion Museum collection.

29. More than three-quarters of the pottery still lying on the mountain consists of undiagnostic medium-coarse body fragments. After sorting, I counted 2,000 sherds and estimated the remainder to number about 11,000.

30. I would like to give warm thanks to Eleni Banou of the 33rd Ephoreia, who tracked the Museum pottery down, and very efficiently facilitated my access. I also thank Eva Grammatikaki, acting head of the Ephoreia, and Eleni

The overwhelming majority of the pottery from the Kamares Cave is in very fresh condition, even though many pieces show traces of burning.[31] A small number are waterworn. Nearly all remains are very fragmentary; only about 50 vases are more than 50% preserved. Of these, 30 are intact or largely complete. However, there are many joining pieces and these make it seem highly likely that many vase fragments are still lying in the cave.[32]

Because of its freshness and frequent joins, it is reasonable to assume that all or most of this pottery had arrived in the cave as parts of whole vases.[33] Indeed, it does not make sense to think that the Minoans would have brought large numbers of unused or little used ceramic fragments to the cave. Thus each pottery fragment or group of joining fragments has been counted as representative of a once complete vessel deposited in the cave.

Hatzaki, then curator of the British School at Knossos, for allowing the transfer of the unregistered pottery to the Stratigraphical Museum at Knossos for study.

The survey of Dawkins and Laistner's dump would not have been possible without the good care of Irini Antonakaki, *epimeletria* for the Mesara, and especially the mountaineering skills and patience of Dimitris Papadovasilakis of Zaros, the archaeological guard who accompanied me. I owe a debt of gratitude to both of them. I would also like to thank the shepherds Barbantonis and Grigoris for gracious hospitality at their respective *mitata* at Kolytos.

31. Myres and Taramelli as well as Dawkins and Laistner comment on the poor preservation of the white and red paint (Myres 1893–1895, 353; Taramelli 1901, 448; Dawkins and Laistner 1912–1913, 3). Some vases, such as teapot HM 503 or bridge-spouted jar HM 9476, described by Dawkins and Laistner (1912–1913, 13, 22, pls. IVa, Xa) as having barely visible white-painted decoration, now have fresh-looking painted patterns, which must mean that they were repainted after their arrival in the Herakleion Museum. Clear evidence of modern repainting has been observed by the author on several other vases in the museum. Nevertheless, the surfaces and edges of the large majority of Kamares Cave pottery fragments are much fresher than those of the pottery normally encountered in settlement sites, including from primary contexts.

It is worth noting that the pottery fragments left exposed for ninety years at Dawkins and Laistner's camp near the Kamares Cave show in general the same extreme freshness as the pottery that had been brought down to the Herakleion Museum. Thus we can conclude that normal exposure to the elements alone—even on a sparsely vegetated mountain slope at c. 1,500 m above sea level—does not cause significant wear to pottery fragments. Such wear must be largely due to human action such as moving and trampling. Considerable water erosion was found on sherds that had washed some distance downslope from the camp. Wear and water erosion were found on a small number of sherds from the camp itself, but their percentage did not exceed that of the worn sherds from the cave. It is reasonable to assume that this wear and water erosion had taken place in the cave prior to excavation.

32. In addition to the c. 50 vases that are currently mendable, 100 more vases have multiple joining pieces. Dawkins and Laistner fruitlessly searched for archaeological remains below boulders by digging deep test trenches near the entrance of the cave, and by splitting and blasting a few blocks inside the cave itself. They concluded that all those boulders must have fallen well before Minoan times, and that the cave in those days looked much the same as today (Dawkins and Laistner 1912–1913, 9–11). The results of the present study suggest, however, that it would be worthwhile to further explore the cave floor, in particular the areas below the boulders in the deepest parts of the cave, where the majority of the pottery was found.

33. My preliminary study of the pottery lying in Dawkins and Laistner's camp on Mt. Ida leads me to believe that there are joins with fragments in the Herakleion Museum, and that many more collar-necked "stamnoid" jars and lids may be mendable. Within the time constraints of this study it was not possible to verify this observation.

CHRONOLOGY OF CAVE USE

Thanks to considerable advances in pottery studies made over the last century we can now refine Dawkins and Laistner's beginning date for the major use of the Kamares Cave from MM I to MM IB. Neolithic and Early Minoan fragments are rare, as the British excavators observed, although the Early Minoan period is better represented than they thought, with remains of 28 vases identified, including EM I and EM II pieces.[34] MM IA pottery is rare as well, represented by about 10 vases. In contrast to these paltry numbers, remains of roughly 1,600 Protopalatial vases have been recovered from the cave.[35] Deposition occurred in every phase of the Protopalatial period, with no convincing evidence for a decrease at any time.[36] Assuming that the number of vases deposited is a reflection of the intensity of activity, one can conclude that the major period of use of the Kamares Cave coincided even more precisely than anticipated with the duration of the First Palace at Phaistos. It now seems even more likely that their fortunes in some way were related.

A second unexpected result was the much better representation of the Neopalatial period than previously believed. Instead of the few pieces reported by Dawkins and Laistner, fragments of over 180 individual vases can now be assigned to this period. Many were closely datable within the MM III (c. 30 vessels), LM IA (c. 10 vessels), and LM IB (c. 30 vessels) phases. It is true that compared to the much greater abundance of Protopalatial pottery there is a steep drop in the deposition of vases in the Neopalatial period, but the change is not as drastic as Dawkins and Laistner thought. Another steep decline took place in LM II and LM III, with remains of only about 15 vases identified. After the Bronze Age, activities at the cave seem to have largely ceased. Six iron spearheads were deposited at an uncertain date, and there was a short revival in the Hellenistic period resulting in the deposition of 5 vases.

NATURE OF CAVE USE

The analysis of vessel shapes has led to some new conclusions regarding the kinds of activities that took place at the cave. Only some preliminary observations are offered here.

Contrary to Watrous' assertion, it is probable that the Kamares Cave was already used for cult during the Early Minoan period. Watrous' claim that it was a seasonal habitation

34. I would like to thank Timothy Campbell-Green, Ph.D student at Sheffield University, for identifying the Early Minoan pottery fragments.

35. Most classes of vases were quantified on the basis of a close examination of fabrics, morphological details, and decoration. For collar-necked "stamnoid" jars and lids, which form the large majority of the c. 13,000 sherds in Dawkins and Laistner's camp, handle counts were taken into account as well; the numbers of collar-necked "stamnoid" jars and lids given here are estimates.

36. About 150 vases are narrowly datable to MM IB, c. 85 to MM IIA, and c. 130 to MM IIB. In addition, c. 75 can be dated to MM IB–MM IIA, and c. 110 to MM II.

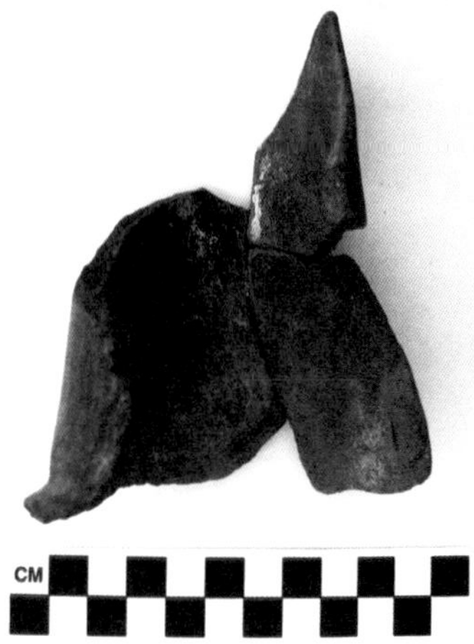

FIG. 3. Interior view of the neck of a large Early Minoan jug [KA03-12-004] from the Kamares Cave, mended from three joining fragments. The estimated length of the neck is 15 cm (A. Van de Moortel).

site in the Neolithic and Early Minoan periods is unconvincing for various reasons.[37] The remoteness and forbidding micro-climate of this wet cave make it seem highly unlikely that it would have been used for habitation. Moreover, the recovered Early Minoan remains are too limited in range to be interpreted as a domestic assemblage. As many as 28 Early Minoan vases were found in the lower and probably also the upper parts of the cave, including the EM I Hagios Onouphrios jug from the inner cave. However, the variety of shapes—8 bowls, 6 jugs, 3 jars, 8 closed vases, and a lid—is much narrower than that of known Early Minoan domestic contexts. Non-pottery objects commonly found in domestic contexts, such as stone grinding slabs, other stone or metal tools, spindle whorls, or loom weights, are entirely lacking in the cave.[38] One could suggest that the Kamares Cave may have served as a short-term shelter for shepherds or hunters seeking a few hours of refuge from the elements. However, the recovered pottery suggests more than casual visits. It includes fragments of two large painted bowls, two large jugs (fig. 3), and three large closed vessels. It is difficult to believe that such large ceramic bowls or even large closed vases would have been carried by shepherds or hunters on their wanderings.

Whereas the narrow range of Early Minoan vessel shapes, and especially the lack of cups, goblets, or cooking pottery, does not accord well with what we know of contemporary domestic assemblages, it closely resembles the range of vase shapes in the Protopalatial pottery assemblage of the cave, which is generally interpreted as the remains of cult. The absence of Early Minoan cups and cooking pottery is echoed by the scarcity of MM IA and Protopalatial cups and cooking vessels, suggesting a high degree of continuity and some change in ritual activities that were specific to the Kamares Cave.[39]

If we turn to the Protopalatial assemblage, a close examination of this pottery prompts us to modify some other observations made by Dawkins and Laistner. Even though unusu-

37. Watrous 1996, 60, 73–4. The idea that Minoan sacred caves were first used for habitation goes back to Nilsson (1950, 56).

38. Cf. Early Minoan domestic assemblages from Myrtos Phournou Koriphi (Warren 1972, 97–240), Trypeti (Vasilakis 1995, 72–3), and Knossos (Wilson 1984; 1985). The two reported Neolithic pottery fragments from the Kamares Cave have not been found among the studied pottery.

39. In contrast, cups figured prominently in Early Minoan mortuary cult, as is shown by their high frequency in Mesara tholos tombs (Branigan 1970, 57). They were also quite prominent in Protopalatial levels at the Psychro Cave and the Idaean Cave (Watrous 1996, 47–8, 58) as well as at the caves at Amnisos and Skoteino (Tyree 2001, 45).

ally rare, the number of cups and bowls belonging to the Protopalatial period is not as negligible as the British excavators thought. Remains of as many as 42 cups and 78 small, medium, and large bowls have now been identified. Yet, their numbers are much lower than those of pouring vessels, which include at least 450 vases (mostly bridge-spouted jars and jugs, with a few rhyta). With a proportion of cups to pouring vessels of almost 1:11, and a proportion of cups and bowls combined to pouring vessels of 1:3.75, the special nature of the cave assemblage can be confirmed. It is indeed very different from a normal household pottery assemblage, which would have several cups or bowls for each pouring vessel.[40]

The relatively low number of cups in comparison to pouring vessels need not signify that more libations than drinking took place at the cave. It can also result from differences in the mode of deposition, visitors taking most cups and bowls with them as they departed while leaving pouring vessels behind, or depositing cups and bowls elsewhere in as yet unexcavated areas of the cave. Another possibility is that visitors used cups made out of perishable material. Yet, an interesting parallel can be drawn with the importance of pouring vessels in Prepalatial and Protopalatial funerary cult assemblages of the Mesara and Archanes, as pointed out by Cultraro. If the pouring of water or other liquids was the principal focus of funerary ceremonies in those periods, as is argued by the author, it may have played an important role in Minoan cave cult as well.[41]

Storage and transport containers were abundantly represented in the cave, as Dawkins and Laistner had already observed. Among the estimated 275 jars there are 55 small to medium and some 210 large jars. The high frequency of small jars in a wide variety of styles is unexpected, and may reflect many events of small-scale deposition. Nearly all large jars are of the collar-necked "stamnoid" type.[42] They either are undecorated or car-

40. For examples of Protopalatial domestic assemblages at Phaistos, see Levi 1976, 422–31, 512–61, 653–79; Van de Moortel 1997, 777–86; Speziale 2001; for Knossos, see Popham 1974; MacGillivray 1998.

41. Cultraro 2000, citing funerary assemblages from Hagia Triada, Koumasa, Archanes, and Kamilari. Especially noteworthy is the close correspondence between the Kamares Cave assemblage and the ceramic assemblages of the *Camerette Sud*, the adjacent paved area, and the annex of nearby Tholos Tomb A at Hagia Triada. Also here the number of pouring vessels (75) far outweighs that of plates (4) and cups (25?). The exact number of cups is not specified by Cultraro, but 18 cups are listed by Banti (1930–1931, 179–80, 217–8) as coming from the annex of Tholos Tomb A and 7 as coming from the *Camerette Sud*. It is unclear whether the quantity listed by Banti represents all or only part of the cups found, but their total number was certainly smaller than that of the pouring vessels (cf. Banti 1930–1931, 160, fig. 4). The *Camerette Sud* seem to have been repositories of pouring vessels, plates, and storage vessels, whereas cups were deposited on top of the paved area outside as well as in the annex of Tholos Tomb A, where rituals may have taken place. Thus it is conceivable that also in the Kamares Cave the bulk of cups and bowls were deposited in different locations from pouring and storage vessels. The Hagia Triada assemblage is dated by Cultraro to MM IA–IIA. A detailed comparison of Minoan funerary and cave cult, apart from their obviously possible chthonic connections, is beyond the scope of the present paper. For a discussion of possible conceptual overlaps between funerary and other areas of Minoan cult, see Peatfield 1990, 124–5.

42. E.g., Dawkins and Laistner 1912–1913, pl. VIIIb–c. For a discussion and illustrations of collar-necked "stamnoid" jars, see Levi and Carinci 1988, 13, pls. 7c–d, 8; Levi 1976, pls. LXXVa, 53c–d, 168c, 169a, c, e–f, 170a–c.

ry simple dark-painted motifs or plastic and impressed rope patterns. Their wide mouths were closed by large lids, of which an estimated 100–200 examples have been found.[43] One lid [HM 31808] has a patch of reddish clay on its interior which may have served to seal it on the jar (fig. 4). Narrow-necked containers (5 narrow-necked jars, c. 30 amphorae, and 3 amphoriskoi) are less common than wide-mouthed jars in the Protopalatial period. The abundance of collar-necked "stamnoid" jars at the cave is unusual and must be related to cult activity. Because of their wide necks, they may have been transport containers for food stuffs consumed or sacrificed during rituals, whereas narrow-necked jars could have transported liquids. Dawkins and Laistner report finding probable remains of grain among the pottery in one of the lower parts of the cave.[44]

An unexpected result of the present study is the identification of large numbers of pithos fragments. Representing an estimated 50 vessels, including at least 5 very large pithoi, this class of storage jar was much more numerous than the "scanty remains" identified by Dawkins and Laistner.[45] The presence of large pithoi at the Kamares Cave is noteworthy given the considerable difficulties involved in bringing them to such a remote and high place.

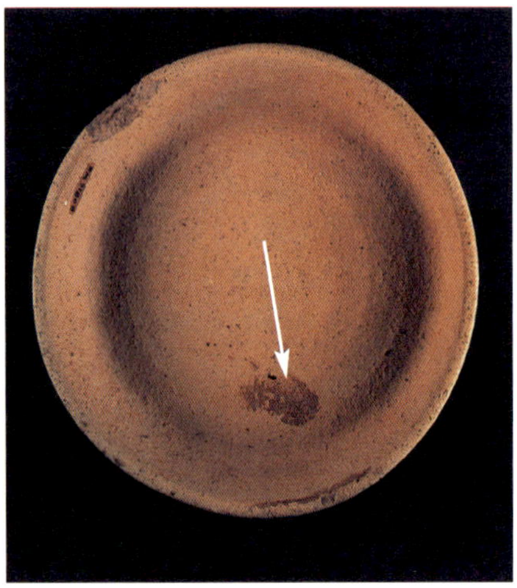

Fig. 4. Interior of lid HM 31808 from the Kamares Cave. The arrow indicates the patch of reddish clay on its interior which may have served to seal the lid on top of a "stamnoid" jar (I. Papadakis-Plumidis).

Equally unexpected is the identification of the remains of some 50 Protopalatial tripod cooking pots, contradicting Dawkins and Laistner's assertion that tripod cooking vessels were not found in the cave.[46] Many show use wear, making it seem likely that eating indeed took place at the cave during Protopalatial times. It is possible, but as yet not proven, that the powdery black earth in which the pottery was found represents the remains of cooking fires (see above).[47]

Lamps are not entirely absent from the cave, as Dawkins and Laistner believed, but they are extremely rare. For the Protopalatial period, only a few fragments belonging to one or two large red-slipped and burnished lamps have been identified. In addition, a MM IB globular bowl and a MM IIB flaring bowl appear to have been reused as lamps. The intact bottom part of a MM IB–MM IIA jug [HM 56] seems to have served the same purpose.[48]

43. Dawkins and Laistner 1912–1913, 27–8, fig. 6.
44. Dawkins and Laistner 1912–1913, 11.
45. Dawkins and Laistner 1912–1913, 30.
46. Remains of as many as 13 cooking pots, including tripod legs, were identified among the pottery left behind in Dawkins and Laistner's camp.
47. More study is needed of the date and spatial distribution of the burned pottery fragments.
48. Dawkins and Laistner 1912–1913, pl. VIIf.

The extreme scarcity of lamps suggests either that another source of artificial lighting was used in the cave, or that most activities took place in the natural semi-dark and dark of the cave. It is unlikely, given the difficult terrain of the cave, that so few ceramic lamps would have been broken if they had been frequently used.

Finally, remains of some special-purpose vessels have been found. Most prominent are a few oval perforated basins or larnakes and slotted jars. (A complete perforated larnax has been published by Dawkins and Laistner and is on display in the Herakleion Museum.[49]) Their function is as yet unclear. They are made of a calcareous coarse fabric and do not bear traces of the scorching that can be associated with incense burning, a use suggested by Dawkins and Laistner. Perhaps they were transport containers for animals, but the absence of lids makes this less likely. Slotted larnakes also have been found in Protopalatial Myrtos-Pyrgos.[50]

Depositions of pottery at the cave underwent some changes in the Neopalatial period. In addition to the pottery finds being much less numerous, the ceramic assemblage is different in its composition, with cups (27) and bowls (9) now occurring in roughly equal number to pouring vessels (34). Especially the number of LM IB cups (17) is striking, exceeding that of narrowly datable LM IB pouring vessels (5) by more than 3:1. The proportion of drinking vessels in the Neopalatial assemblage of the Kamares Cave is comparable to that of the Protopalatial and Neopalatial assemblages of the caves at Psychro, Amnisos, and Skoteino.[51]

Transport and storage containers are still deposited at the Kamares Cave in the Neopalatial period, forming a larger percentage of the total number of vases than before (29% as opposed to 19% in the Protopalatial assemblage). They include jars (7 small, 35 larger), amphorae (7), amphoriskoi (1), and perhaps pithoi (2). Collar-necked "stamnoid" jars and lids are absent, even though they still were produced in the western Mesara.[52]

There are remains of 4 to 5 Neopalatial tripod cooking pots in the Kamares Cave, including one large example. Even though much less numerous than in the Protopalatial period, Neopalatial cooking pots make up a roughly similar percentage (3%) of the overall assemblage. It seems that eating retained its importance at the cave. Clay lamps continue to be extremely rare. We have remains of a small Neopalatial pedestal lamp and a handleless flaring lamp as well as a possible fragment of a little hand lamp.

Contrary to Dawkins and Laistner's assertion that Late Minoan deposition was confined

49. Dawkins and Laistner 1912–1913, 29–30, fig. 7a, c.

50. Cadogan 1977–1978, 74.

51. Tyree 2001, 45.

52. Pernier and Banti 1951, 366, fig. 232d; stamnos fragments were found in the advanced to final LM IA kiln dump at Kommos (Van de Moortel 2001, 82–3, fig. 37.56), and a lid similar to many Protopalatial stamnos lids from the Kamares Cave was found in a final LM IA to early LM IB context at Kommos (Van de Moortel 1997, 200, fig. 72 [C9465]).

to an area close to the cave entrance, the results of the present study indicate that it took place in the upper as well as lower reaches of the outer chamber and possibly even in the inner cave.[53] Already Taramelli reported finding Late Minoan remains deep down in the outer chamber and he may have found some in the inner cave as well.[54] LM I and LM III fragments have now been identified in nearly all units of unregistered sherds at the Herakleion Museum, including those labeled as coming from deep parts of the outer chamber.[55] Some mixing between units could of course have occurred in the 90 years since their excavation, but the presence of Late Minoan pottery in those lower units is too widespread to be ascribed to mere error.

There is no unambiguous evidence for LM II deposition in the cave. Most interesting is a previously unreported neck fragment from a Palace Style jar, possibly found by Taramelli in the inner cave, which cannot be dated more closely than LM IB–LM IIIA1 (fig. 5). This substantial fragment, preserving about one-third of the circumference of the neck, must be part of a once complete jar brought to the cave. Since Palace Style jars are nearly always found in elite contexts, the presence of this jar fragment may well be an indication of elite sponsorship of the Kamares Cave.[56] The piece is likely to be of Knossian manufacture, and may reflect Knossian interest in the cult site. It must be pointed out, however, that several fragments of Palace Style jars occurred in LM III contexts at Kommos.[57] Thus it cannot be ruled out that the Kamares Cave jar had been deposited by a member of the local elite.

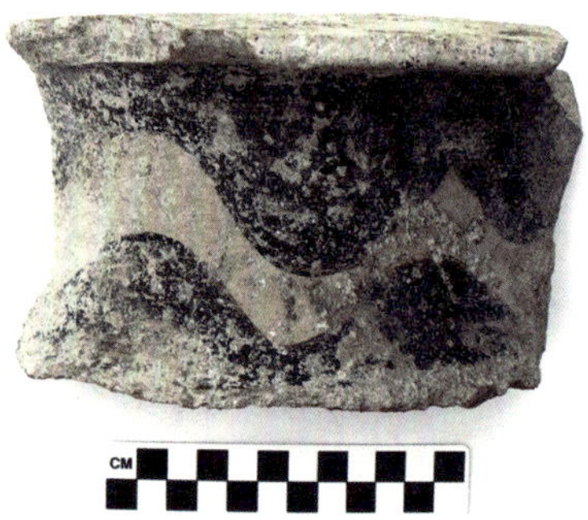

Fig. 5. Neck fragment of a LM IB–LM IIIA1 Palace Style jar [KA03-Unid.C-011] from the Kamares Cave (A. Van de Moortel).

The small size of the group of deposited vases datable within the LM III period shows a clear decrease in importance of the sanctuary. Single

53. Dawkins and Laistner 1912–1913, 9.

54. Taramelli 1901, 448–9, fig. 4. Dawkins and Laistner may have drawn their conclusion without having seen Taramelli's pottery. This would also explain their omission of some remarkable pieces, such as the neck of an LM IB–IIIA1 Palace Style jar [KA03-Unid.C-011], now stored in a unit of unknown provenance, labeled "Unidentified C" by the present author (fig. 5). Lightly covered with calcareous concretion, this jar neck may have been among the lime-encrusted pottery found by Taramelli in the inner cave (1901, 447).

55. These are the units labeled "Hole near Cave C, Pit 10, and Pit 12."

56. The neck fragment of the Palace Style jar is discussed in note 54 supra. For a discussion of find contexts of Palace Style jars, see Niemeier 1985, 191. Palace Style jar fragments were found in rather modest private residences on the Hilltop and Central Hillside at Kommos (Oblique House, Southeast Rooms, and House with the Snake Tube, respectively), but they are highly fragmentary and not unquestionably in primary contexts. Thus it is hazardous to draw conclusions regarding the social context of their use (Watrous 1992, nos. 555, 727, 797, 799, 838, 1034, 1057. See also Nixon 1996; MacEnroe 1996.)

57. Watrous 1992 (see supra n. 56).

fragments of a large decorated conical rhyton and a decorated kylix are suggestive of at least one pouring and drinking event. In addition, there are 3 to 6 small and medium stirrup jars.[58] A small series of similar ordinary wide-mouthed jugs and a cooking pot with circular-sectioned legs may be contemporary. The scarcity of decorated fine tableware and the utilitarian quality of the jugs, if indeed they belong to this period, are a far cry from the large numbers of highly decorated pouring and drinking vessels of the Neopalatial and especially the Protopalatial periods. They suggest that the cave's importance had declined to the point that it was visited only by inhabitants of the immediate vicinity.[59] The sanctuary may well have returned to its Prepalatial status. Any interest by the ruling elite of the western Mesara or Knossos, if it existed before, has now ceased.

Post-Bronze Age depositions are rare, with six iron spearheads of uncertain date and five pottery fragments datable to the Hellenistic period. The latter include two similar thymiateria (incense burners), a large bowl, a possible base support, and a fragment of a large, closed vase decorated with a relief appliqué of a Papposilenos figure.[60] Since they are obviously cult paraphernalia, the Hellenistic pieces signal a short revival of religious activity in the cave. Their exact findspot within the cave is unknown.

Whereas the presence and number of vessel types in each period gives us valuable evidence for depositions in the cave, differential wear patterns on vases provide clues about their use before being deposited. A detailed discussion of use wear is beyond the scope of this paper, but it can already be reported that most Protopalatial vases show evidence of no or very light use. In this respect they strongly differ from the pottery that usually is found in habitation sites. Even though the same shapes were used in contemporary settlements, the results of the present study suggest that many Protopalatial vases had been acquired specifically to be deposited in the Kamares Cave.

58. Kanta (1980, 112) believes that two small stirrup jars HM 90 and HM 92, described by Dawkins and Laistner (1912–1913, fig. 5a–b) as coming from the cave, derive instead from Halbherr's exploration of the Mycenaean cemetery of Kamares (for a description of this cemetery, see Taramelli 1901, 439–43). HM 92 reportedly carries the label "Kamares, Halbherr's excavation." These two vases were not among the material examined in the present study. Kanta dates HM 92 to LM IIIA and HM 90 to LM IIIB.

59. Two LM III stirrup jars may be of east Cretan origin, but that does not mean that they were brought by an east Cretan worshipper, since east Cretan pottery was imported into the Mesara at that time (Watrous 1992, 153). Similarly, the decorated LM III vases may be Knossian, but could have been acquired in the western Mesara (see infra). Taramelli reports finding a Mycenaean settlement near the tholos tomb cemetery southwest of the present-day village of Kamares, a 4-hour walk downslope from the cave (1901, 439–43). He saw stirrup jars among the surface remains.

60. I am much obliged to Peter Callaghan of the University of Sydney for identifying these Hellenistic fragments and discussing their significance with me.

MANUFACTURING TRADITION

MACROSCOPIC ANALYSES have shown that not only shape and decoration but also fabric recipes and other manufacturing practices of most Protopalatial and Neopalatial vases from the Kamares Cave are identical to those of the pottery excavated in the towns and civic buildings of Phaistos, Kommos, and Hagia Triada.[61] There are also general similarities and some close morphological and decorative resemblances with vases from Mesara tholos tombs, but the latter have been too poorly published to allow for detailed comparisons.[62] Based on these observations it is safe to conclude that the bulk of the Kamares Cave pottery of these periods—utilitarian as well as higher-quality vases—originated in the western Mesara and was produced by the same potters who also supplied those towns. There is no evidence to support the thesis that there were potters who produced solely for the Kamares Cave and the Phaistian palace.

Thus it appears that we must abandon the traditional view that the presence of high-quality pottery in the cave in itself is evidence for the palatial character of the cave cult. Certainly, the orientation of the Central Court of the Phaistian palace suggests a close re-

61. For descriptions of MM IIB–LM IB pottery manufacturing practices in the western Mesara and comparisons with Knossos, see Van de Moortel 1997. My conclusions are based on twelve years of experience processing and studying the excavation pottery from Kommos as well as on visual examination of pottery groups from Phaistos and Hagia Triada. For Protopalatial manufacturing practices at Phaistos, see Levi and Carinci 1988.

62. Pottery from smaller habitation sites and tombs in the western Mesara has been poorly published. The few available images of Middle Minoan tholos tomb vases show mostly MM IA and IB shapes. These include highly decorated pieces. Few vases are datable to MM IIA and B (MM IIB: Xanthoudides 1971, pl. XXXV.5123, pl. XLV.5702; and a teacup from the shrine at Koumasa, pl. XXXIII.5001). It is conceivable, in my opinion, that few highly decorated MM IIA and IIB vases were recovered because they belonged to the upper depositional layers and had been looted, destroyed by roof fall, or damaged by exposure (cf. Branigan 1970, 56). Without further study it is impossible to assess whether the tomb vases had been produced by the same potters who supplied the three major Mesara towns, but some similarities can already be indicated. Similar in shape and decoration are: two MM I ridged jugs from the tholos tomb at Drakones (Xanthoudides 1971, pl. XLI.4953, 4955), a jug from Patrikies (Levi 1976, pl. 16c), and jugs HM 9490 and HM 9491 from the Kamares Cave; a conical cup (Xanthoudides 1971, pl. VI.5069) and carinated cup from the tholos tomb at Porti (Xanthoudides 1971, pl. XXXVIB.5120), and MM IB and IIA conical cups (Levi 1976, pl. 35d, 145m; Levi and Carinci 1988, 236–7) and an MM IIA carinated cup, respectively, from Phaistos (Levi 1976, pl. 134a). Closely related in shape and decorative syntax are: three-handled globular barbotine jugs from Koumasa (Xanthoudides 1971, pl. V) and MM IB and IIA examples from Phaistos (Levi 1976, pl. 23b–c, f, 81); a flaring bowl from Porti (Xanthoudides 1971, pl. VI.5082) and an MM IIA example from Phaistos (Levi 1976, pl. 142o); a tumbler from Platanos (Xanthoudides 1971, pl. IX.6862) and an MM IB tumbler from Phaistos (Levi 1976, pl. 31d). Similarities in shape: a teacup from the shrine at Koumasa (Xanthoudides 1971, pl. XXXIII.5001) and MM IIB teacups from Phaistos (Levi 1976, pl. 124) and Kommos (Betancourt 1990, fig. 21.370–1); teapots from Drakones (Xanthoudides 1971, pl. XLI.4962, 4964, 5682) and MM IA examples from Patrikies (Levi 1976, pl. 15a–h) and the Kamares Cave. "Horned" vases such as those from Kalathiana (Xanthoudides 1971, pl. XLV.5703, 5704) have been found in MM IIB contexts at the Phaistos palace and room LXXX west of the West Court (Levi 1976, pls. 149a, c, e, g, 175a; Levi and Carinci 1988, 256–7), but similar vases occur at Knossos (Evans 1928, figs. 176f, 179, dated by Evans to MM IIIB) and Malia.

lationship between palace and cave, and the chronology of cave use points to a link between the fortunes of sanctuary and palace. However, there is no evidence that there ever was palatial control over the production of pottery used in the cave, nor is there any support for Walberg's statement that the cave was mainly visited by the inhabitants of the Phaistian palace, i.e., that most of the pottery was deposited by palace residents. At the most, it seems that the palatial elite would have patronized and strongly encouraged cult activity at the cave.

POTTERY FROM OUTSIDE THE WESTERN MESARA

IN ADDITION to the masses of local pottery, there are almost 120 vases, mostly of Protopalatial date, with fabrics and technical details that are not local to the western Mesara. They were imported from various regions on Crete or from the nearby island of Gavdos. For the Protopalatial period at least 23 vases (1 large bowl, 16 or more collared-necked "stamnoid" jars [fig. 6], 1 closed vase, 3 pithoi, and 2 lids) are from Gavdos, located some 70 km southwest of the Mesara coast, and visible from the Kamares Cave.[63] As many as 46 vases (1 bowl, 41 trefoil-mouthed small jugs, 3 small closed vessels, and a lid) as well as one or both of the preserved heads of bull figurines have been tentatively identified as coming from the Pediada region in north-central Crete.[64] Fragments of a tray and 9 closed vases can be identified as east Cretan. These imported Protopalatial vases total almost 100, constituting about 6% of that period's assemblage.

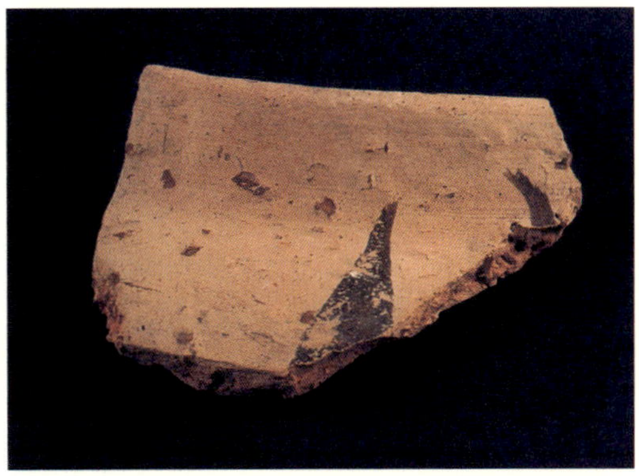

FIG. 6. Neck fragment of a Protopalatial collar-necked "stamnoid" jar with the angular coarse temper typical of Gavdos (I. Papadakis-Plumidis).

In the subsequent MM III phase there seems to be a temporary decline in imports, with only one non-local piece (a conical cup) identified among the 30 vases datable to this phase. Imports pick up again in LM IA and IB, when they make up almost half of the assemblage. A clear shift is noticeable in the provenance of those Neopalatial imports. Whereas 3 out of 4 non-local vases in the LM IA phase come from east Crete (1 bowl, 1 amphoriskos, and 1 closed vase), all 12 LM IB imports are probably Knossian (8 teacups, 3 jugs, and 1 closed vase). Contacts with Gavdos did not entirely cease, as is shown by the presence of a single Neopalatial jar from that island. The preponderance of Knossian vases

63. Vases with similar fabrics found at Kommos have been identified by Katerina Kopaka and Christina Papadaki of the University of Rethymnon as coming from Gavdos.

64. I thank Kostis Christakis for these identifications.

continues in LM II–III, when all decorated vases seem to be either Knossian (Palace Style jar, pyxis, kylix, and conical rhyton) or east Cretan (2 LM III stirrup jars).

All this non-local pottery consists of cups, pouring and storage vases, representing similar functions to the Mesara pottery. Its presence could mean that worshippers came to the cave from these various places, but this is not necessarily so. Imports from the same regions have been found in the western Mesara, and especially at Kommos, its maritime port.[65] Diachronic changes in the frequencies of imports at the cave even follow closely those observed at Kommos. Thus it is conceivable that those non-local vases were brought to the cave by inhabitants of the Mesara.

The situation seems to be somewhat different for the Knossian vases. Their presence at the cave from the LM IB phase onward is much more prominent than in the settlements, and may signal Knossian interest in the sanctuary. On the other hand, it is possible that the Knossian vases were highly appreciated by the local inhabitants and preferred by them for deposition in the cave. Supporting this idea is the fact that, with exception of the Palace Style jar, none of the Knossian vases are decorated in the Special Palatial Tradition, which has often been associated with Knossian palatial production and elite consumption.

THE KAMARES CAVE AND THE PHAISTIAN PALACE

FINALLY, let us briefly connect the history of the Kamares Cave with major developments that took place in central Crete at the transition from the Protopalatial to the Neopalatial period. Most archaeologists presently working in the Mesara believe that Phaistos suffered a period of political turmoil and weakened palatial power after the final destruction of the First Palace. According to some, this may have led to a Knossian takeover of the western Mesara in the mature phase of LM IA.[66] This would explain the dramatic increase of Knossian influence on the material culture of this region, including record keeping, symbols of power, architecture, and wall painting. Through my own research I have come to the conclusion that at the beginning of the Neopalatial period, the potters of the Mesara had already abandoned earlier economic practices and adopted the Knossian mode of production.[67] This can be seen as an even earlier sign of Knossian cultural preeminence.

The sharp decline in importance of the Kamares Cave occurred at that very same time, at the beginning of the Neopalatial period. Since the rise and decline of the cave cult coincided exactly with the fortunes of the Phaistian palace, as shown by the present study, and the palatial elite attached great importance to the cave cult, as suggested by the orientation

65. Betancourt 1990, *passim*; Watrous 1992, 150–3. Imported pottery from the large civic buildings at Kommos will be published by the present author (Building AA) and Jeremy B. Rutter (Buildings T and P). Protopalatial trefoil-mouthed Pediada jugs at Phaistos are described by Levi and Carinci (1988, 217–8). I thank F. Carinci for this reference.
66. E.g., D'Agata 1989; La Rosa 1989; 1995.
67. Van de Moortel 1997; 2002; (forthcoming).

of the Central Court to the cave, it is argued here that the decline of the Kamares Cave and its subsequent lack of recovery after the final destruction of the First Palace at Phaistos can be seen as yet another strong sign of serious trouble for the Phaistian palatial elite.

WORKS CITED

Banti, L. 1930–1931. "La grande tomba a tholos di Haghia Triadha," *ASAtene* 13–14: 155–251.

Betancourt, P.P. 1990. *Kommos*. Vol. 2, *The Final Neolithic through Middle Minoan III Pottery*. Princeton, NJ: Princeton University Press.

Branigan, K. 1970. *The Tombs of Mesara: A Study of Funerary Architecture and Ritual in Southern Crete, 2800–1700 B.C.* London: Gerald Duckworth.

Cadogan, G. 1977–1978. "Pyrgos, Crete, 1970-7." *AR* 24: 70–84.

Cherry, J.F. 1986. "Polities and Palaces: Some Problems in Minoan State Formation." In *Peer Polity Interaction and Socio-Political Change,* edited by C. Renfrew and J.F. Cherry, 19–45. New Directions in Archaeology. Cambridge: Cambridge University Press.

Cultraro, M. 2000. "La brocchetta dei vivi per la sete dei morti: riconsiderazione delle camerette a sud della grande tholos di Haghia Triada." In *Πεπραγμένα Η' Διεθνούς Κρητολογικού Συνεδρίου Ηράκλειο, 9-14 Σεπτεμβρίου 1996.* Vol. A1, *Προϊστορική και Αρχαία Ελληνική Περίοδος*, 309–26. Heraklion: Etairia Kretikon Istorikon Meleton.

D'Agata, A.L. 1989. "Some MM IIIB/LM IA Pottery from Haghia Triada." In *Transition: Le monde égéen du bronze moyen au bronze recent. Actes de la deuxième Rencontre égéenne internationale de l'Université de Liège (18–20 avril 1988),* edited by R. Laffineur, 93–7. *Aegaeum* 3. Liège: Université de l'Etat à Liège.

Dawkins, R.M. and M.L.W. Laistner. 1912–1913. "The Excavation of the Kamares Cave in Crete." *BSA* 19: 1–34.

Evans, A. 1928. *The Palace of Minos at Knossos*. Vol. 2. London: Macmillan.

Faure, P. 1964. *Fonctions des cavernes crétoises*. École française d'Athènes. Travaux et mémoires 14. Paris: E. de Boccard.

Graham, J.W. 1987. *The Palaces of Crete*, rev. ed. Princeton, NJ: Princeton University Press.

Kanta, A. 1980. *The Late Minoan III Period in Crete: A Survey of Sites, Pottery and Their Distribution. SIMA* 58. Göteborg: Paul Åströms.

La Rosa, V. 1989. "Nouvelles données du Bronze Moyen au Bronze Récent à Haghia Triada." In *Transition: Le monde égéen du bronze moyen au bronze recent. Actes de la deuxième Rencontre égéenne internationale de l'Université de Liège (18–20 avril 1988),* edited by R. Laffineur, 81–92. *Aegaeum* 3. Liège: Université de l'Etat à Liège.

———. 1995. "A Hypothesis on Earthquakes and Political Power in Minoan Crete." *Annali di Geofisica* 38: 881–91.

Levi, D. 1976. *Festòs e la civiltà minoica*. Vol. 1. Incunabula Graeca 60. Rome: Edizioni dell'Ateneo.

Levi, D. and F. Carinci 1988. *Festòs e la civiltà minoica*. Vol. 2, pt. 2. Incunabula Graeca 77. Roma: Edizioni dell'Ateneo.

MacEnroe, J. 1996. "The Late Minoan Period." In *Kommos*. Vol. 1, *The Kommos Region and Houses of the Minoan Town.* Part 2, *The Minoan Hilltop and Hillside Houses*, edited by J.W. Shaw and M.C. Shaw, 199–235. Princeton, NJ: Princeton University Press.

MacGillivray, J.A. 1986. Review of *Provincial Middle Minoan Pottery*, by G. Walberg. *JHS* 106: 249–50.

———. 1998. *Knossos: Pottery Groups of the Old Palace Period. BSA* Studies 5. London: British School at Athens.

Mariani, L. 1895. "Antichità cretesi: Note sulla ceramica cretese, 1. Vasi di Kamares." *MonAnt* 6: 333–48.

Myres, J.L. 1893–1895. "Prehistoric Polychrome Pottery from Kamárais in Crete." *Proceedings of the Society of Antiquaries of London* 15, 2nd series: 351–6.

Niemeier, W.-D. 1985. *Die Palaststilkeramik von Knossos: Stil, Chronologie und historischer Kontext. AF* 13. Berlin: Gebr. Mann.

Nilsson, M.P. 1950. *The Minoan-Mycenaean Religion and Its Survival in Greek Religion*. Lund: C.W.K. Gleerup.

Nixon, L.F. 1996. "The Oblique House and the Southeast Rooms." In *Kommos*. Vol. 1, *The Kommos Region and Houses of the Minoan Town*. Part 2, *The Minoan Hilltop and Hillside Houses*, edited by J.W. Shaw and M.C. Shaw, 59–76. Princeton, NJ: Princeton University Press.

Peatfield, A.A.D. 1990. "Minoan Peak Sanctuaries: History and Society." *OpAth* 18: 117–31.

Pernier, L. and L. Banti. 1951. *Il palazzo minoico di Festòs*. Vol. 2, *Il secondo palazzo*. Rome: Libreria dello Stato.

Popham, M.R. 1974. "Trial KV (1969), a Middle Minoan Building at Knossos." *BSA* 69: 181–94.

Speziale, A. 2001. "Il MMII: La casa LXXXI–LXXXV, XCIV–XCV." In *I centro anni dello scavo di Festòs, Giornate lincee, Rome, 13–14 dicembre 2000*, 157–67. Atti dei Convegni Lincei 173. Rome: Accademia Nazionale dei Lincei.

Taramelli, A. 1901. "Cretan Expedition XX: A Visit to the Grotto of Camares on Mount Ida." *AJA* 5: 437–51.

Tyree, E.L. 2001. "Diachronic Changes in Minoan Cave Cult." In *POTNIA: Deities and Religion in the Aegean Bronze Age. Proceedings of the 8th International Aegean Conference, Göteborg, Göteborg University, 12*–15 April 2000, edited by R. Laffineur and R. Hägg, 39–50. *Aegaeum* 22. Liège: Université de Liège.

Van de Moortel, A. 1997. "The Transition from the Protopalatial to the Neopalatial Society in South-Central Crete: A Ceramic Perspective." Ph.D. diss., Bryn Mawr College.

———. 2001. "The Area Around the Kiln, and the Pottery from the Kiln and the Kiln Dump." In *A LM IA Ceramic Kiln in South-Central Crete,* by J.W. Shaw, A. Van de Moortel, P.M. Day and V. Kilikoglou, 25–110. *Hesperia* Suppl. 30. Princeton, NJ: American School of Classical Studies at Athens.

———. 2002. "Pottery as a Barometer of Economic Change: From the Protopalatial to the Neopalatial Society in Central Crete." In *Labyrinth Revisited: Rethinking 'Minoan' Archaeology,* edited by Y. Hamilakis, 189–211. Oxford: Oxbow Books.

———. Forthcoming. "Adopting Knossian Ways: Neopalatial versus Protopalatial Pottery Production in the Western Mesara." In *Proceedings of the 9th International Congress of Cretan Studies, Elounda, 1–6 October 2001.*

Vasilakis, A. 1995. "Τρυπητή 1986–1991." In *Πεπραγμένα του Ζ' Διεθνούς Κρητολογικού Συνεδρίου*. Vol. A1, *Τμήμα Αρχαιολογικό*, edited by N.E. Papadogiannakis, 69–74. Rethymnon: Iera Mitropolis Rethymnis & Aulopotamou.

Walberg, G. 1983. *Provincial Middle Minoan Pottery.* Mainz on Rhine: Philipp von Zabern.

———. 1987. "Palatial and Provincial Workshops in the Middle Minoan Period." In *The Function of the Minoan Palaces. Proceedings of the Fourth International Symposium at the Swedish Institute in Athens, 10–16 June 1984*, edited by R. Hägg and N. Marinatos, 281–5. *SkrAth* 4, 35. Stockholm: Svenska Institutet i Athen.

Warren, P. 1972. *Myrtos: An Early Bronze Age Settlement in Crete. BSA* Suppl. 7. Oxford: British School of Archaeology at Athens and Thames and Hudson.

Watrous, L.V. 1992. *Kommos.* Vol. 3, *The Late Bronze Age Pottery*. Princeton, NJ: Princeton University Press.

———. 1996. *The Cave Sanctuary of Zeus at Psychro: A Study of Extra-Urban Sanctuaries in Minoan and Early Iron Age Crete. Aegaeum* 15. Liège: Université de Liège.

Wilson, D.E. 1984. "The Early Minoan IIA West Court House at Knossos." Ph.D. diss., University of Cincinnati.

———. 1985. "The Pottery and Architecture of the EM IIA West Court House at Knossos." *BSA* 80: 281–364.

Xanthoudides, S. 1971. Reprint. *The Vaulted Tombs of Mesara.* Farnborough: Gregg. Original edition, Liverpool: University Press of Liverpool; London: Hodder and Stoughton, 1924.

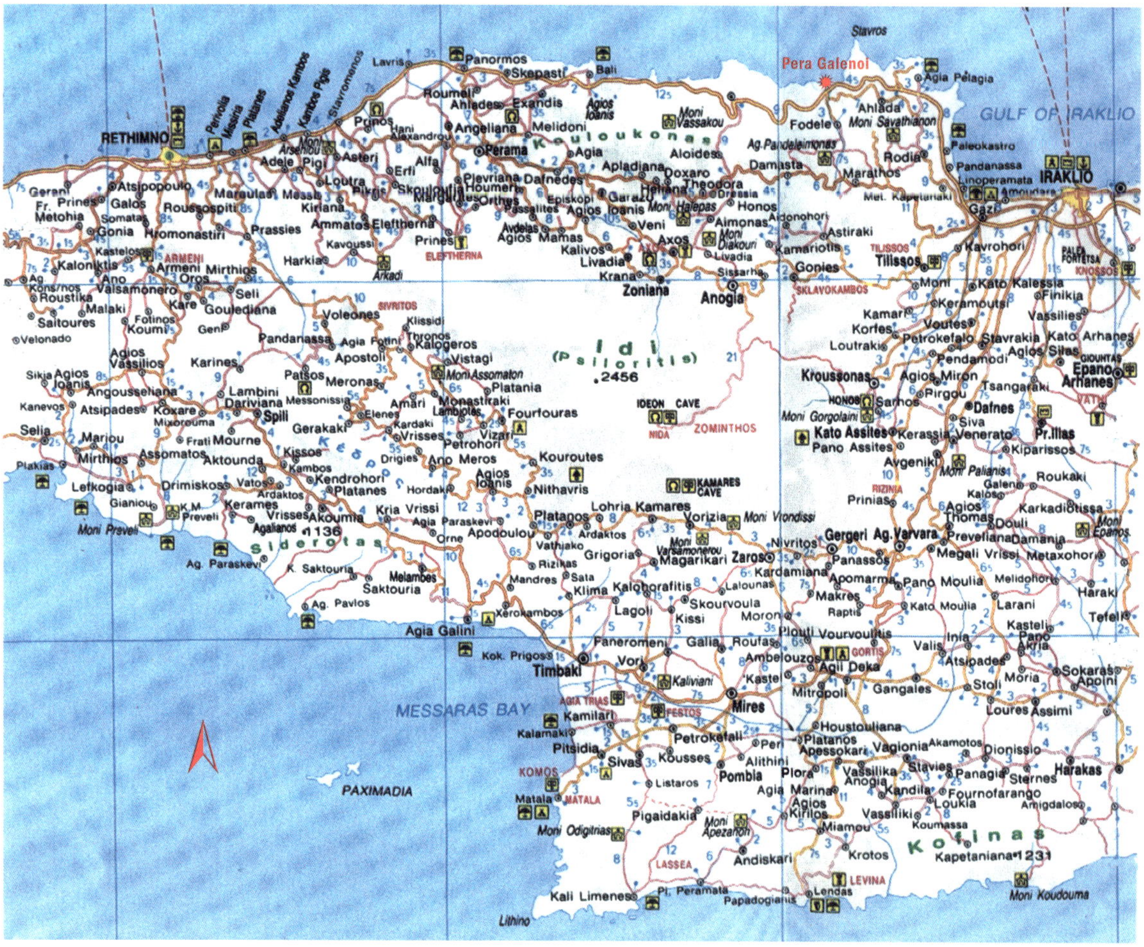

Fig. 1. Map of Central Crete.

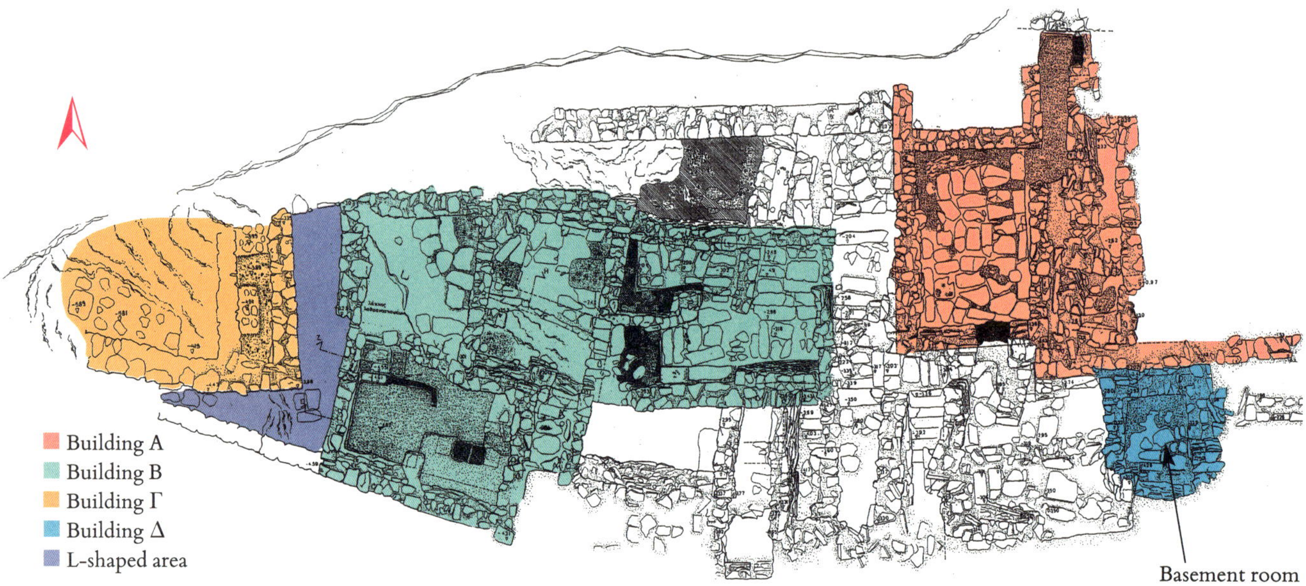

Fig. 2. Pera Galenoi. Ground plan of the excavated area.

PROVINCIAL MIDDLE MINOAN POTTERY: THE CASE OF PERA GALENOI

ELENI S. BANOU & ELENI TSIVILIKA

THE MINOAN SITE OF PERA GALENOI[1] is situated along the north coast of Crete at the natural border between the prefectures of Herakleion and Rethymnon (4 km west of the village of Fodele, fig. 1). The headland on which the ancient site is situated commands a medium-sized, wind-protected harbor, which is formed at the foot of a picturesque valley traversed today by a creek, a flood river in antiquity.

A small-scale survey conducted concurrently with the excavation by the authors has indicated that the ancient site extends over two hills, Kephali Soudas and Tartaroi, that flank the natural harbor, as well as over the northernmost tip of the cliffs east of the harbor at the site called Trachiloi.[2] Illicit excavation that occurred at the site in 1992 compelled the 25th Ephoreia of Prehistoric and Classical Antiquities to initiate a series of rescue campaigns in 1993 and 1995.[3]

Systematic excavations, initiated in 1998 and continuing to date on the northern headland of Kephali Soudas, have brought to light four buildings (two completely uncovered and a third and fourth partially excavated) on the summit of the hill—Buildings Delta (Δ), Alpha (A), Beta (B) and Gamma (Γ) and from east to west, i.e., the sequence in which one encounters the buildings walking toward the summit from the east (fig. 2).[4]

Eleni Banou and Eleni Tsivilika direct the excavation at Pera Galenoi. Nikitas Lianeris, a specialist in archaeology of the Neolithic period, was one of the trench-masters. The excavation to date (campaigns for 1993, 1995, 1998, 2000, 2001, 2002, 2003) is financially supported by the Institute for Aegean Prehistory and the Psycha Foundation (Greek Ministry of Culture). Special thanks are extended to Maria Adreadaki-Vlazaki, director of the 25th Ephoreia of Prehistoric and Classical Antiquities, for her constant aid and concern, and to Nikos Minos, director of the Conservation Department of the Ministry of Culture, for his support in the conservation of the material. Finally, thanks are expressed to the staff of the Rethymnon Museum where the material is kept. The present study of the pottery by no means claims to be exhaustive, since the material is still being processed in the Rethymnon Museum, but it is a preliminary discussion of the subject.

1. The name of the site probably derives from the name of the Venetian family of "Galenoi" of the thirteenth century A.D.; see Platakis 1975, 43–4.
2. The site was first discovered by Eleni Tsivilika in 1983; see Tsivilika 1983, 374.
3. Banou and Tsivilika 1993; Tsivilika and Banou 1994–1996, 293–4.
4. Banou and Tsivilika 2002, 295–8; and Tsivilika and Banou 1998.

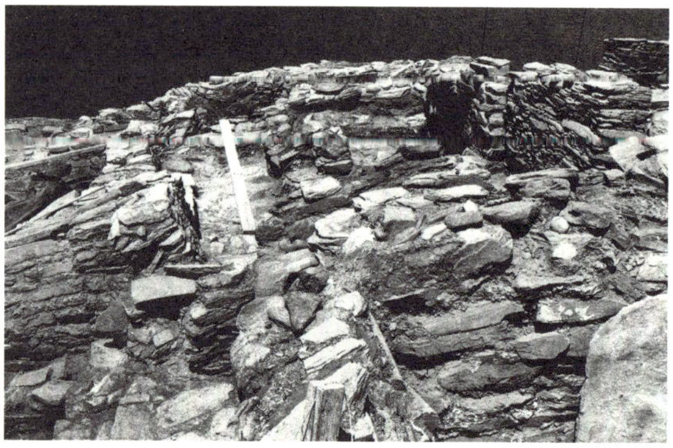

Fig. 3. General view of Pera Galenoi from the east. In the background, a small room with a bench.

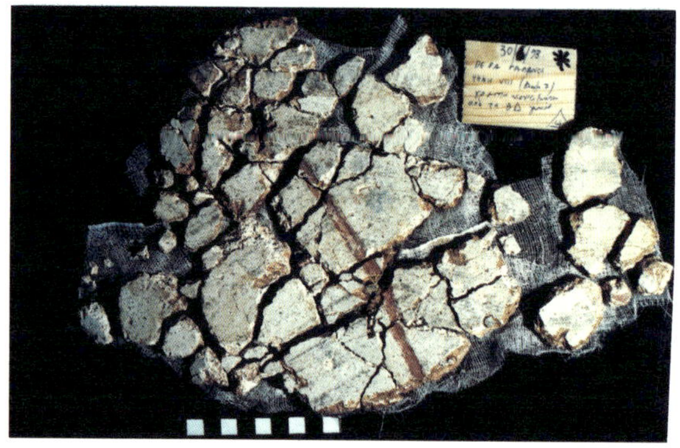

Fig. 4. Fragments of painted plaster.

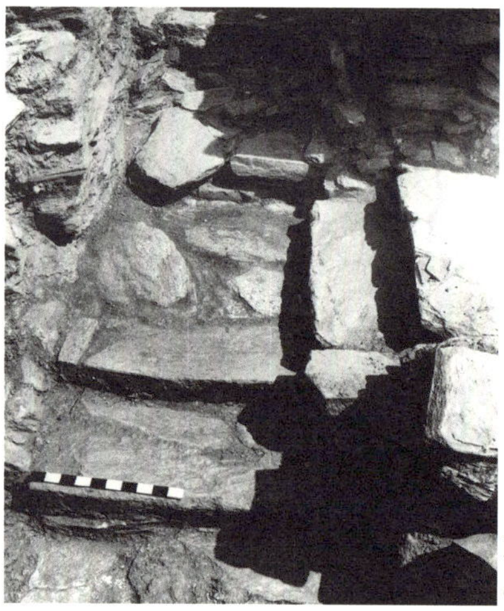

Fig. 5. The central staircase.

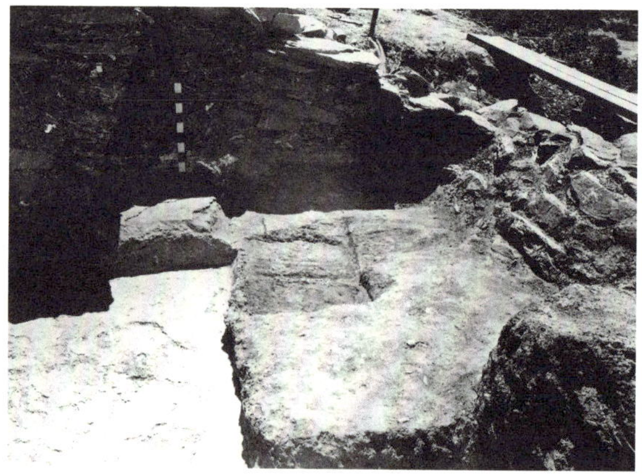

Fig. 6. The lustral basin or adyton from the west. In the foreground, the low platform-bench.

At least one room of Building A to the north and possibly part of the western settlement, west of Building Γ, has been lost to erosion. The walls, impressively preserved at places to the height of 2.10 m, are made of local phyllite stone (fig. 3). Some architectural features such as the benches and partition walls in Building B are made entirely of mud brick. All rooms are nicely paved with flagstones with plastered joints. Plaster fragments painted with red bands and brush strokes imitating marble veneering demonstrate that plaster was lavishly used to coat wall and possibly floor surfaces (fig. 4). Other architectural features such as stone staircases conforming to the steep incline of the ground were used to give access to higher levels (fig. 5). One room in Building B exhibited architectural elements resembling a lustral basin or adyton (fig. 6), and a room in Building A contained cult furnishings, including stone offering tables (more than six offering tables were found in this house), one of which is illustrated in figure 7, perhaps suggesting that certain rooms of Buildings A and B could have been used for religious purposes as well as for secular activities.

Since the very beginning of our work we have believed that we were dealing with a site of potential significance, which merited intensive excavation and study to explore issues such as: 1) the actual character of the Minoan settlement and the role it played in connection with other known (excavated) Minoan sites in the vicinity (i.e., Hagia Pelagia to the east and Tylissos and Sklavokambos to the south), and 2) the site's possible affiliation with any of the well-known major palatial centers (i.e., Phaistos or Knossos).

The study of the pottery from Kephali Soudas at Pera Galenoi is still in a preliminary stage. Nevertheless, it looks quite promising as it provides information on regional ceramic styles and on intra-Cretan and seaborne trade with the Aegean.

The pottery deposits examined here come primarily from two areas: an L-shaped area, which seems to be an alley between Buildings B and Γ, and a basement room in Building Δ. The pottery from the alley includes the earliest ceramic styles found at the site to date; the deposit from the basement room is a destruction deposit, which dates the severe earthquake that destroyed the settlement.

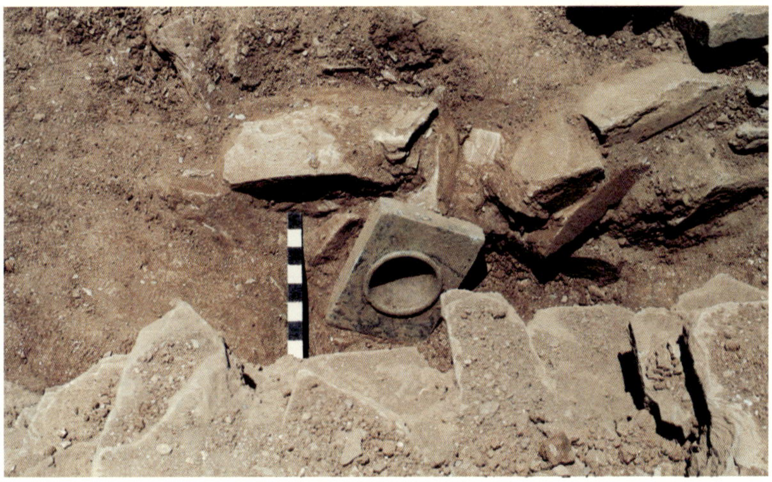

Fig. 7.
Building B. Stone offering table.

THE POTTERY FROM THE L-SHAPED AREA

A large amount of pottery (approximately 150 kg) was found scattered in an L-shaped space (on the ground plan, far west, fig. 2) measuring 9 m (length) by 1.50 m (width) at its northern branch. The actual character of the deposit cannot be determined with certainty at present, as the excavation here is not complete. One suggestion sees it as a dump or a rubble fill to raise the surface of this space (perhaps once used as a room and then later as an alley) after room cleaning and reorganization activities that had taken place at the site (this is clearly visible in the architecture).[5] Another suggestion views the L-shaped area as an outdoor space

5. Clear signs of architectural alterations and additions are visible in space 7, where the wall north of the staircase has been added and possibly the staircase itself; in room 9 the southern opening has been blocked with consecutive layers of large mud bricks; in room (corridor) 12b an opening at its northeastern end has also been blocked with layers of mud brick.

for activities (perhaps rituals) directly connected with adjacent room 3 (the so-called Adyton) in Building B to the east, since a number of cups had been inverted along the west wall of the Adyton. Finally, accumulation of pottery by other means cannot be ruled out.

Nevertheless, the preliminary examination of the pottery from the alley indicates that this deposit was created more or less at one time and not over a long period, since a number of physical joins connect some of the sherds from the four separately excavated layers.

The pottery from this space is abundant and generally fragmentary, although a number of vessels could be restored (mainly saucers, cups and plates made of coarse fabric). The pottery comprises three basic fabric categories: 1) Red Coarse Fabric, which outnumbers all others, consisting of reddish-orange and reddish-brown clay (for the fire-resistant vases), well fired and slightly tempered with phyllite or quartzite inclusions. A subclass of category "1" is a group of vases in brownish-red gritty fabric with small inclusions of silver mica (see below). 2) Buff Coarse Fabric of yellowish-buff clay, also very well fired, with many quartzite inclusions. 3) Fine fabric pottery made from light-colored or pinkish, highly refined clay. A specific source for all fabrics cannot yet be determined since no such investigation has been conducted in the surrounding region to date. Nevertheless, red clay beds are expected to be found in the vicinity, if we judge from the red color of the clay bricks used in the Minoan houses of Pera Galenoi.

A variety of shapes mainly, though not exclusively, for culinary use were recognized from this space; they include a number of restorable cups, conical and carinated, which were found placed along the walls of this space; tripod vessels (trays and cooking pots); and a large number of plates and lamps. Other shapes include jugs and storage vases (of the latter no complete example has survived).

Contacts with areas of the eastern Mediterranean are suggested by imports from the Syro-Palestinian region.

An MM IIA *terminus post quem* for the deposit is suggested by the absence of any distinctive features of the MM I ceramic style—that is handmade pottery, Barbotine Ware, pottery of the Polychrome Geometric style, and particularly the cup shapes with strap and loop handles as defined by Walberg and MacGillivray.[6] Furthermore, not one sherd has yet been uncovered decorated in the so-called White-spotted Style, which is considered to be characteristic of MM IIIA ceramics, thus perhaps indicating the lower chronological limit of this group of vessels.[7] Lastly, all the complete or restorable datable vessels (mainly cups) belong to the MM IIB period.

6. Walberg 1983; MacGillivray 1998, 68–76.
7. Warren and Hankey 1989; Catling et al. 1979, fig. 18.

CATALOGUE

MM IIA

Fine Fabric

Some features that stylistically may be assigned to the MM IIA period are found at the site, such as a fine example of a base sherd of the so-called Eggshell Ware decorated on the underside of the base with white paint, perhaps petals (fig. 8).

Fig. 8 [**RM 27003**]. Cup, base sherd. D of base: 4.5 cm. Fine fabric (pink). Eggshell Ware. Monochrome. Added white (fugitive) petals(?).
Comments: Although the profile of the vessel is missing it is probably a rounded cup like all other known examples of Eggshell Ware; this ware was undoubtedly the finest pottery made in Crete to fulfill palatial needs and is considered the hallmark of the MM IIA period.

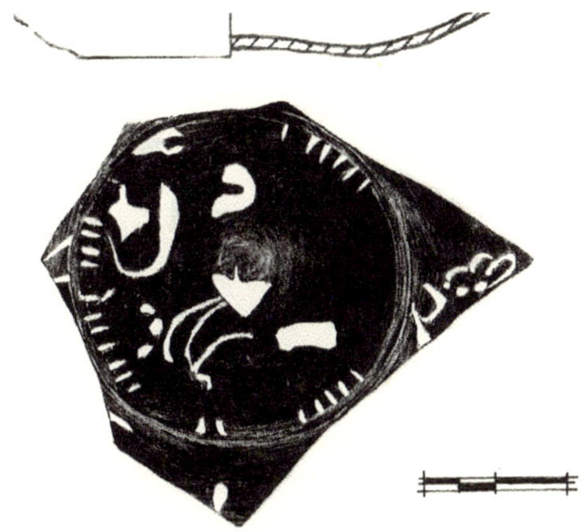

Fig. 8. L-shaped area. MM IIA Eggshell Ware.

MM IIB

Brownish-red Gritty Fabric

A few of the numerous cups of all shapes are made of hard, well-baked, slightly tempered gritty fabric (brownish-red with tiny flecks of silver mica). They seem to conform to the Gritty Fabric Class at Knossos as defined by MacGillivray[8]—a few cups with sharp carination and ridged walls characterized by randomly displaced grooves on the upper part of the body, above the carination (fig. 9); a tall conical cup also with ridged walls and raised base (fig. 10d); and several shallow bowls/saucers (fig. 11). The cups, which may be viewed as a variation of the Shallow Grooved Ware from Knossos (not necessarily of micaceous fabric), are known from the Early Chamber beneath the West Court and from the Royal Pottery Stores at the palace at Knossos dated to MM IIA[9] and from the MM II phase (peri-

8. MacGillivray 1998, 89.
9. MacGillivray 1998, pls. 40–1 and 125 respectively.

ods 1 and 2) at Phaistos and Malia.[10] The origin of these vessels undoubtedly lies within Crete since these shapes are typically Minoan. It is of interest that a group of vessels in red micaceous fabric occurs at Knossos in deposits that span the Old Palace period. These Knossian vessels, however, are not considered local; MacGillivray conjectured a Pediada (central Crete) origin as they bear striking similarities in fabric and shape to vessels found in the Trapeza Cave at Lassithi, Myrtos-Pyrgos and those found at Kastelli-Pediada.[11]

One of the rare pieces among this mass of pottery is a wheel-made pyxis sherd in gritty fabric with decoration imitating the mottled effect of Vasiliki Ware (fig. 12). Recent investigation in the Pediada region by Rethemiotakis and Christakis indicates that this pseudo-mottled style was quite fashionable in central Crete during the Old Palace period.[12] If we accept the Pediada region as a likely source for the pyxis, then it fits well to suggest that the group of micaceous vessels mentioned above are also from there. Whether the introduction of these vessels came directly from the Pediada region or via Knossos is certainly premature to assess in light of the present evidence.

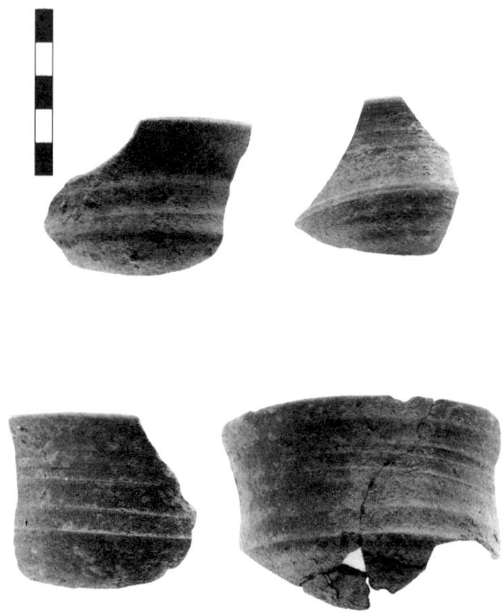

FIG. 9. L-shaped area. MM IIA carinated cups.

Fig. 9 [**RM 26990 α–δ**]. Four cup rim sherds. Red gritty fabric with flecks of silver mica. D of rim: ranging from 8 to 11.2 cm. Ridged thin walls. Well-baked fabric.

Fig. 10a [**RM 26979**]. Conical cup, complete. Reddish-brown fabric with flecks of silver mica. D of rim: 8.4 cm; D of base: 3.7 cm; H: 6.5 cm. Wall ridged from manufacture. Raised base.

Fig. 10b [**RM 26980**]. Conical cup, almost complete. Reddish-brown fabric with flecks of silver mica. D of rim: 8.9 cm; D of base: 4.9 cm; H: 5.5 cm.

Fig. 10c [**RM 26981**]. Conical cup, almost complete. Yellowish-red fabric. D of rim: 8.9 cm; D of base: 4.8 cm; H: 6.8 cm.

Fig. 10d [**RM 26982**]. Conical cup, complete profile. Reddish-brown fabric with flecks of silver mica. D of rim: 8.4 cm; D of base: 3.7 cm; H: 6.5 cm. Half of body is restored. Wall ridged from manufacture. Raised base.

Fig. 11a. Bowl/saucer, complete. Reddish-brown fabric with flecks of silver mica. D of rim: 10 cm; D of base: 2.9 cm; H: 3.5 cm. Outturned flat rim; small ring base.

Fig. 11b. Bowl/saucer, complete. Reddish-brown fabric with flecks of silver mica. D of rim: 10 cm; D of base: 2.9 cm; H: 2.5 cm. Outturned flat rim; small ring base.

10. Phaistos: Fiandra 1980; Malia: Stürmer 1993; Pelon 1970, pl. X.3–4, cups with ridged upper walls are dated to the MM IIB period.
11. See supra n. 8.
12. Rethemiotakis and Christakis 2004.

Fig. 11c. Bowl/saucer, almost complete. Reddish-brown fabric with flecks of silver mica. D of rim: 10 cm; D of base: 2.9 cm; H: 3.5 cm. Outturned flat rim; small ring base.

Fig. 12 [**RM 26989**]. Pyxis, rim and handle sherd. Reddish-brown fabric with small quartzite inclusions. Max pres H: 10 cm. Small straight rim; vertical handle; straight wall. Pseudo-mottled effect.
Comments: Similarly manufactured vessels are known from the Pediada district.

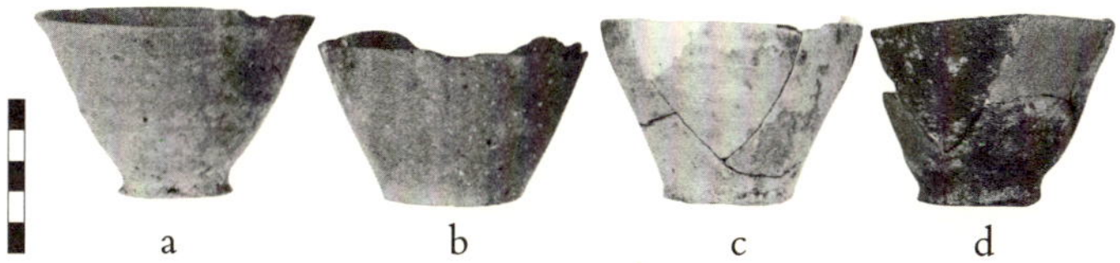

Fig. 10. L-shaped area. Conical cups with raised bases.

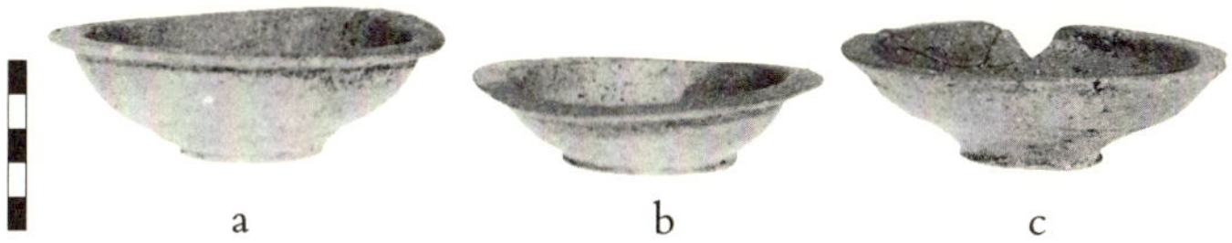

Fig. 11. L-shaped area. Bowls/saucers.

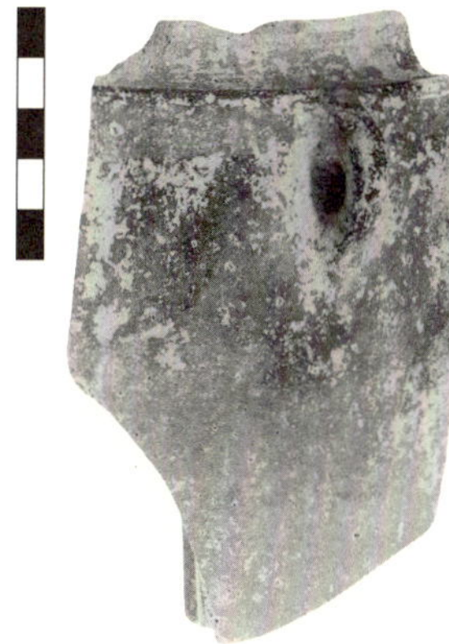

Fig. 12.
L-shaped area. MM II pseudo-Vassiliki ware.

Fine Fabric

Cups in fine buff fabric, either miniature with a small upright handle (fig. 15b) or straight-sided with a flat base and thin walls (fig. 14), were present in the deposit. They find parallels in the Loomweight Basement deposit from the palace at Knossos,[13] in the Trial KV deposits at Knossos[14] and also in the Phaistian deposits of Levi's phase II, and they may be dated to the MM IIB period. Very few painted sherds have been found in this mass of pottery. The bottom sherd in figure 16 in fine orange fabric is decorated with a white band and splashes of paint in MM IIB style as encountered in the Loomweight deposit and at Phaistos.[15]

Fig. 14a [**RM 26986**]. Straight-sided cup, almost complete. Rim mended. Fine, brownish-yellow fabric. D of rim: 11 cm; D of base: 7.5 cm; H: 8.2 cm. Flat base; ribbon handle; thin walls.

Fig. 14b [**RM 26985**]. Straight-sided cup, base preserved. Fine, reddish-yellow fabric. D of base: 7 cm.

Fig. 15b. Miniature cup, three-quarters preserved, complete profile. Fine, yellowish fabric. D of rim: 3 cm; D of base: 1.8 cm; H: 2.5 cm. Small upright handle.

Fig. 16b. Closed vessel, body sherd. Fine, reddish-yellow fabric. Max pres H: 3 cm. Splashes in dark-on-light with bands in added white.

13. MacGillivray 1998, pl. 128.
14. Popham 1974, fig. 6.10–4.
15. Knossos: MacGillivray 1998, pl. 129.840 (on Coarse Ware); Phaistos: Levi 1976, pl. 95c.

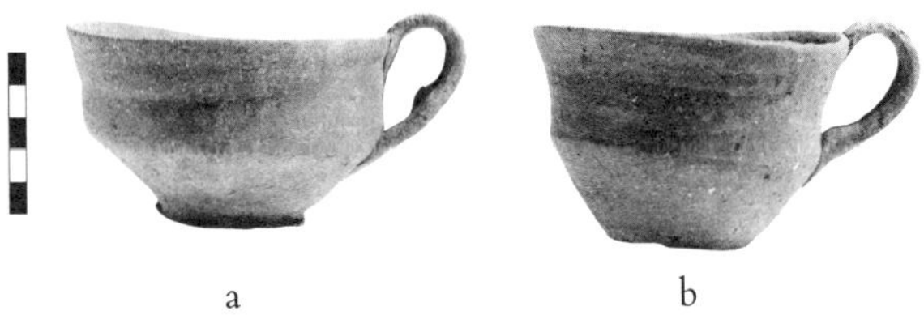

FIG. 13. L-shaped area. MM IIB–IIIA cups with slight carination.

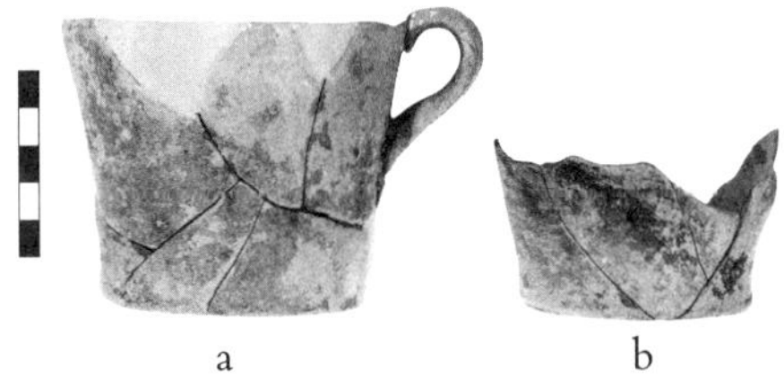

FIG. 14. L-shaped area. MM IIIA straight-sided cups.

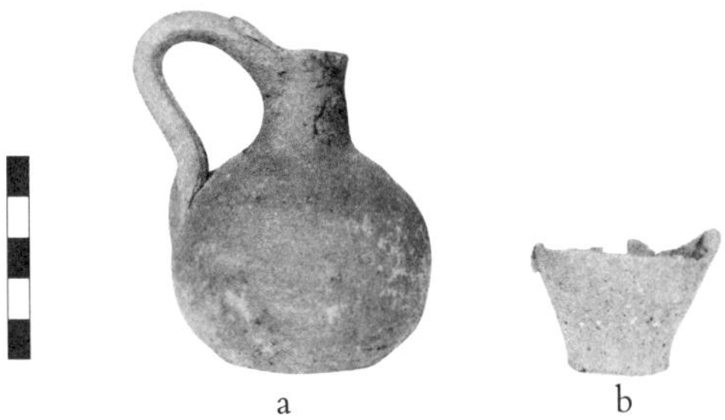

FIG. 15. L-shaped area. MM IIB juglet and miniature cup.

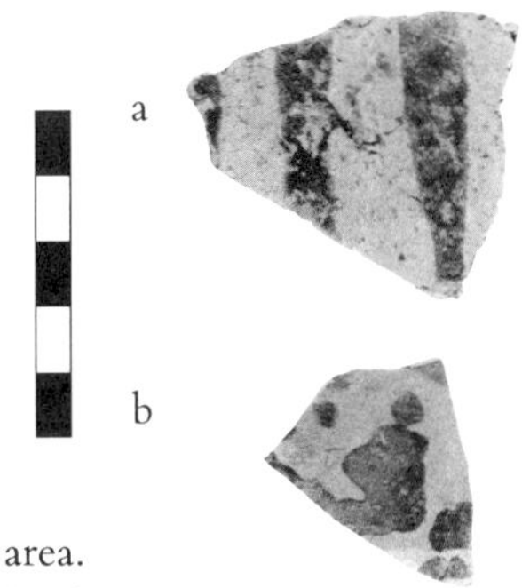

FIG. 16. L-shaped area. MM IIB painted sherds.

Coarse Fabric

CUPS. A large number of fragmentary and restorable cups in the deposit belong to the one-handled, bell-shaped type; they are modeled in a reddish-brown, crudely-made fabric, usually tempered with small white (quartzite) grits. The cups often have ridges on the exterior and they bear a ribbon-type handle and sometimes a small ring base (fig. 13).

JUGS. Juglets are plain with globular bodies and cylindrical necks (fig. 15a) and are exactly paralleled in the Phaistian deposits of Levi's phase Ib and the deposit from the Trial KV trench (1969) at Knossos.[16]

Fig. 13a [**RM 26988**]. Carinated cup, complete. Coarse fabric with minor white grits. D of rim: 10 cm; D of base: 3.8 cm; H: 6.5 cm. Rounded carination; small ring base; vertical strap handle.

Fig. 15a. Juglet, complete. Reddish-brown, gritty fabric with small quartzite inclusions. Max D: 6 cm; H (including handle): 7.5 cm. Globular body; cylindrical neck; round-sectioned handle rising above rim; plastic knob on handle; flat base.

Coarse Buff Fabric

The sherd illustrated in figure 16a is of coarse buff fabric with yellowish-white slip with dark-on-light trickle decoration, the latter being widespread in Crete in the MM IIB and III periods.[17]

Fig. 16a. Closed vessel, body sherd. A coarse buff fabric. Max pres H: 10 cm. Dull, reddish-brown paint; trickle decoration.

16. Popham 1974, fig. 6.23–5.
17. Walberg 1976; Betancourt 1990, 40–1.

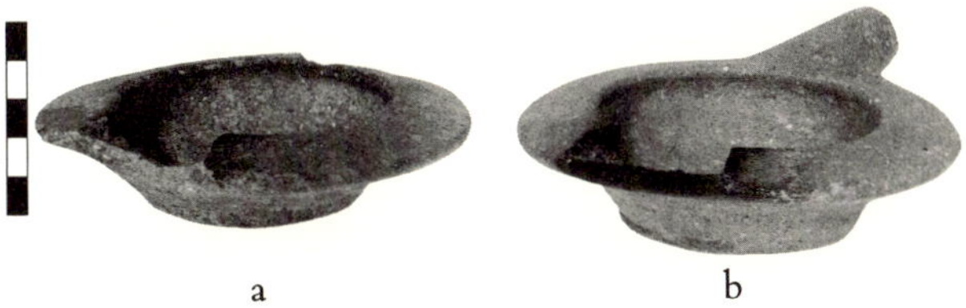

FIG. 17. L-shaped area. MM IIB hand lamps.

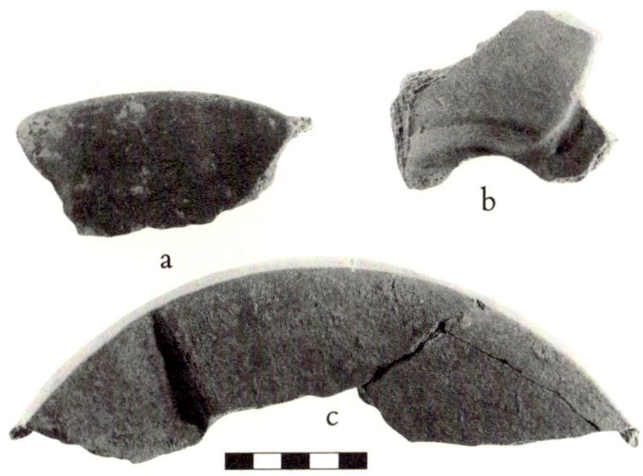

FIG. 18. L-shaped area. MMIIB–IIIA pedestal lamps.

Coarse Red Fabric

In coarse red fabric, two MM IIB lamp types have been recognized: 1) a small one with a flat, outturned rim and pan-type handle (fig. 17a, b) and 2) a large pedestal lamp (fig. 18). Of the latter type, only rim fragments have survived. Comparable specimens (mainly type "1") are known from the Old Palace period deposits at the palace at Knossos,[18] Phaistos[19] and the Trial KV trench destruction deposit at Knossos,[20] ranging chronologically from MM IA to MM IIB. Another type of vessel with a low pedestal base and a central depression with flaring rim may be a lamp or a fruitstand (fig. 19). Comparable vases were found in Phaistian deposits from Levi's phases Ib and II,[21] and from MM III deposits at Kommos.[22]

In the same fabric, two sherds (fig. 20b, c), one probably from a cooking tray and the other from a cup, are worth mentioning as they bear potters' marks consisting of at least five cut marks of diamond shape and three shallow cuts respectively. Similar marks are known from Keos in Middle Cycladic levels.[23] In this deposit the presence of restorable or complete plates, like the example illustrated in figure 35, calls for further discussion. The plates range in diameter from 12–16 cm; they are quite rare in regular house deposits although it is (and it should have been) a common shape.

Fig. 17a. Hand lamp, complete except for handle and tip of spout. Reddish-brown, coarse fabric. D of rim: 8 cm. Traces of burning around periphery of rim.

Fig. 17b. Hand lamp, complete except for tip of handle. D of rim: 10 cm. Traces of heavy burning around spout.

Fig. 18a–c. Three sherds of pedestal lamps. Reddish-brown, coarse fabric. D of rim 18c: 11 cm. Wide spout opening.

18. MacGillivray 1998, 87 and fig. 2.24.
19. Levi 1976, pls. 152–3.
20. Popham 1974, fig. 8.9.
21. Levi 1976, pls. 60f, 151, 182.
22. Betancourt 1990, fig. 34.727.
23. Bikaki 1984, pls. 3.IV.31, 17.IV.31–32.

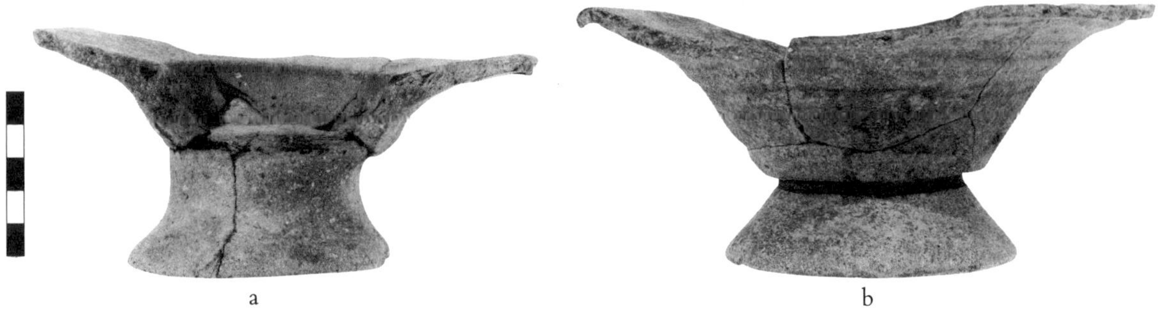

FIG. 19. L-shaped area. MM II footed lamps(?).

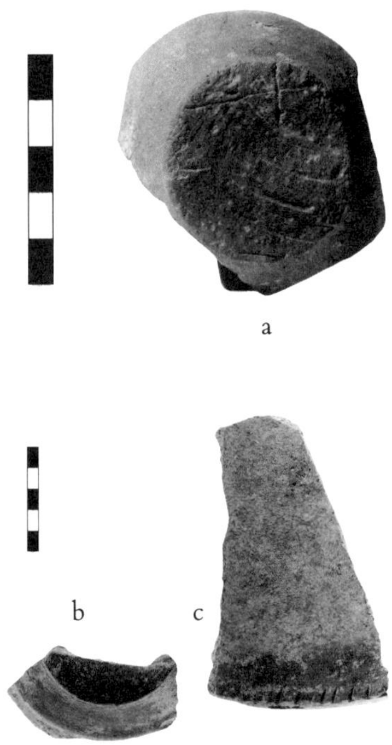

FIG. 20. L-shaped area. Vessels with potter's marks.

Fig. 19a. Open, low pedestal vase, three-quarters preserved, complete profile. Reddish-brown fabric, with grits. D of rim: 10.6 cm; D of base: 5.4 cm. Circular central depression.
Comments: The absence of comparable vessels from the Knossian deposits and its presence in the Mesara region (Phaistos and Kommos) suggest that the introduction of this shape at Pera Galenoi was probably via south Crete.

Fig. 19b. Similar to 19a. D of rim: 12.2cm; D of base: 6.3 cm.

Fig. 20a. Cup(?), base sherd. Coarse, reddish-brown fabric. D of base: 12 cm. A potter's mark consisting of a lightly cut cross; impressions from the cut string are visible.

Fig. 20b [**RM 27001**]. Open vessel, base sherd. Coarse, reddish-brown fabric. D of base: 10 cm. A potter's mark consisting of deep-cut strokes around edge of base.

Fig. 20c [**RM 27002**]. Carinated cup, base and body sherd. Coarse, reddish-brown fabric. D of base: 20 cm. A potter's mark consisting of deep-cut strokes around edge of base.

Fig. 35. Plate, complete. Coarse, reddish-brown fabric with white inclusions. D: 25 cm; H: 2 cm. Rounded rim. Slipped inside, rough underside.
Parallels: Identical plates have been found at the palace of Galatas.[24]

Non-Cretan Fabrics

Two unmistakably non-Minoan sherds were exceptional among the rest of the material (fig. 21). They are made of a distinctive soft porous matrix with sandy grits. The exterior has a pinkish-buff slip. They seem to be part of the same vase, in all probability a Syrian amphora; unfortunately it is much too fragmentary to be compared to Amiran's typology.[25] This is extremely important evidence for the site's role and position in Minoan international trade during the Old Palace period. Not many examples of Canaanite or Syrian amphorae dating to the Old Palace period are known from Crete; the earliest examples are

24. Rethemiotakis 1994, pl. 228.
25. Amiran 1970.

this one from Pera Galenoi and one specimen from the Old Palace deposit from Knossos.[26]

Ceramic imports from the eastern Mediterranean become more popular in MM III–LM IA contexts such as those from Kommos,[27] Pseira and Mochlos,[28] and from outside Crete at Thera.[29]

Fig. 21. Closed vessel, two body sherds. Soft, porous, red fabric with brown matrix. One of the sherds preserves traces of a thin pink slip. Unlike any Cretan fabric; probably from a Canaanite/Syrian amphora.

DATE

Although the decorated vases from this large deposit are very few (a fact that does not facilitate the task of dating) it seems that the lower chronological limit of the pottery from the L-shaped area does not post-date the MM IIB ceramic style; this is established mainly through correlations with the crude pottery from the Loomweight Basement deposit of the palace and the Trial KV trench destruction deposit at Knossos. Cups, the best indicators we have, belong to the carinated or slightly carinated type (MM IIB) or to the saucer type, which is a very shallow vessel comparable to those in the deposits from Knossos and Phaistos. Cups with grooved or stepped walls either decorated or plain with white spots (usually taken as a characteristic feature of MM IIIA ceramic style)[30] are absent. Worth noting are the thin-walled carinated cups and open vessels decorated with splash decoration in dark paint and added white, a crude style quite popular at Knossos and also perhaps at Phaistos.

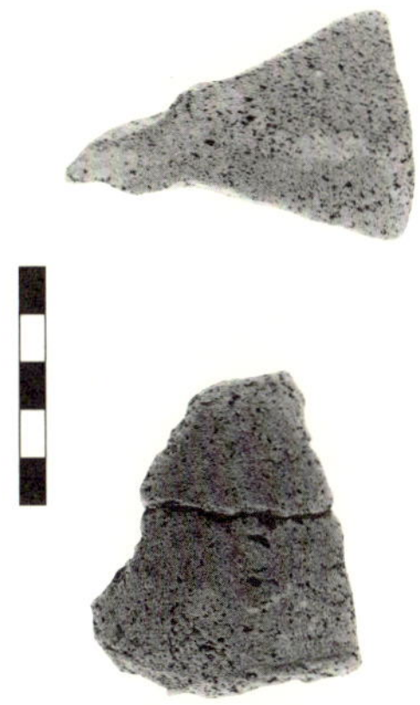

FIG. 21. L-shaped area. Canaanite/Syrian sherds.

BUILDING Δ BASEMENT ROOM FLOOR DEPOSIT

A MEDIUM-SIZED DEPOSIT from a basement room in Building Δ was excavated in 2001; it comprised a mass of material with many joins between the separately excavated layers that constituted a floor deposit. Over sixty vases have been restored from the layers near and on the floor of a 2x3 m room, which was nicely paved with flagstones and equipped with a small bench and a plaster drain along its southern entrance. Vessels in all fabric categories were present, with an overwhelming majority in the brownish-red gritty fabric. Stylistically, the deposit was homogenous, including mainly plain vases. The few decorated

26. MacGillivray 1998, fig. 2.26 (MM IIB–IIIA context).

27. Watrous 1992, 156 no. 1929, fig. 69, pl. 51 (Anatolian LM IB).

28. Banou 1992; Betancourt and Banou 1991, 107–10.

29. Marinatos 1976, 15, pl. 49b (Syrian amphora).

30. MacGillivray 1998, 65, where he claims on ceramic evidence that "the style came into existence before the end of the MM IIB period."

vases were in the Light-on-Dark Style of the MM II–III period, with very few sherds in the Dark-on-Light of the transitional MM III LM IA. No imports from outside Crete were recognized in this deposit.

CATALOGUE

MM III–LM IA

Fine Fabric

DECORATED VASES. A jug in fine fabric (fig. 22)—the finest piece in the deposit—is decorated in Light-on-Dark Style with lilies and geometric designs (cross-hatching and rock patterns). This style surpasses the surface pattern style of MM IIB and becomes more naturalistic using many more motifs still in Light-on-Dark Style. A few specimens of this class of pottery are known from the MM IIB–III deposits from Poros Herakleiou,[31] Kommos[32] and from deposits of period MM III at Phaistos.[33] A comparable specimen in shape and style dated to MM III comes from the House of the Ramp at Phaistos.[34] Our jug represents a good example of the new pictorial style with a specific desire for naturalistic plant motifs and it could be dated independently from its context to the MM IIIB period. Despite the lack of a beak it clearly is a libation jug akin to the alabaster libation jug from the palace at Zakros redated recently to LM IA.[35]

Another interesting piece in Light-on-Dark Style is a rounded cup (fig. 23) with spirals painted in white, a painted cross on the underside and a potter's mark (fig. 23b). The mark consists of an incised column of two chevrons. Similar marks are known from Phylakopi and Keos.[36] Sherds in figure 37 appear to belong to a cup with white-spotted decoration on the upper part of the body, to a bridge-spouted jar, and to a large closed vessel with very distinctively ridged walls.

Fig. 22 [**RM 27033**]. Jug, complete. Fine buff fabric; black and white paint. D of rim: 9.5 cm; D of base: 8 cm; H (including handle): 21.9. Wide mouth; tubular neck; distinctive ridge around neck; compressed globular body; vertical, round-sectioned handle starting from inner part of rim; low ring base. Decorated in light-on-dark; handle and rim painted in added white; solid black neck; upper shoulder with lily flowers and white-spotted decoration; middle zone with rock pattern; lower zone with cross-hatched semicircles in added white.
Parallels: The closest parallel comes from the House of the Ramp at Phaistos.[37]

31. Dimopoulou 1994, pl. 230; Metaxa-Muhly 1992.
32. Betancourt 1990, 40–1, figs. 30–1.
33. Levi 1976.
34. Carinci 2001, fig. 25.
35. Platonos-Giota 1995, 788.
36. Bikaki 1984, pl. 11.VI.18.
37. Carinci 2001, fig. 25.

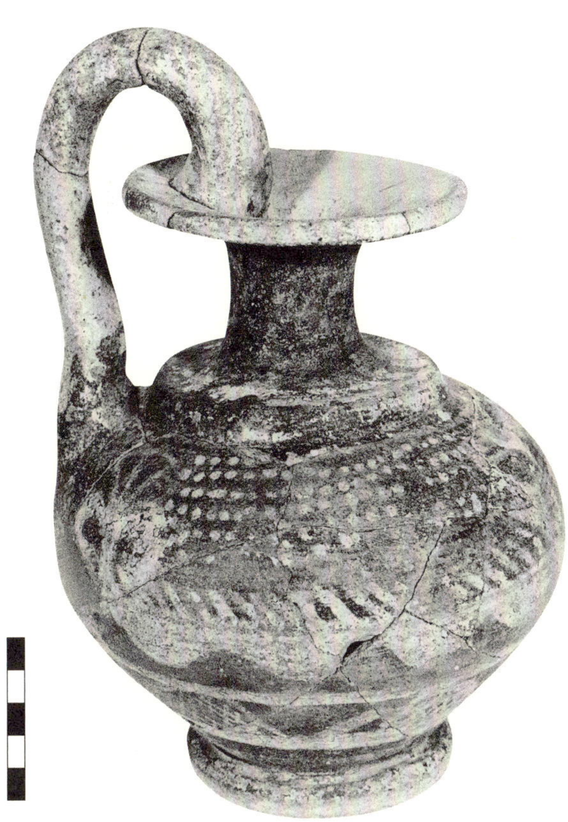

FIG. 22. Building Δ. MM III jug decorated with lilies.

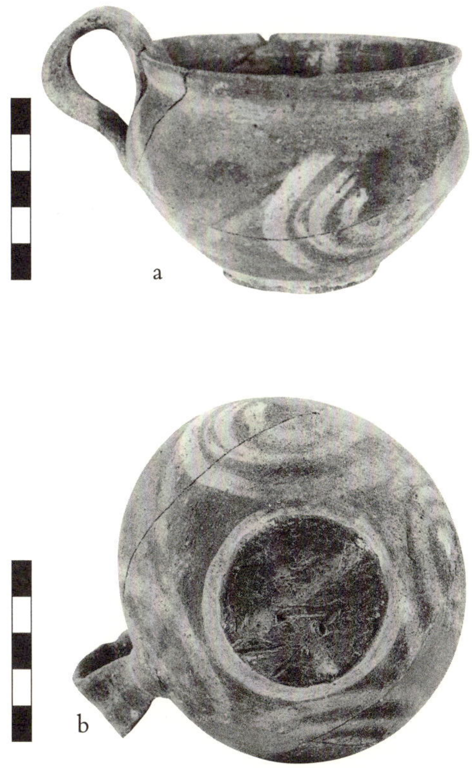

FIG. 23. (a) Building Δ. MM III–LM IA rounded cup with spirals in added white; (b) Building Δ. Detail of the same cup. Underside of base with potter's mark.

Fig. 23 a–b [**RM 27034**]. Rounded cup, complete. Fine buff fabric. D of rim: 8.5 cm; D of base: 4 cm; H: 6 cm. Offset rim; rounded body; vertical strap handle; small ring base. Decoration in light-on-dark; running spirals; band at rim; band at base; strokes on handle; a cross in added white on underside; potter's mark on underside consisting of two deep-cut chevrons.
Comments: This is the typical MM III rounded cup shape. The light-on-dark decoration brings the cup stylistically closer to the MM III tradition.[38]

Coarse Ware

CUPS. Cups in all shapes such as shallow conical cups, straight-sided cups and handleless bell cups made of well-baked, brownish-orange fabric, sometimes gritty but not micaceous, as in the previously described deposit, outnumber all other vessel types.

SHALLOW CUPS. Shallow cups in less gritty fabric than the MM II ones linger on (fig. 24, top vessels, fig. 25a, fig. 26a). Their height usually ranges between 3 and 3.9 cm and their rim diameter from 10 to 13.5 cm. More than 12 specimens were present in the deposit.

38. Betancourt 1985; Popham 1967.

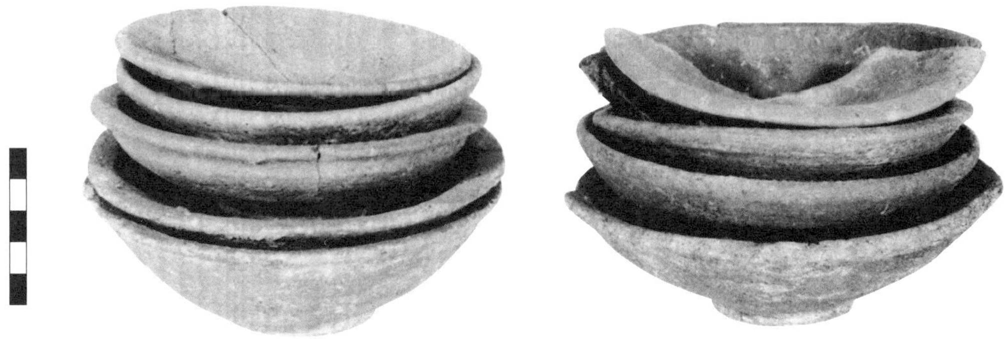

Fig. 24. Building Δ. MM III shallow cups and conical cups.

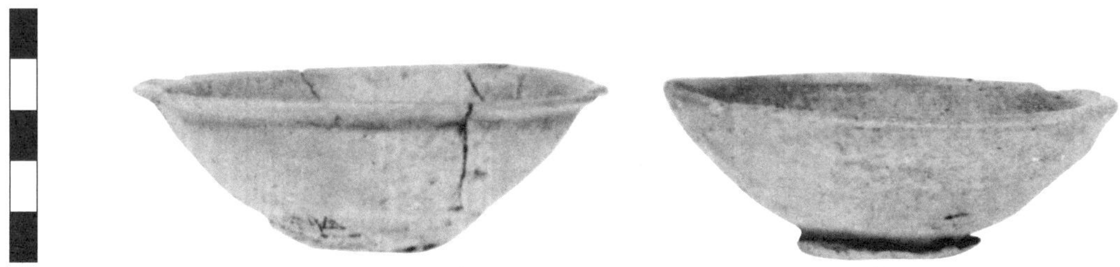

a b

Fig. 25. Building Δ. MM III–LM IA shallow cup and conical cup.

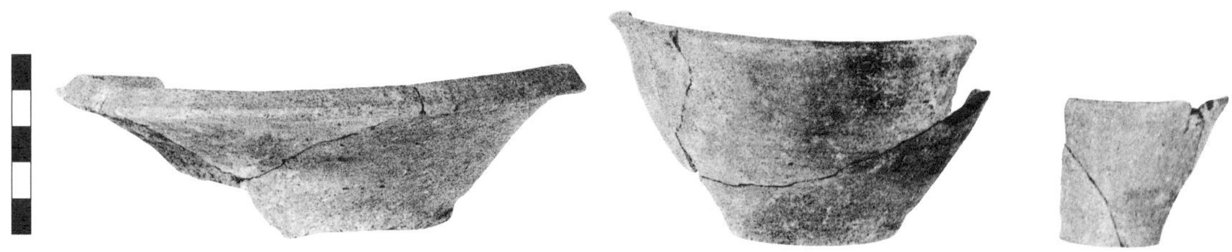

a b c

Fig. 26. Building Δ. MM III–LM IA conical cups.

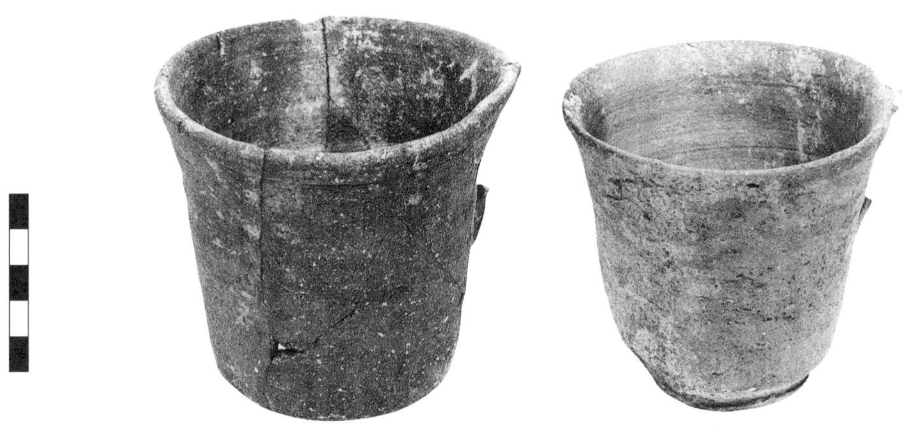

a b

Fig. 27. Building Δ. MM III–LM IA straight-sided cups.

CONICAL CUPS. Type 1. Conical cups of type 1 are crudely made of coarse fabric with a small ring base and round-sectioned straight rim (fig. 24). More than 22 examples were counted in the deposit. Their rim diameter usually ranges from 11 to 12.5 cm and their height does not surpass 4 cm.

Type 2. The second type of conical cup is made of very gritty fabric (fig. 25b and fig. 26a), and has a pure conical profile and square-sectioned straight rim; rim diameter ranges from 9 to 10 cm.

Type 3. Another shape in this deposit is the handleless bell cup or ogival cup of reddish-brown coarse fabric (fig. 30); these cups, reaching 7.5 cm, are usually taller than the typical conical cups. Similar cups are encountered in the previously described deposit dated to the MM II–IIIA period and in deposit A (MM IIIA) of the Acropolis House at Knossos; their percentage increases during MM IIIB–LM IA, as exemplified by the E and F ceramic deposits from the Acropolis Houses at Knossos.[39]

STRAIGHT-SIDED CUPS. The straight-sided cup, either plain or decorated, is the second most popular shape in this deposit. In MM III the shape acquires a beveled or a small ring base with walls slightly ridged from the fast wheel (fig. 27). The height of the plain, straight-sided cup ranges from 7 to 8.3 cm and the rim diameter is, as in most straight-sided cups, around 10 cm.

A smaller version of this cup bears decoration in white, usually a lip band or a loop around the handle (fig. 28). Similarly decorated cups have been found in deposits from the Unexplored Mansion dated by Popham to MM IIIB–LM IA.[40] A few specimens of these decorated cups have grooved walls and are decorated in the White-spotted Style on the lip zone (fig. 29a). Comparable cups are known from the MM III deposits at Anemospilia[41] and from the MM IIIB deposit D of the Acropolis Houses at Knossos.[42] However, the stepped walls of the cups, as they appear in the Knossian and Poros deposits, are not present in any deposit hitherto excavated at Pera Galenoi.[43]

BOWL/RHYTON. What seems to be a rarely encountered shape is a handleless bowl/rhyton in coarse fabric (fig. 31a and b), possibly a translation in clay of the stone "bird's nest bowl."

JUGS. The small crudely-made juglets (fig. 32a) and the spouted large version (fig. 32b), both encountered in the MM IIB deposit from the L-shaped area, which in essence belong

39. Catling et al. 1979, fig. 27.

40. Popham 1984, pl. 142.2, 10, 11.

41. Sakellarakis and Sapouna-Sakellaraki 1997, fig. 385 and fig. 383, respectively.

42. Catling et al. 1979, fig. 16.6, fig. 35.235.

43. Metaxa-Muhly 1992.

to the Old Palace tradition, are also present in this floor deposit. Both shapes also appear in the pottery from the Kalpadakis plot at Archanes, dated to the MM IIIB period.[44]

LAMPS. The hand lamp (fig. 38), which has already been encountered in the MM IIB deposit from Pera Galenoi as described above remains unchanged.

KALATHOS. The open conical kalathos illustrated in figure 36 was found preserved intact in an upright position a few centimeters above the paved floor.

BRIDGE-SPOUTED JARS. Two complete examples of bridge-spouted jars in coarse fabric (fig. 33a and b), one plain and the other decorated in Light-on-Dark Style, may be assigned to the transitional MM IIIB–LM IA period.

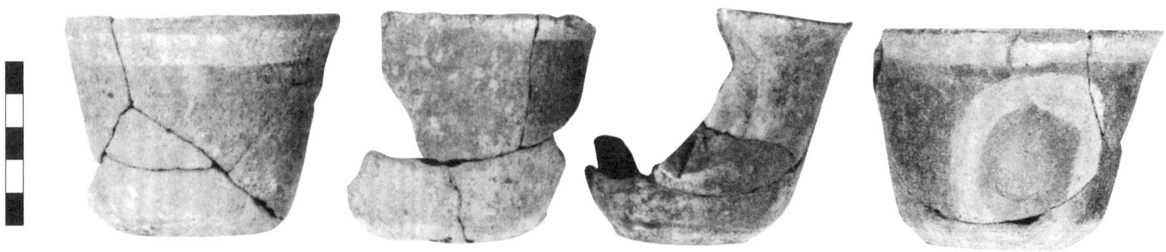

FIG. 28. Building Δ. MM III–LM IA straight-sided cups with white decoration.

Fig. 24. Shallow cups and conical cups, complete. Red coarse fabric with tiny grits. D of rim: 10–13.5 cm; D of base: 2–3 cm; H: 3.3–4.1 cm.

Fig. 25a [**RM 27010α**]. Shallow cup, complete. Reddish-brown fabric with tiny inclusions. D of rim: 12.3 cm; D of base: 5.8 cm; H: 3 cm. Outturned rim.

Fig. 25b. Conical cup, complete. D of rim: 12 cm; D of base: 4.2 cm; H: 3.3 cm. Small ring base.

Fig. 26a [**RM 27010β**]. Conical cup, complete profile. D of rim: 12 cm; D of base: 4.2 cm; H: 3.3 cm. Flat base; outturned rim.

Fig. 26b. Conical cup, half preserved, complete profile. D of rim: 9.6 cm; D of base: 4 cm; H: 5 cm.

Fig. 26c. Cup, half preserved, complete profile. D of rim: 4.6 cm; D of base: 2 cm; H: 3 cm.

Fig. 27a [**RM 27008**]. Straight-sided cup, complete except for handle. Grayish-brown, coarse fabric. D of rim: 11 cm; D of base: 4 cm; H: 8 cm. Oval mouth; beveled base.

Fig. 27b. Straight-sided cup, complete except for handle. Grayish-brown, coarse fabric with white inclusions. D of rim: 11 cm; D of base: 3.8 cm; H: 7.7 cm. Oval mouth; small ring base.

Fig. 28a [**RM 27023**]. Straight-sided cup, complete except for handle. Reddish-brown, coarse fabric with white inclusions. D of rim: 9 cm; D of base: 5 cm; H: 7 cm. Small, beveled base. White band at rim; white loop around handle.

Fig. 28b–d. Similar to 28a, but less complete.

44. Sakellarakis and Sapouna-Sakellaraki 1997, figs. 397–8.

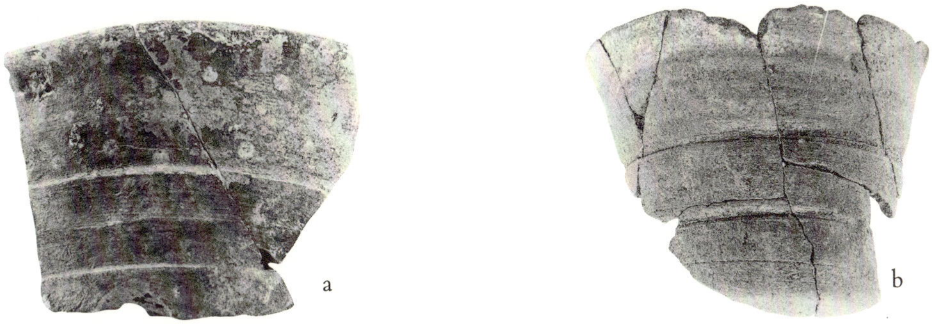

a b

Fig. 29. Building Δ. MM III–LM IA cups with white spotted decoration and grooved walls.

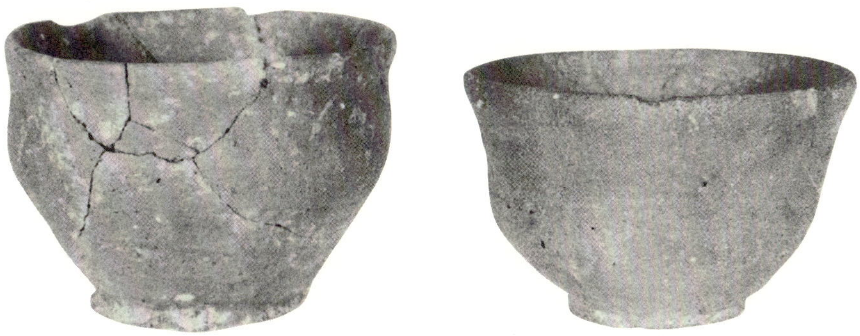

a b

Fig. 30. Building Δ. MM III–LM IA handless ogival cups.

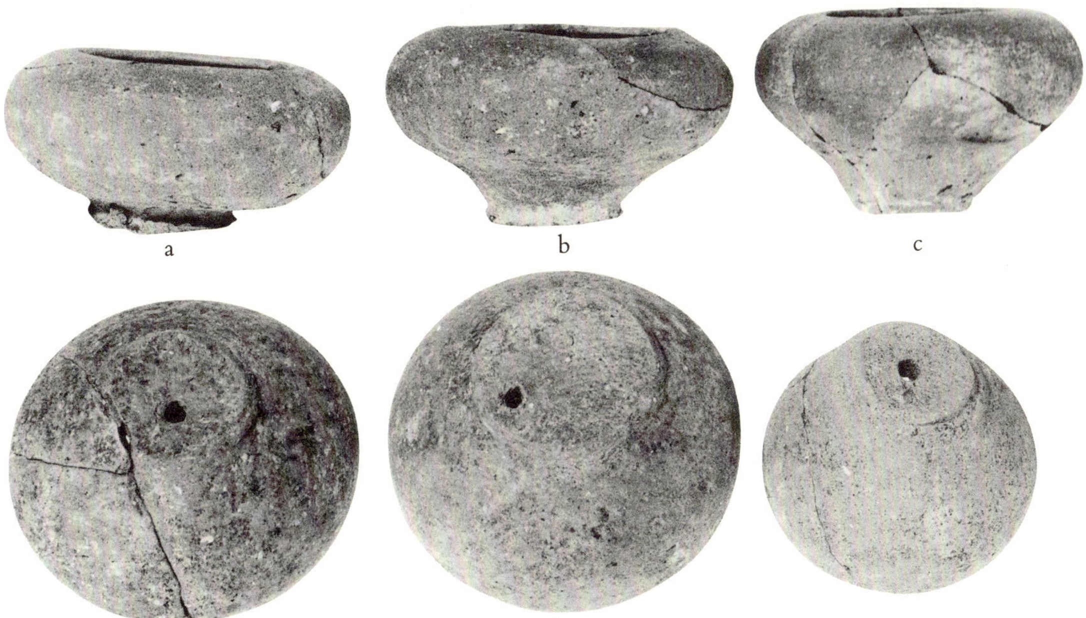

a b c

a b c

Fig. 31. Building Δ. MM III–LM IA bowls/rhyta.

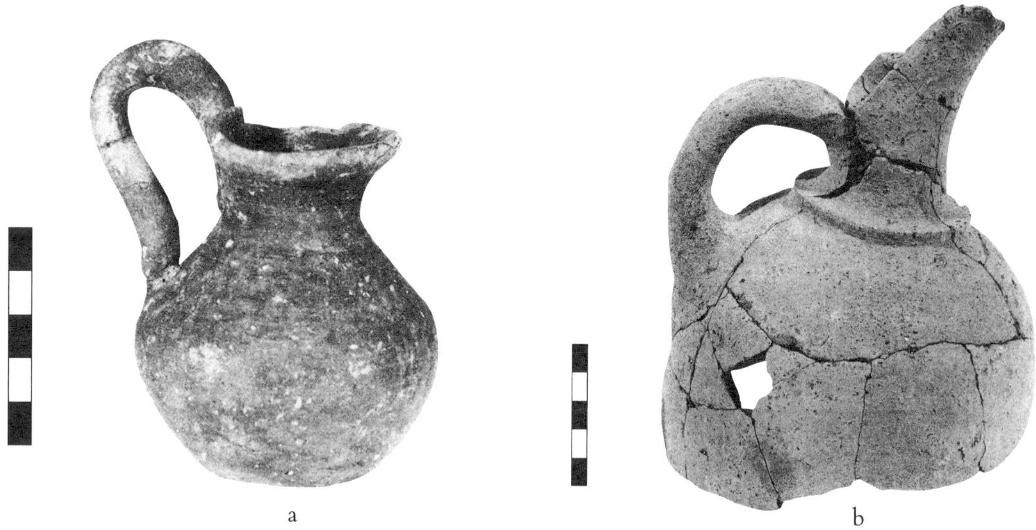

a b

Fig. 32. Building Δ. MM III–LM IA juglet and jug.

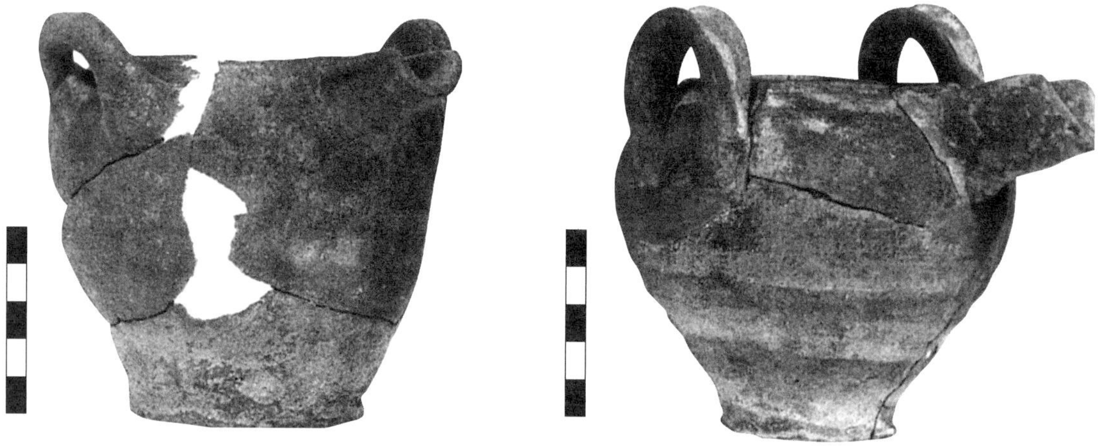

a b

Fig. 33. Building Δ. Bridge-spouted jars.

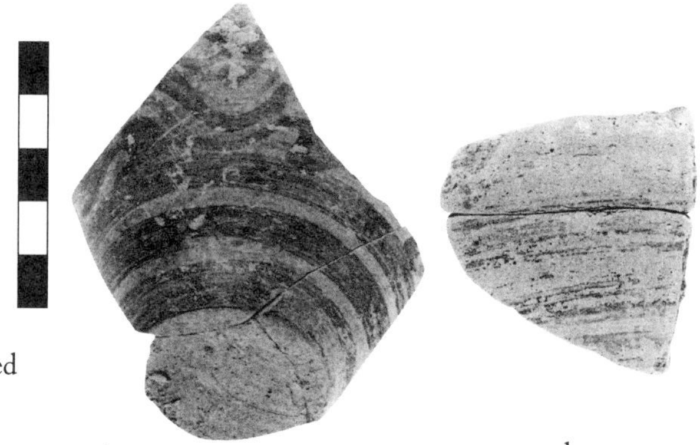

a b

Fig. 34. Building Δ. MM III–LM IA sherds decorated in dark-on-light.

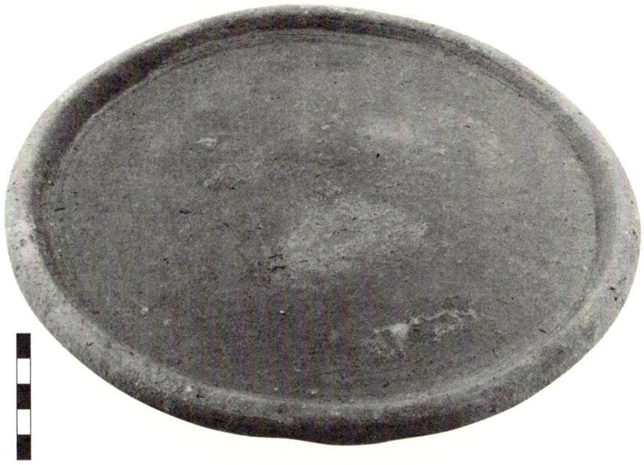

Fig. 35. L-shaped area. Serving dish.

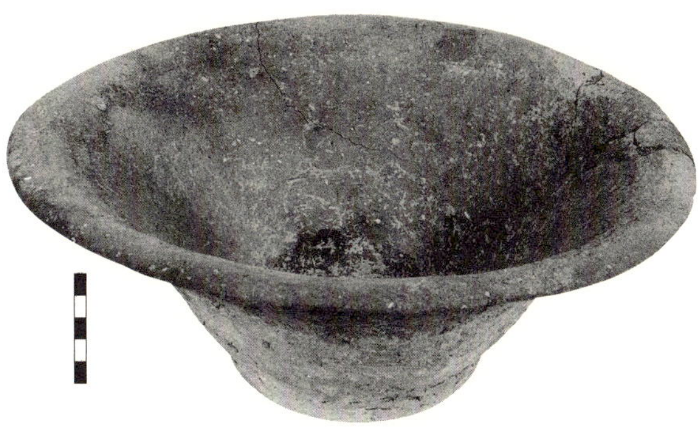

Fig. 36. Building Δ. Kalathos.

Fig. 29a. Straight-sided cup, rim sherd. Grayish-brown, coarse fabric. Max pres dimension: 8 cm. Thick rounded rim; grooved wall. Decoration in White-spotted Style.

Fig. 29b. Straight-sided cup, complete profile. Reddish-brown, coarse fabric. Max pres dimension: 6.5 cm. Straight rim; two grooves on wall. White band at rim.

Fig. 30a [**RM 27039**]. Ogival cup, complete. Reddish-brown, coarse fabric with white inclusions. D of rim: 10 cm; D of base: 4.5 cm; H: 7.8 cm.

Fig. 30b. Similar to 30a.

Fig. 31a [**RM 27030α–γ**]. Bowl/rhyton, complete. Reddish-brown, coarse fabric with white inclusions. D of rim: 6.7 cm; D of base: 4.5 cm; H: 5 cm. Inturned rim; small ring base; pouring hole on underside of base.

Fig. 31b–c. Similar to 31a, but slightly taller.

Fig. 32a [**RM 27042**]. Jug, complete. Reddish-brown, coarse fabric with white inclusions. Max D: 4 cm; H: 7.5 cm. Cylindrical neck; globular body; round-sectioned vertical handle rising above rim; flat base. *Comments*: Similar jugs are common in Old Palace deposits.

Fig 32b [**RM 27009**]. Jug, upper body preserved. Buff, coarse fabric. Max pres dimension: 12.5 cm. Beaked spout; ridge at neck; ovoid body; vertical handle starting from mid neck.

Fig. 33a [**RM 27005**]. Bridge-spouted jar, complete profile. Partially restored. Reddish-brown, coarse fabric. Max D: 10 cm; D of base: 6.3 cm; H: 10.5 cm. Ovoid body; large, thick spout; round-sectioned handles.

Fig. 33b [**RM 27006**]. Bridge-spouted jar, complete. Reddish-brown, coarse fabric. Max D: 12 cm; D of base: 5.2 cm; H: 12.2 cm. Globular body; large spout; grooved handles. Decoration in Light-on-Dark Style: festoons and bands at lower body in added white.

Fig. 36 [**RM 27032**]. Kalathos, complete. Reddish-brown, coarse fabric. D of rim: 28.6 cm; D of base: 10.2 cm; H: 11 cm. Rounded flaring rim.

Fig. 38 [**RM 27043**]. Hand lamp, complete. D of rim: 11.5 cm; D of base: 5 cm; H: 6.5 cm.

MM III–LM IA

Fine Fabric

Sherds belonging to two different cups are decorated in Light-on-Dark Style (fig. 34); the left sherd shows branches with ivy leaves, and the right sherd is decorated with a spiral in very fugitive color. The former has an exact parallel in the pottery of the Stratigraphical Museum site, dated by Warren to the MM IIIB–LM IA transitional phase.[45]

Fig. 34a. Open vessel (cup?), base sherd. Reddish-yellow fabric. Max D: 6 cm. Decoration in dark-on-light: bands at base; interlocking(?) papyri.

Fig. 34b. Open vessel (cup?), body sherd. Fine buff fabric. Max D: 4 cm. Decoration in dark-on-light: bands; running spirals.

Fig. 37a [**RM 27011**]. Bridge-spouted jar, rim and handle sherd. Max D: 6.4 cm.

Fig. 37b [**RM 27013**]. Closed vessel, body sherd. Coarse, reddish-yellow fabric. Max D: 16 cm. Grooved wall. Dark paint; decoration in White-spotted Style: bands in white.

Fig. 37c [**RM 27012**]. Cup, rim sherd. Fine buff fabric. Max D: 5.4 cm.

Crucibles

The conservation work conducted in the Rethymnon Museum laboratory during the summer of 2003 revealed fragments of a roughly-made, round vessel of very crude, dark red coarse fabric. When these fragments were joined, they created the rim and parts of the upper body of an open vessel with extremely thick walls (fig. 39). There is no doubt that this partially restored vessel belongs to a crucible. Fragments of at least three more crucibles were recognized, but only one was partially restored. Crucible fragments from MM III contexts have been found at Kommos.[46]

Fig. 39 [**RM 27047**]. Crucible, rim sherds. Mended from eight fragments. Red fabric with tiny quartzite inclusions. D of rim: 22 cm. Straight rim; thick walls.

This is a find of immense importance in determining the *raison d'être* of the site, which will be discussed below.

DATE

If a deposit is dated by the latest style pottery found in it, then stylistically the basement room deposit could be placed early (due to the lack of many decorated sherds in Dark-on-Light Style) in the transitional MM IIIB–LM IA ceramic phase. In the discussion of the chronology of this deposit two points should not elude our attention: 1) the absence of any Ripple Ware (which nevertheless has been detected in small quantities elsewhere at the site of Pera Galenoi); and 2) the fact that the latest style in this deposit is represented by sherd material only. In the chronological sequence of the published settlement contexts, the Pera Galenoi floor deposit from the basement room finds its best parallels in the Strati-

45. Warren 1991, fig. 10.G, I.

46. Blitzer 1995.

graphical Museum site deposit, the Acropolis House deposits C and D, the Anemospilia deposit, the Archanes Kalpadakis plot deposits, and the deposits from the Central Hillside House at Kommos. From outside Crete, it may be compared with the seismic destruction deposit from the West House at Thera.[47]

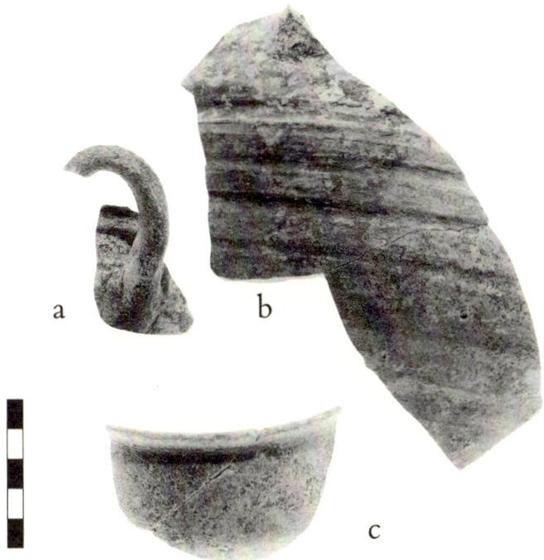

FIG. 37. Building Δ. MM III painted sherds.

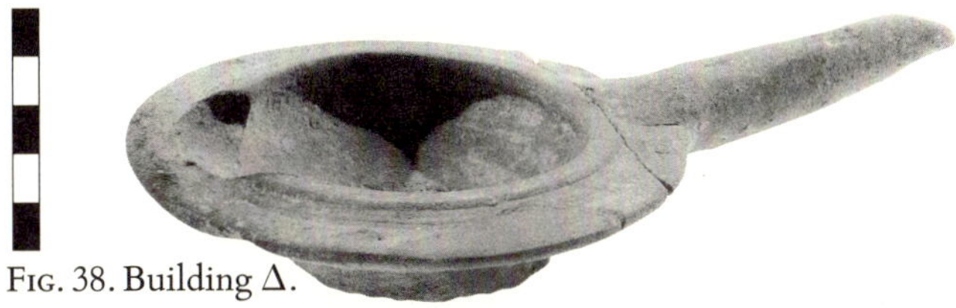

FIG. 38. Building Δ. Hand lamp.

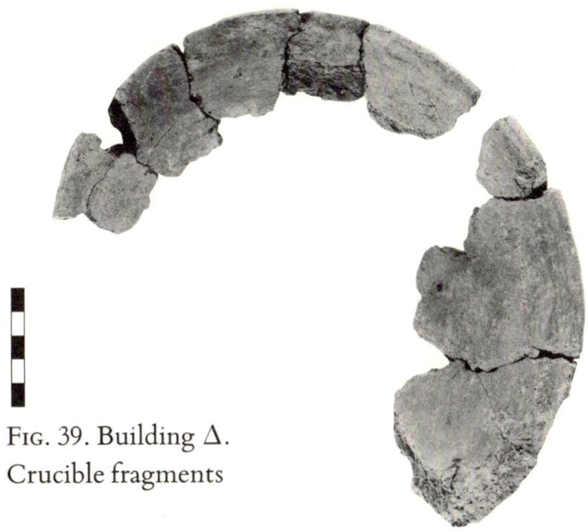

FIG. 39. Building Δ. Crucible fragments

CONCLUSIONS

THE POTTERY examined in this article permits some preliminary observations:

1) According to the pottery studied to date, the site seems to have been established sometime early in the MM II period (MM IIA?). The reasons why the Minoans chose this particular area can only be surmised. The site is naturally wind-protected and a suitable coastal settlement. It also happens to be located near metal resources (iron ores, see below).

2) The typical fabric of the site during the Old Palace period is brownish clay with small grits including an interesting group of vessels made of brownish-red clay with tiny flecks of silver mica. Aleydis Van de Moortel has informed me that a peculiar group of micaceous pottery appeared in Old Palace deposits at Kommos and hence, she wonders whether the Pera Galenoi area may be the source for this unusual pottery at Kommos.[48] On the other hand, as already mentioned, MacGillivray reports a group of vessels with silver mica from Knossos, probably originating from the Pediada region. Further investiga-

47. Marthari 1984; 1990.

48. Personal communication of 5 January 2003.

tion and regional pottery studies will probably clarify this question. Pottery is mainly undecorated and limited in quantity, relative to the hitherto excavated locations. In fact, some of the excavated areas were completely devoid of pottery, which may suggest that the inhabitants abandoned the site, taking their belongings with them.

3) Contacts with central Crete and the eastern Mediterranean seem to have been established subsequent to the foundation of the site. However, contacts with south-central Crete (e.g., Phaistos) should not be overlooked.[49] A specific shape such as the low pedestal lamp, present in Phaistian and Galenian deposits may be an indication of direct contact with the Mesara during the Old Palace period.

4) The pottery from the Building Δ basement room floor deposit that dates the earthquake destruction to the MM III–LM IA period, specifically the cups with grooved or stepped walls in White-spotted Style and the straight-sided cups with white loop decoration around the handles, exemplify certain similarities with the north-central Cretan ceramic styles and shapes.

5) The crucible fragments (and copper lump fragments) clearly point to smelting processes and copper production at the site of Pera Galenoi. Geological data from the Kouloukonas Mountains near Sisses in the Rethymnon district and the nearby Talaia Mountains (named after the legendary giant Talos, guardian of Crete) collected by Georgiadou-Dikaioulia and Dermitzakis indicate that the local phyllites and the carbonate rocks include iron ore and mixed sulphides, such as galena, shalerite and pyrite.[50] Additionally, there are signs of intensive exploitation of these mineral resources in antiquity. However, according to these geological studies copper ores have not yet been detected in this part of Crete. Therefore the vexing question of the origin of the copper that was being processed at Pera Galenoi during the Bronze Age remains unanswered.[51]

In conclusion, the seismic destruction that put an end to the site's existence occurred sometime early in the transitional MM IIIB–LM IA period and may be equated with the destruction horizon at other Cretan sites, and may have been contemporary to the Theran seismic destruction. The destruction from the severe earthquake, so vividly evident in the tumbled walls, is responsible for the abandonment of the Minoan settlement at Pera Galenoi, which possibly just preceded the final destruction. Because it may have been too arduous to repair the settlement, it was finally completely abandoned by the beginning of LM IA.

49. A. Van de Moortel in the discussion following the presentation of the paper remarked that the early (Old Palace period) pottery looked Phaistian to her, suggesting possible contacts of Pera Galenoi with this southern region.

50. Georgiadou-Dikaioukia et al. 1995, 111–21.

51. There is an ongoing program conducted by the National Center of Scientific Research "Demokritos" and the University of Crete which aims at tracing possible ancient copper ores or copper mines in the area of the mountain of Talaia. Should future geological investigation detect copper ores in the geographical region between Bali and Fodele, this may answer the question as to why the Minoan port of Pera Galenoi was originally established in this particular area.

WORKS CITED

Amiran, R. 1970. *Ancient Pottery of the Holy Land: From Its Beginnings in the Neolithic Period to the End of the Iron Age*. New Brunswick, NJ: Rutgers University Press.

Banou, E. 1992. "Pottery Groups from the West Side of Area A at Pseira, Crete." Ph.D. diss., University of Pennsylvania.

Banou, E. and E. Tsivilika. 1993. "ΚΕ΄ Εφορεία Προϊστορικών και Κλασικών Αρχαιοτήτων: Πέρα Γαλήνοι." *ArchDelt* 48, B2: 488–9.

———. 2002. "Αρχαιολογικές Ειδήσεις: Πέρα Γαλήνοι." *Κρητική Εστία* 9: 295–8.

Betancourt, P.P. 1985. *The History of Minoan Pottery*. Princeton, NJ: Princeton University Press.

———. 1990. *Kommos*. Vol. 2, *The Final Neolithic through Middle Minoan III Pottery*. Princeton, NJ: Princeton University Press.

Betancourt, P.P. and E. Banou. 1991. "Pseira and Minoan Sea-Trade." In *THALASSA: L'Egée Prehistorique et la Mer. Actes de la troisième Rencontre égéenne internationale de l'Université de Liège (23–25 avril 1990)*, edited by R. Laffineur and L. Basch, 107–10, *Aegaeum* 7. Liège: Université de Liège.

Bikaki, A.H. 1984. *Keos*. Vol. 4, *Ayia Irini: The Potters' Marks*. Mainz on Rhine: Philipp von Zabern.

Blitzer, H. 1995. "Minoan Implements and Industries." In *Kommos*. Vol. 1, *The Kommos Region and Houses of the Minoan Town*. Part 1, *The Kommos Region, Ecology, and Minoan Industries*, edited by J.W. Shaw and M.C. Shaw, 403–535. Princeton, NJ: Princeton University Press.

Carinci, F.M. 2001. "La casa a sud della rampa e il Medio Minoico III a Festòs." In *I cento anni dello scavo di Festòs: Giornate lincee, Roma, 13–14 dicembre 2000*, 203–41. Atti dei Convegni Lincei 173. Rome: Accademia Nazionale dei Lincei.

Catling, E.A., H.W Catling and D. Smyth. 1979. "Knossos 1975: Middle Minoan III and Late Minoan I Houses by the Acropolis." *BSA* 74: 1–80.

Dimopoulou, N. 1994. "ΚΓ΄ Εφορεία Προϊστορικών και Κλασικών Αρχαιοτήτων: Πόρος Ηρακλείου." *ArchDelt* 49, B2: 707–11.

Fiandra, E. 1980. "Precisazioni sul MM IIA a Festòs." In *Πεπραγμένα του Δ΄Διεθνοῦς Κρητολογικοῦ Συνεδρίου (Ηράκλειο, 29 Αυγούστου–3 Σεπτεμβρίου 1976)*, Vol. A1, *Προϊστορικοί καί 'Αρχαίοι Χρόνοι*, 169–96. Athens: Panepistemion Kretes.

Georgiades-Dikeoulia, E., M. Stamatakis and M. Dermitzakis. 1995. "Συμβολή στη γνώση της γεωλογίας των κυριοτέρων ορυκτών πρώτων υλών της νήσου Κρήτης." In *Πεπραγμένα του Ζ' Διεθνούς Κρητολογικού Συνεδρίου*. Vol. A1: *Τμήμα Αρχαιολογικό*, edited by N.E. Papadogiannakis, 111–23. Rethymnon: Iera Mitropolis Rethymnis & Aulopotamou.

Levi, D. 1976. *Festòs e la civiltà minoica*. Vol. 1. Incunabula Graeca 60. Rome: Edizioni dell'Ateneo.

MacGillivray, J.A. 1998. *Knossos: Pottery Groups of the Old Palace Period. BSA* Studies 5. London: British School at Athens.

Marinatos, S. 1976. *Excavations at Thera*. Vol. 7, *1973 Season*. 'Αρχαίοι Τόποι καί Μουσεία τῆς 'Ελλάδος 4. Athens: En Athenais Archaiologike Hetaireia.

Marthari, M. 1984. "The Destruction of the Town at Akrotiri, Thera at the Beginning of LC I: Definition and Chronology." In *The Prehistoric Cyclades. Contributions to a Workshop on Cycladic Chronology*, edited by J.A. MacGillivray and R.L.N. Barber, 119–33. Edinburgh: Department of Classical Archaeology, University of Edinburgh.

———. 1990. "The Chronology of the Last Phases of Occupation at Akrotiri in the Light of the Evidence from the West House Pottery Groups." In *Thera and the Aegean World III. Proceedings of the Third International Congress, Santorini, Greece, 3–9 September 1989*. Vol. 3, *Chronology*, edited by D.A. Hardy and A.C. Renfrew, 57–70. London: Thera Foundation.

Metaxa-Muhly, P. 1992. *Μινωικός Λαξευτός Τάφος στον Πόρο Ηρακλείου*. Βιβλιοθήκη της ἐν 'Αθήναις 'Αρχαιολογικής 'Εταιρείας 129, Athens: En Athenais Archaiologike Hetaireia.

Pelon, O. 1970. *Fouilles exécutées à Mallia*. Vol. 3, *Exploration des maisons et quartiers d'habitation (1963–1966)*. *ÉtCrét* 16. Paris: Paul Geuthner.

Platakis, E.K. 1975. "Οἱ Μονές τοῦ Ἀγ. Αντωνίου στούς Γαλήνούς καί τοῦ Αγίου Παντελεήμονος στή Φόδελε." *Kretologia* 1: 37–90.

Platonos-Giota, M. 1995. "Σπονδική τελετουργική πρόχους." In *Πεπραγμένα του Ζ' Διεθνούς Κρητολογικού Συνεδρίου*. Vol. A2, *Τμήμα Αρχαιολογικό*, edited by N.E. Papadogiannakis, 777–88. Rethymnon: Iera Mitropolis Rethymnis & Aulopotamou.

Popham, M.R. 1967. "Late Minoan Pottery, A Summary." *BSA* 62: 337–51.

———. 1974. "Trial KV (1969), a Middle Minoan Building at Knossos." *BSA* 69: 181–94.

———. 1984. *The Minoan Unexplored Mansion at Knossos*. *BSA* Suppl. 17, Oxford: British School of Archaeology at Athens and Thames and Hudson.

Rethemiotakis, G. 1994. "ΚΓ΄ Εφορεία Προϊστορικών και Κλασικών Αρχαιοτήτων: Γαλατάς Πεδιάδος (Σχέδ. 1.)" *ArchDelt* 49, B2: 701–7.

Rethemiotakis, G. and K.S. Christakis. 2004. "Cultural Interaction between Knossos and Pediada: The Evidence from the Middle Minoan IB Pottery." In *Knossos: Palace, City, State. Proceedings of the Conference in Herakleion Organised by the British School at Athens and the 23rd Ephoreia of Prehistoric and Classical Antiquities of Herakleion, in November 2000, for the Centenary of Sir Arthur Evans's Excavations at Knossos*, edited by G. Cadogan, E. Hatzaki and A. Vasilakis, 169–75. *BSA* Studies 12. London: British School at Athens.

Sakellarakis, Y. and E. Sapouna-Sakellaraki. 1997. *Archanes: Minoan Crete in a New Light*. Athens: Ammos.

Stürmer, V. 1993. "La céramique de Chrysolakkos: Catalogue et réexamen." *BCH* 117: 123–87.

Tsivilika, E. 1983. "ΚΕ΄ Εφορεία Προϊστορικών και Κλασικών Αρχαιοτήτων: Επιφανειακές Έρευνες – Τυχαία Ευρήματα." *ArchDelt* 38, B2: 374.

Tsivilika, E. and E. Banou. 1994–1996. "Αρχαιολογικές Ειδήσεις 1992–1994: Πέρα Γαλήνοι." *Κρητική Εστία* 5: 293–4.

Tsivilika, E., and E. Banou. 1999. "Επαρχία Μυλοποτάμου. Πέρα Γαληνοι." *ArchDelt* 53, B3: 873–4.

Walberg, G. 1976. *Kamares: A Study of the Character of Palatial Middle Minoan Pottery*. Acta Universitatis Upsaliensis. Boreas 8. Uppsala: [Universitet]; Stockholm: Almqvist & Wikell.

———. 1983. *Provincial Middle Minoan Pottery*. Mainz on Rhine: Philipp von Zabern.

Warren, P. 1991. "A New Minoan Deposit from Knossos, c. 1600 B.C., and Its Wider Relations." *BSA* 86: 319–40.

Warren, P. and V. Hankey. 1989. *Aegean Bronze Age Chronology*. Bristol: Bristol Classical Press.

Watrous, L.V. 1992. *Kommos*. Vol. 3, *The Late Bronze Age Pottery*. Princeton, NJ: Princeton University Press.

TRADITIONS AND TRENDS IN THE PRODUCTION AND CONSUMPTION OF STORAGE CONTAINERS IN PROTO-PALATIAL AND NEOPALATIAL CRETE

KOSTANDINOS S. CHRISTAKIS

MINOAN FINE WARE HAS MONOPOLIZED scientific interest for many decades. Its stylistic variation has been employed for establishing chronological sequences and defining cultural horizons. However, in the last few years, innovative approaches to pottery have increased our awareness concerning the importance of utilitarian ware in Minoan society. Utilitarian pottery is now being used for understanding complex regional and inter-regional patterns of ceramic production and consumption and their relationship to Minoan economic, political and cultural conditions.

This paper is an attempt to elucidate traditions and trends in the production and consumption of pithoi, the most distinctive utilitarian form in the Minoan ceramic repertoire, within the cultural frameworks of Protopalatial and Neopalatial Crete.[1] Selected pithos assemblages from elite, domestic and burial contexts all over Crete have been studied in terms of morphology and style, of fabric and manufacturing technique, and of functional properties and contextual associations. Variations in fabric types discussed here are based on visual analysis without the aid of ceramic petrography. Particular attention is also paid to the isolation of similar microfinishing details in the manufacturing process. The technique of

It is a pleasure to offer this paper to Philip Betancourt as a tribute to a scholar who has worked with exemplary fashion in changing the way we view Minoan civilization. My debt is great to James Muhly for the invitation to contribute to this significant publication. Thanks are due to Vance Watrous for reading a version of this paper at the Gold Metal Colloquium in honor of Philip Betancourt in New Orleans on 5 January 2003. Many institutions and excavators gave me permission to study unpublished and published material. I would like to thank the Greek Ministry of Culture, the Council of the British School at Athens, the Archaeological Society at Athens, the Scuola Archaeologica Italiana di Atene, the American School of Classical Studies at Athens, the École Française d'Athènes, the late N. Platon, and A. Lembesi, E. Hallager, B. Hallager, A. Zois, Y. Tzedakis, A. Kanta, L. Godart, K. Kopaka, V. La Rosa, S. Hood, G. Rethemiotakis, N. Dimopoulou, J.-C. Poursat, N. Panagiotakis, M. Tsipopoulou, L. Platon, H. Sackett, and C. Davaras. Many thanks to Nikoletta Ntolia for the drawings.

1. This paper summarizes the results of a study on Minoan storage containers. A more thorough discussion appears in the monograph by the present author, entitled *Cretan Bronze Age Pithoi. Traditions and Trends in the Production and Consumption of Storage Containers in Bronze Age Crete*. Prehistory Monographs 18. Philadelphia: INSTAP Academic Press (2005).

building the coils for the manufacture of the pithos, the means of attaching rims, handles and spouts, the surface levigation, and the execution of painted, impressed and incised decorative patterns can all provide the detailed and specific information to highlight manufacturing processes shared among potting groups active in a certain contextual framework. These observations are of crucial importance in order to distinguish potting groups in a regional setting, where discrimination on the basis of fabric is often difficult. Identical manufacturing idiosyncrasies observed in the production of limited assemblages of pithoi may be interpreted as the presence of the same potter or group of potters.

The present discussion is based on the assumption that the distribution of similar morphological, technological and functional attributes that exist within the same spatial and temporal framework will reflect local traditions in the production and consumption of these storage containers.[2] Regions where the same tradition is reported are envisioned as cultural, but not necessarily sociopolitical, units. Of course, traditions were not static through time. They changed according to diachronic shifts in consumption needs or were affected by the exchange of potting ideas.

THE PROTOPALATIAL PERIOD

The picture for the Protopalatial period (Middle Minoan IB–Middle Minoan IIB) tends to be patchy because of a lack of representative ceramic data. The main body of evidence comes from the Protopalatial settlements of the western Mesara (Phaistos and Kommos) and the Amari Valley (Monastiraki and Apodoulou), the north-central (Knossos, Archanes and Galatas) and east-central (Malia, Myrtos-Pyrgos and Pacheia Ammos) areas of Crete. Information from the other Protopalatial sites on the island is at present too limited for the local potting traits to be considered.

Potting groups active in the area of the Mesara made pithoi distinctive in their originality in morphological and decorative attributes (fig. 1). The pithoi produced here are ovoid with narrow mouths and distinct collars, numerous handles below the rims and narrow bases. Decoration is simple or absent. Ropework is not common and is placed mostly near the base. Incised patterns are occasionally displayed in the same position. Complex painted decoration is displayed only on pithoi from the palace of Phaistos. Pithoi, irrespective of their context, were manufactured with a high level of care. Surfaces are very well finished; coil joins are smoothed over, with the rims, handles and spouts well integrated.

Phaistos seems to be the most important center of production in the western Mesara. Workshops located in the vicinity of the settlement provided the palatial elite with stan-

2. On potting traditions, see Dobres and Hoffman 1994; Stark 1998; Gosselain 1998.

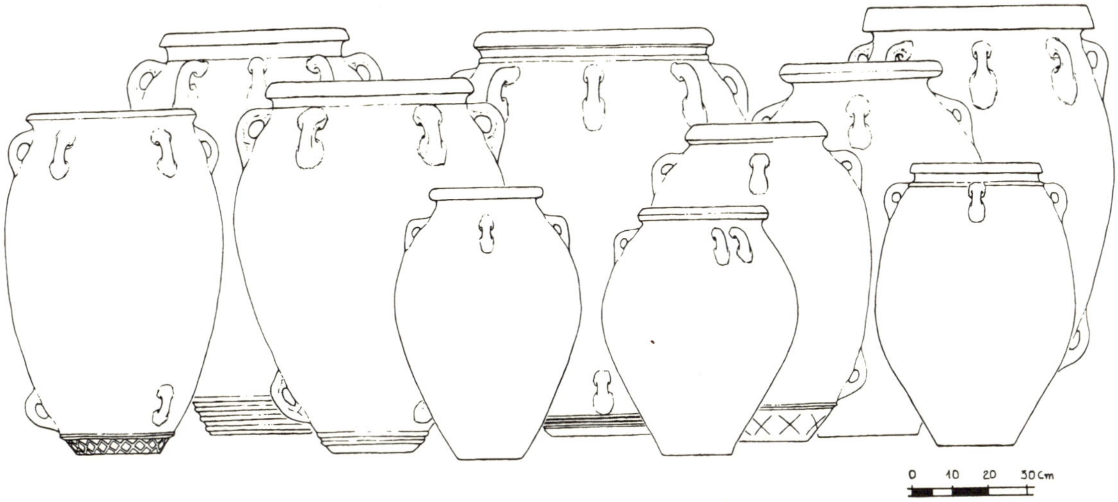

FIG. 1. Pithoi produced in south-central Crete during the Protopalatial Period.

dardized and elaborately decorated storage containers, manufactured and finished with extreme care. About 72% of the pithoi consumed at the palace are enhanced with elaborate painted patterns,[3] while only 18% and 10% feature trickle decoration and ropework respectively.[4] The standardization in morphology and style, in forming techniques and fabrics, let alone the skillful execution of painted motifs and the considerable investment of labor, all indicate production in specialized workshops and elite groups eager to display their status.

The pithoi consumed at Kommos were very similar to those used at Phaistos.[5] Decoration, however, is simpler at Kommos and there are differences in the execution of morphological attributes. The potting tradition of the Mesara had a great impact on the local pithos production of the Amari Valley; the potters in the Amari Valley imitated Phaistian prototypes.[6] Indeed, the degree of similarity in microfinishing details on some pithoi from Phaistos and the Amari Valley has led to the suggestion of itinerant potting groups.[7] Painted decoration at Amari, however, is limited to simple trickle decoration. Those storage containers decorated with elaborate painted patterns look to be imported directly from the area of Phaistos.

Some morphological features typical of the Mesara also occur on pithoi produced and consumed in the area of north-central Crete (mostly in the area of Knossos and the southern part of the Pediada Plain). The recovery of two almost identical pithoi—one from the

3. Levi 1976, pls. 48, 50–1, 53, 168, LXXII–LXXIII, LXXVI.

4. Levi 1976, pls. 47, 167, 169.

5. Betancourt 1990, figs. 28–9, 36.

6. E.g., Godart and Tzedakis 1992, pls. LXXI.1, LXXII.1–2, LXXIV.1.

7. Christakis 1996.

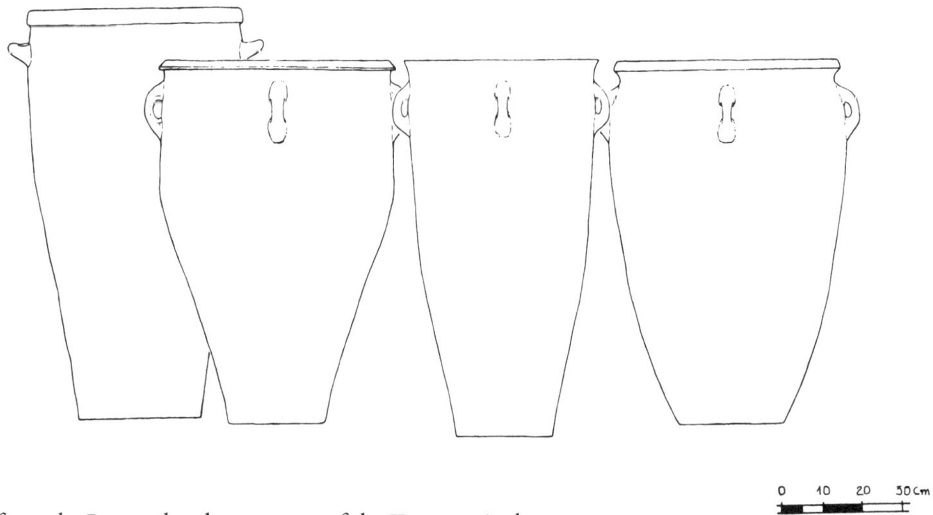

FIG. 2. Pithoi from the Protopalatial cemeteries of the Knossos-Archanes area.

Knossos Royal Road Excavation [SMP 4181] and the other from Poros[8]—with morphological attributes and painted patterns (petaloid loops) completely in the Phaistian tradition but manufactured in the local clay of north-central Crete might argue for the movement of potters from the Mesara to the area of Knossos and Poros, or a close imitation of Phaistian pithoi by a potter of north-central Crete. Pithoi produced at Phaistos—all products of much labor and time—have been found nearby at Monastiraki and Apodoulou,[9] farther afield at Knossos and Myrtos-Pyrgos,[10] and even outside Crete at Akrotiri.[11] Pithoi produced somewhere in the Mesara have also turned up in the southern Pediada and on the island of Gavdos.

Pithos makers working in the region of north-central Crete show less care and attention in the process of manufacture compared to those active in the Mesara. Groups of potters working in the areas of Knossos and Archanes produced both ovoid and elongated ovoid pithoi with either a wide or narrow mouth, two rows of four vertical handles and a wide base. Decoration is limited to ropework arranged above and below the handles while painted decorations are infrequent. Elaborate painted patterns, as displayed on pithoi from the Mesara, are rare, occurring only on some pithoi decorated in the Kamares Style from Knossos.[12]

Conical pithoi, like those shown in figure 2, were very common at the cemeteries of Ailias Knossos and Archanes-Phourni, as well as in burials at Poros and in a newly excavated burial enclosure at Aitania. At Ailias, these pithoi represent about 92% of the total bur-

8. Psychoyoudakis Plot, Trench XIV, N. Dimopoulou excavations.

9. Godart and Tzedakis 1992, pl. LXXIII.

10. The evidence from Knossos is unpublished; for Phaistian pithoi at Myrtos-Pyrgos, see Knappett 1997, fig. 15.

11. Nikolakopoulou (forthcoming).

12. Evans 1928, pl. IX.

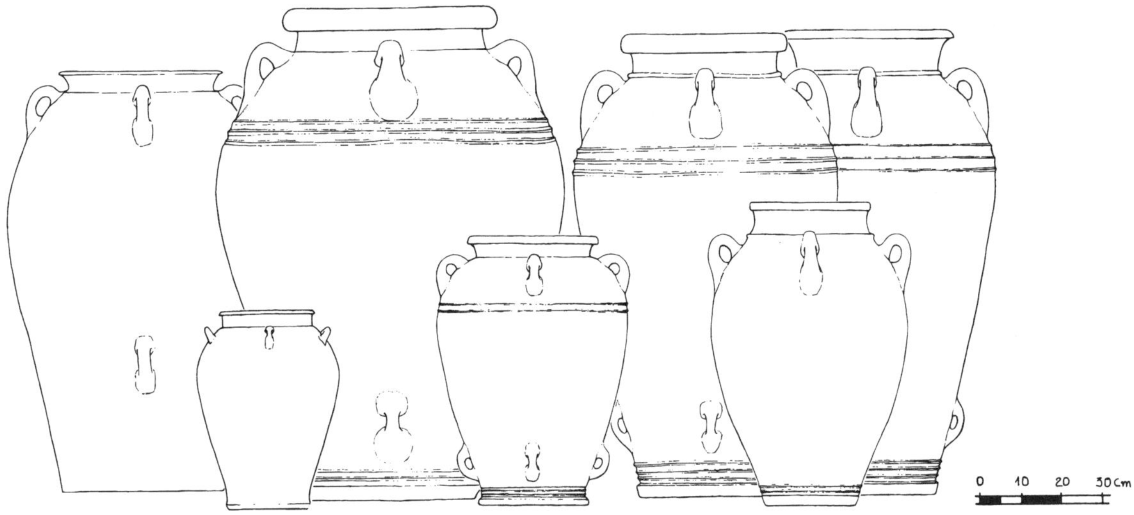

FIG. 3. Pithoi produced in east-central Crete during the Protopalatial period.

ial receptacles. The high standardization achieved in morphological and decorative attributes, as well as formation techniques and fabrics, all point to specialized potting groups. Morphological details typical of pithoi produced in the area of the Mesara were occasionally displayed on some north-central pithoi. It is not entirely certain whether these attributes make up an integral part of a north-central pithos potting tradition or are due to the exchange of potting ideas between the potters active in these two regions.

Potters working in the area of the Pediada followed their own potting trends, which are different from those of the other Protopalatial centers of Crete.[13] Here the morphological and decorative features of Prepalatial pithoi continue into the next period. Some pithos fragments recovered on Protopalatial sites located in the northern and southern areas of the Pediada display morphological and decorative features typical of the Knossos-Archanes and the Mesara potting traditions respectively.

Plentiful pithos assemblages of the Protopalatial period come from Malia, Myrtos-Pyrgos and the area of the Isthmus of Ierapetra. Piriform pithoi with narrow mouths and high collars, decorated with rows of ridges set near the handles and above the bases, are typical types of storage containers used at these sites (fig. 3). Small- and medium-sized piriform and ovoid pithoi with narrow mouths, high collars and one row of handles (vertical or vertical juxtaposed with horizontal) also appear.[14] Ropework and complex painted decorations are not frequent. Painted motifs, however, although simple were still original in conception and syntax. They are usually displayed on piriform and ovoid pithoi of small and medium size.[15]

13. Rethemiotakis and Christakis 2004.

14. Seager 1916, pls. V, VII, XI.

15. Seager 1916, pls. VII, XI, XIIIa, XVII; van Effenterre and van Effenterre 1976, pl. XV.

Specialized pithos workshops were active in the northern part of the Isthmus. Peter Day has shown that large storage jars from a production center in the Gournia/Kalo Chorio area were shipped to coastal sites of east Crete.[16] It is also argued that pithoi produced both in the area of the south coast and the Mirabello were transported to Malia, where they appear in Quartier Mu.[17] I am skeptical concerning the claims of the distribution to Malia of pithoi produced somewhere on the south coast: the morphological and stylistic features of pithoi used in Quartier Mu do not occur on pithoi from the south coast. Potting groups working with local clays were active in the region of Myrtos-Pyrgos.[18] Storage containers produced in east-central Crete betray considerably little care in manufacture compared with those produced in the Mesara.

THE NEOPALATIAL PERIOD

The picture changes during the Neopalatial period (MM III–LM IB); new morphological, stylistic and functional attributes are now introduced. Workshops are producing pithoi with an increased storage capability, highlighting the intensification of staple storage activities, especially in the central sector of societal organization.[19] Potting groups working in the area of the Mesara during the MM III period continued to follow the morphological and stylistic trends of the Protopalatial period.[20] There is, however, a considerable drop in labor input. Morphological details are hastily executed and painted decorations are simplified and repetitive. The departure from the labor-intensive pithos production of the Protopalatial period may reflect the adoption of a cost-controlling approach to pithos production already observed by Van de Moortel for the pottery production of the Neopalatial Mesara.[21] The production of pithoi embellished with complex ropework,[22] a trend not particularly frequent in the area of the Mesara during the Protopalatial period, is here interpreted as the first sign of infiltration of potting trends from north-central Crete.

New types of large pithoi appeared in the area of north-central Crete in the same period (fig. 4). Although similar in many morphological and decorative attributes to pithoi produced during the Protopalatial period, they differ in the increased capacity that varies from 100 to 580 liters. Ropework is now more complex than before in conception and arrangement. Variations in finishing details and fabrics indicate the presence of different potting groups working close to the major settlements of the region. Patterns of production and

16. Day 1991, 173, 213–20.
17. Knappett 1997, 178–9.
18. Knappett 1997, 180.
19. Christakis 1999a; 1999b.
20. Levi and Carinci 1988, 9–11.
21. Van de Moortel 2002.
22. Levi 1976, 489–505, pls. 758, 763; Pernier 1935, 277–8, 331, figs. 159–61, 197; Palio 2001, 398, fig. 47e.

consumption can be complex even at the same site. For instance, three different potting groups produced the pithoi used at Galatas Pediados during the MM III period. Two imitated Knossian prototypes. The first of these employed local clays similar to those used in the area of Knossos-Archanes, while the second preferred the characteristic orange and red clays of the Pediada. The care taken in manufacture also varies. Pithoi of the first group are more carefully executed than those of the second. The third group followed the local potting tradition of the Pediada, which displays original decorative and morphological attributes.

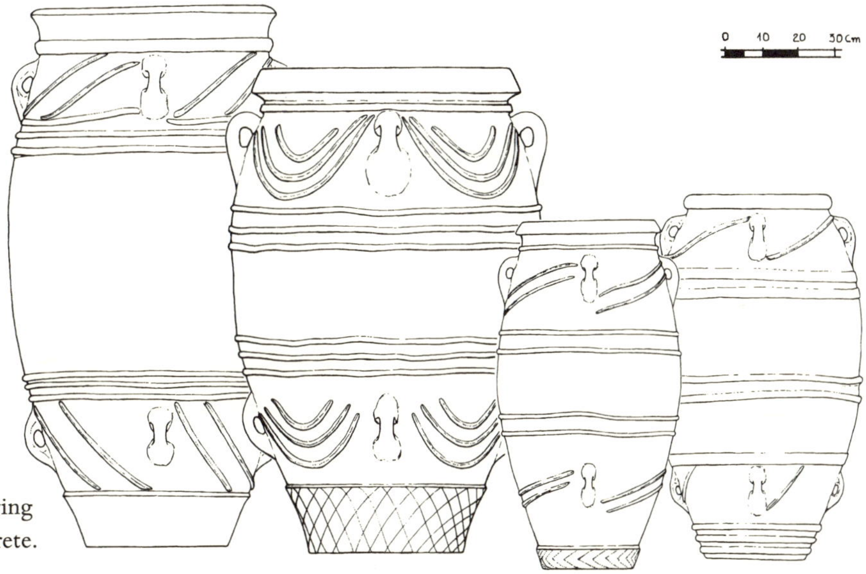

Fig. 4. Pithoi produced during MM III in north-central Crete.

Distinctive products of a Knossian workshop active during the MM III period are the pithoi decorated with knobs.[23] The excessive dimensions, the rows of handles and the complex knobbed and rope decoration distinguish these pithoi. The uniformity of morphological and decorative features, construction technique, microfinishing detail and fabric suggest the activity of a single potting group or even of just one potter. A sizable fragment from a knobbed pithos—perhaps of larger dimensions than those recovered in the Knossian palace—was found in N. Panagiotakis' survey at Katalagari, near Archanes. Its morphological and decorative attributes are almost identical to those of the Knossian pithoi. There is also great similarity in the microfinishing details. Although the evidence from Katalagari is very fragmentary, it could argue for the activity of a Knossian itinerant potter.

A new type of large, ovoid pithos with a wide mouth and decorated with horizontal and wavy rows of raised bands appeared in north-central and south-central Crete during the LM I period (fig. 5). It is *par excellence* the storage container favored in palatial and elite contexts. Its capacity varies from 250 to 580 liters. This new type of pithos was invented

23. Evans 1921, 231–5; 1930, 18–25; for an MM III date, see Christakis 1999a, 361.

by the north-central potters: its morphological and decorative attributes are drawn in part from the local MM III tradition of north-central Crete. The amount of care spent in the manufacture of these pithoi is low. Surfaces are not smoothed, coil joins are obvious, appendages are neither regular nor carefully attached, and the incisions on raised bands are hastily made. The overall impression points to a desire to reduce time and labor costs.

The impact of this new storage technology was decisive in the area of south-central Crete: local potters went over to the north-central potting trends. If governing elites were somehow involved in the control of the organization of pottery production, it is very tempting to see this infiltration of north-central potting traditions as the result of changes in administrative involvement after the weakening of the Phaistian palatial authority in the course of the Neopalatial period.[24]

Outside Crete, morphological and decorative attributes of these new pithoi were adopted in the pithos production at the Late Cycladic settlement of Akrotiri. Here, the large, elongated-ovoid pithoi with their squared rims, two rows of handles and decoration of horizontal rows of raised bands with vertical incisions recall many of the morphological and decorative attributes displayed on pithoi in figure 5.[25] This constitutes a good case of how potting trends can travel over long distances and become incorporated into local potting traditions.

Many centers of production were required to serve each of the major towns of north-central and south-central Crete. The most important and influential potting center was that of Knossos. The LM I pithoi recovered within the palace are specimens in which much labor was invested; they are manufactured with considerable care and embellished

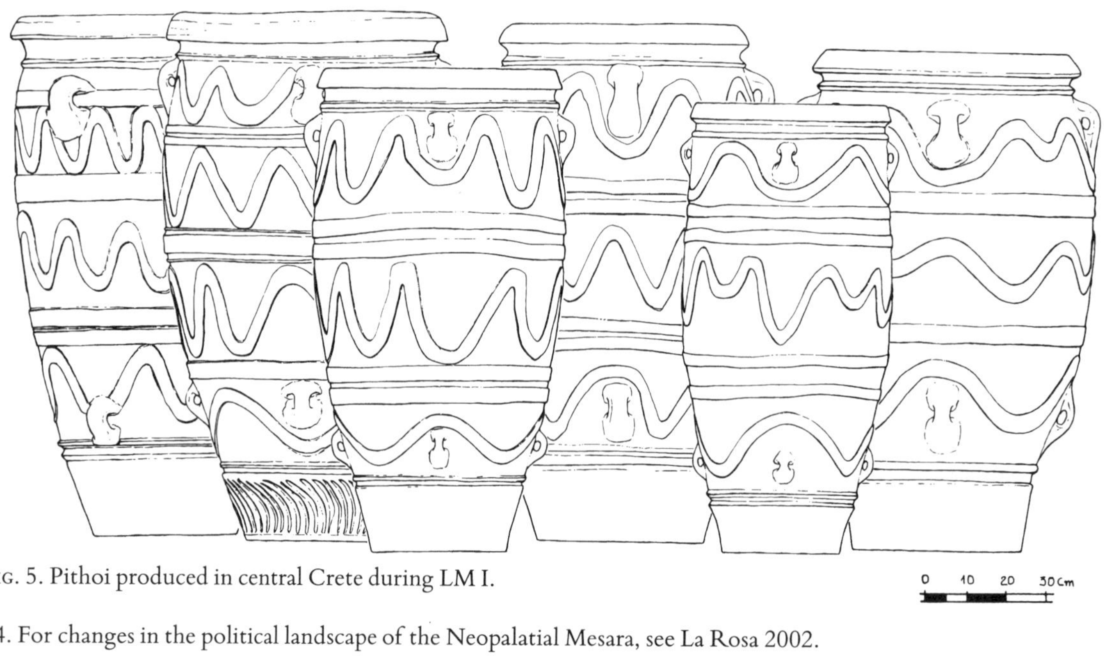

FIG. 5. Pithoi produced in central Crete during LM I.

24. For changes in the political landscape of the Neopalatial Mesara, see La Rosa 2002.

25. Most of these pithoi are unpublished. One is shown in Michailidou 1990, fig. 7.

with original and even unique appliqué patterns. Similar pithoi used in the Knossian settlement betray less care in preparation, and their decorative patterns are simple and repetitive. These stylistic and technological differences between pithoi used in the palace as opposed to the settlement suggest specialized modes of production and distribution, according to the demands of consumption.

The highly labor-intensive pithoi used in the palace of Knossos are probably part of a well-planned "scenographic setting" for the display of the stored staples. The high quality in the construction of the Knossian storerooms (gypsum floors, walls lined with gypsum slabs, gypsum jamb bases, finely plastered walls with frescoes), the pithoi of high craftsmanship, the architectural planning and lighting configurations all interacted to create impressive and luxurious contexts. Patterns of accessibility to the stores are very carefully organized: an interest in facilitating the movement in and out of commodities and in controlling access to stored wealth, as well as the direct communication to ritual (the Central Sanctuary Complex) and political spaces (the Throne Room Complex) are the main concerns. It is very likely that palatial elites sought to make a public show of their stored wealth. Display of wealth can establish, maintain and change social relations.[26]

The impact of Knossian palatial workshops on the pithos production of central Crete is noteworthy. Knossian decorative styles were imitated, although not successfully, by potters working in the area of Archanes, the northern part of the Pediada, the area of Viannos and at Hagia Triada. A large Knossian pithos, decorated with raised bands with circle impressions, similar to those used in the West Magazines of the palace of Knossos was shipped as far as Petras.

Distinctive products of Knossian potting groups, active during LM I, are also the so-called Palatial Style Jars: small- and medium-sized storage containers with morphological features similar to the well-known Palace Style jars of the LM II period.[27] The recovery of such pithoi—produced in north-central Crete—in the Late Cycladic IA context of Akrotiri, shows that the production of Palatial Style Jars started as early as LM IA. They are distinctive in their high quality of manufacture and the originality and complexity of the decorative compositions. The best specimens are found at Knossos, which seems to be the main center of production and use of these sumptuous containers. Palatial Style Jars, products of Knossian workshops, have been found so far, at House A at Tylissos[28] and at Zakros.[29] Fragmentary jars, products of a local workshop, come from the palace of Archanes.[30]

Palatial Style Jars similar to those produced in north-central Crete were also produced

26. Earle 1997; Hendon 2000.

27. Niemeier 1985.

28. Hazzidakis 1921, pl. XXIV.

29. N. Platon 1971, 123.

30. Sapouna-Sakellaraki 1988–1989; Sakellarakis and Sapouna-Sakellaraki 1997, fig. 422.

in the areas of the Isthmus,[31] at Zakros[32] and at Palaikastro.[33] The jars consumed in the east Crete area have a row of four vertical handles on the shoulder and a funnel-like high collar. The painted patterns are typical of the region.[34] It is argued that many of these jars consumed in eastern contexts were produced in a Zakrian workshop.[35] A fragmentary Palatial Style Jar from House II at Petras[36] was produced in a workshop other than those active in the area of Zakros: the fabric of the pithos, the surface treatment and the execution of the painted patterns are all different from those of the pithoi used at Gournia and Zakros.[37] Therefore, there very likely exists a workshop or a single potter, somewhere in the hinterland of Petras, who imitated the products of the workshops of Zakros. A study of the fabrics of these containers may reveal complex patterns of production and distribution within the area of east Crete.

On account of their material, technological knowledge and heavy labor investment, Palatial Style Jars, and painted pithoi in general, especially in circumstances of intense social interaction, can become indicators of social status and may convey ritual meaning. It is not by chance that many of these pithoi were placed in spaces where they could easily be viewed. Arthur Evans, for instance, considered that Palatial Style Jars were for display and believed these pots came from the upper rooms of the palace of Knossos.[38] A similar contextual distribution has also been observed for the pithoi from the palatial complexes at Archanes[39] and Zakros,[40] and the Unexplored Mansion.[41]

Many of the morphological features of the Palatial Style Jars are displayed in a class of pithoi with an extremely accentuated piriform body and embellished with complex painted patterns (fig. 6). The main center(s) of production of these pithoi was/were in north-central Crete, though a few with similar morphological attributes were also produced in south-central Crete.[42] Three almost identical pithoi of this class are reported: one recovered from the Northeast House at Knossos[43] and two from Building AD North at Pseira.[44] These were products of a Knossian workshop and perhaps by the same potter;

31. Hawes et al. 1908, pl. K; Betancourt 1983, pl. 5.54; Seager 1909, fig. 19; 1910, fig. 14.
32. N. Platon 1964, pls. 173β, 177β; 1966, pls. 156α, γ, 159α.
33. Bosanquet and Dawkins 1923, fig. 29.
34. Silverman 1978.
35. L. Platon 2002.
36. Tsipopoulou and Hallager 1996, fig. 7e.
37. M. Tsipopoulou, personal communication 2003.
38. Popham 1970, 50.
39. Sapouna-Sakellaraki 1988–1989; Sakellarakis and Sapouna-Sakellaraki 1997, 107–10.
40. N. Platon 1971, 115–20.
41. Popham 1984, 172.
42. Cf. Halbherr et al. 1977, fig. 93.
43. Evans 1928, fig. 245.
44. Betancourt and Davaras 1995, fig. 45.

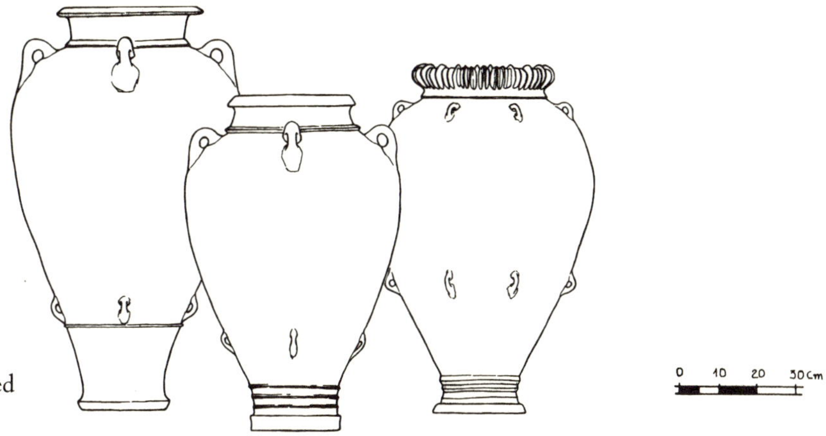

FIG. 6. Piriform pithoi produced in central Crete during LM I.

those recovered at Pseira were probably shipped from Knossos. Two fragmentary pithoi with morphological and stylistic attributes similar to pithoi of this class were found at the mansion of Nerokourou.[45] Production in a workshop of north-central Crete seems possible although this suggestion has to be petrographically tested.

Pithos workshops were also located in the areas of Archanes, Tylissos and in the Pediada region. Potting groups serving the settlement of Archanes exploited the same ceramic environment, located around Mt. Juktas, as did those working for the Knossian clientele.[46] Despite the interaction between these production units, the pithoi produced for Archanes were manufactured with less care, and with decorative patterns that were simple and repetitive. Production in the area of Tylissos is less influenced by Knossian trends. Some of the morphological and stylistic attributes appearing on pithoi used in the stores of the large mansions of this settlement were original and are confined to this site.

Potters working in south-central Crete during LM I were influenced by the trends of north-central Crete. Large, ovoid pithoi, decorated with raised appliqué bands with vertical, herringbone and impressed patterns, are now widely used. Protopalatial morphological traits survived only in very few types.[47] It is, however, difficult to isolate centers of production active during the Neopalatial period because of the limited number of pithoi dated to this period in the area of south-central Crete. Differences in the execution of morphological and decorative features observed in some pithoi from Phaistos (the palace) and Hagia Triada (the palatial building) might point to production from separate potting groups, each distributing its own output to one of these sites.

Potting groups working in the area of Hagia Triada are strongly influenced by Knossian pithos-manufacturing approaches.[48] Potters adopt decorative patterns similar to those

45. Kanta and Rochetti 1989, 115.

46. Day 1988.

47. E.g., La Rosa and Cucuzza 2001, figs. 273, 275.

48. The body of evidence from Hagia Triada is rather limited. Most of the pithoi were destroyed in World War II.

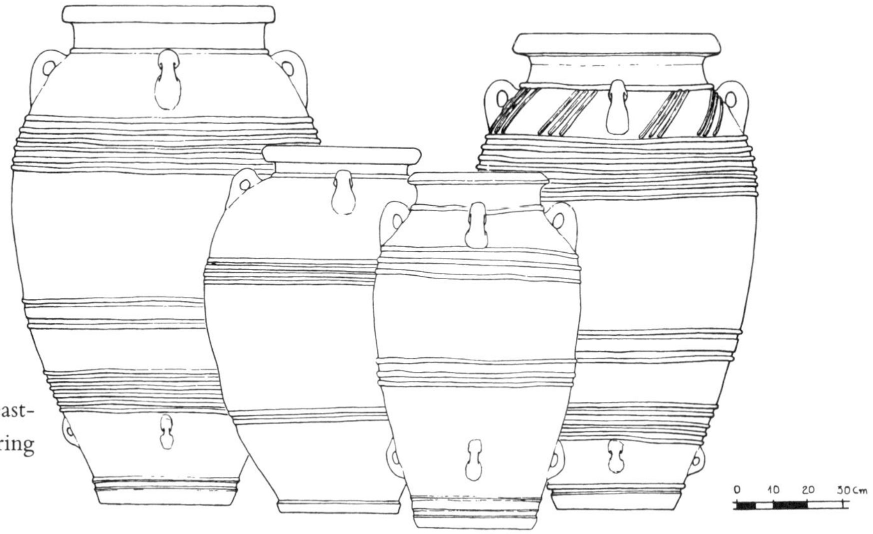

FIG. 7. Pithoi produced in east-central and east Crete during the Neopalatial period.

displayed on pithoi from Knossos: the most obvious instance of this is the imitation of the Knossian medallion pithoi by a potter working in the area of Hagia Triada.[49] He produced two pithoi decorated with medallions and raised bands with spiral stamp impressions very similar to those produced by the Knossian workshop. Though similar in basic morphological and decorative aspects to the Knossian specimens, they are different in fabric, the quality of execution, which is less accurate, and some decorative attributes. The pithoi decorated with medallions from Hagia Triada were produced either by a local potter who imitated the Knossian pieces or by an itinerant potter from north-central Crete.

The basic morphological and decorative features of LM I pithoi used in the mansion of Kannia Mitropolis are similar to those from the rest of the Mesara. They differ, however, in their execution, which inevitably implies the activity of potting groups other than those working in the other LM I contexts of the Mesara. In addition, some types of raised-band patterns on the pithoi used in the stores of the mansion are exclusive to them. Three different groups of production have been isolated on the basis of idiosyncrasies in the manufacturing process.

Contrary to the circumstances operating in south-central Crete, potters working in east-central and east Crete followed their local traditions, which were quite different from those of the north-central area. Pithoi such as those described above were almost unknown in east-central and east Crete: here pithoi continue to be mostly decorated with ropework. Those decorated with complex patterns of raised bands are extremely rare.[50]

The characteristic storage container in most LM I contexts is the large- and medium-

49. Halbherr et al. 1977, 141–2, 288.

50. The most decorative example is the large pithos with complex, appliqué raised-band decorations recovered in room XXVIII of the Malia palace, Chapouthier and Demargne 1942, pl. xiii; see also Pelon 1997, 351–2, figs. 16–7.

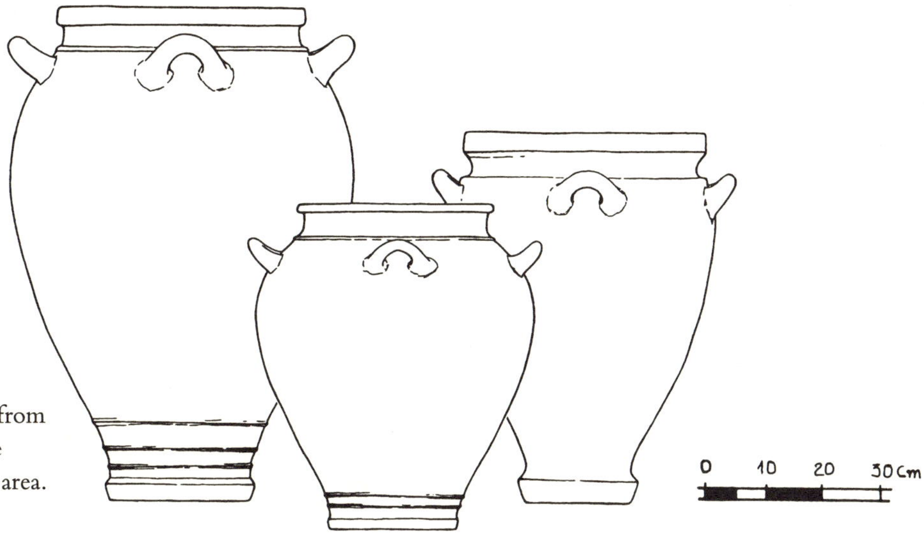

Fig. 8. Burial pithoi from the cemeteries of the Isthmus of Ierapetra area.

sized piriform pithos with a narrow mouth, high collar and overlapping rim and two rows of vertical handles (fig. 7). Rows of ropework occur in complex arrangements. Similar morphological features were already observed in the few pithoi that may be assigned to the MM III period. Medium- and small-sized piriform pithoi with extremely narrow mouths, high collars and one row of vertical handles on the shoulders appear. The consumption of these pithoi is mostly confined to the area of east Crete. They were also widely reported in the area of the Isthmus and occasionally appeared in other locations in east-central Crete. Potting groups were active close to major towns of the region, with further centers of production located in the area of the Isthmus.

A distinctive product of workshops active in the area of the Isthmus is the piriform pithos with a wide mouth and distinct collar used in the burial contexts of Pacheia Ammos and Sphoungaras (fig. 8).[51] The standardization in morphology, style, forming details and fabric, as well as the high investment of labor for the production of these pithoi, all point to production by potting groups specializing in the manufacture of sumptuous burial containers.

These pithoi represent a very low proportion of the total number of burial receptacles used at these sites: at the cemetery of Pacheia Ammos they represent about 13% of the total, and at the cemetery of Sphoungaras about 20%. The low percentage of painted pithoi certainly highlights the semiotic value of these specimens in the local societies. Not by chance, it has been argued that these pithoi were displayed in the funeral processions of the prosperous deceased.[52]

Small- and medium-sized piriform pithoi with narrow mouths, high collars and one

51. Seager 1916, pls. I, IV, VI, VIII, X, XIV, XVII, XX; Hall 1912, 62–3, figs. 34–5.
52. Hall 1912, 65.

row of handles (vertical or vertical juxtaposed with horizontal) on the shoulders are particularly frequent at Gournia, Pseira and Mochlos.[53] Their fabric suggests production in the Mirabello area. Similar pithoi were also reported in many sites of east-central and east Crete. I would suggest that some of them, on the basis of fabric, were produced in the area of the Isthmus. Larger pithoi produced in the Isthmus were also distributed in coastal settlements of the Siteia area in the east.[54] Pithoi manufactured in a center near Myrtos were used in the mansion of Makrygialos.[55]

The evidence from the area of west Crete is rather limited: there are few Minoan contexts fully excavated and even fewer published. LM I pithoi produced by local workshops are highly standardized in their morphological and decorative features (fig. 9). Potters use a very restricted potting vocabulary confined exclusively to this region. The typical storage container is ovoid with a low-bellied body and wide mouth. The handles are arranged in two rows: one of four vertical handles below the rim and another of two horizontal handles at the maximum diameter. These pithoi are decorated with closely-spaced horizontal rows of ropes/bands. The present-day production processes of ovoid, low-bellied pithoi in the village of Agii Pantes in west Crete[56] are quite different from those known in the other Cretan potting centers such as Thrapsano, Margarites and Kendri. Might this point to some survival of the Minoan potting tradition?

The adoption of morphological and decorative attributes from other pithos potting traditions is rather limited. With some rare exceptions, pithoi like those from the other LM I contexts do not occur on the western part of the island.[57] Only during LM III (especially during LM IIIB and IIIC) do some morphological and decorative attributes recalling those produced in other parts of the island appear in west Crete. Two production units, active during LM I, have been isolated so far on the basis of morphological differences, forming details and fabric: one sent its output to the building at Vrises and the other to Nerokourou.

The impact of west Cretan potting trends on the rest of the island was limited. Pithos fragments from the north and south areas of the Rethymnon district show some influence. Outside Crete, morphological and decorative attributes typical of west Crete are seen in the local pithos production on the island of Gavdos. A similar situation is noted at the Late Cycladic settlement of Akrotiri.[58] Direct influence on local production from potters of west Crete, perhaps even the import of pithoi from there, could account for this.

53. E.g., Soles and Davaras 1994, pls. 93b, c, d, 106a.

54. Day 1991, 27, 176.

55. Day 1995, 165.

56. Cf. Sklavenitis 1996, 85, fig. 3.

57. Kanta and Rocchetti 1989, 115, 150–1.

58. Nikolakopoulou (forthcoming).

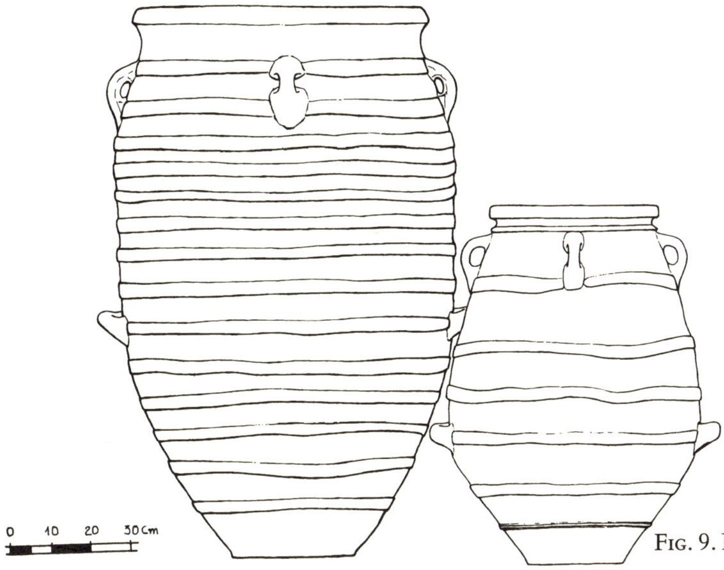

FIG. 9. Pithoi produced in west Crete during LM I.

CONCLUSIONS

THE ABOVE DISCUSSION has revealed the marked differences in morphology, style and manufacture observed in pithos assemblages from the regional contexts of Protopalatial and Neopalatial Crete. A narrow range of interrelated morphological and technological parameters deeply rooted in regional potting traditions inspired potters' choices. Potting traditions were not static but subject to change. The exchange of ideas on potting technologies between different groups, the adoption or imitation of morphological and stylistic traits from different potting regions, changes in administrative involvement in pottery production, and the intra-regional distribution of finished products created a multilayered process of interaction.

Variation in the idiosyncratic manufacturing practices for pithoi from the different contexts of the same region indicates the existence of workshops serving each of the major towns. Yet the internal homogeneity displayed within the pithos assemblages consumed in each of these contexts indicates that some of the workshops produced pithoi on a substantial scale. The decentralized production of storage containers, close to the centers of consumption, is therefore the main mode of production throughout the Bronze Age. The bulkiness of pithoi favors this decentralized pattern of production and distribution. Petrographic analyses of selected pithos assemblages, however, have also shown the distribution of pithoi (even bulky ones) over long distances, not only within Crete but also throughout the Aegean.

The degree to which pithos workshops were controlled from the central sector of state organization is difficult to ascertain from present knowledge. The common "mental template" held by pithos makers working in the same regional framework appears to be the result of accumulated knowledge and experience transmitted from generation to generation. Palatial authorities may have played a crucial role in this process by promoting and regulating stylistic and technological standards in order to set cultural and social boundaries. Is it accidental that regionalism in the production and consumption of pithoi is highly emphasized during the Palatial period, while after the destruction of the palatial political systems trends in pithos manufacture assume more unified expressions? There are no grounds, however, to assume the direct control of a governing elite over potters manufacturing storage containers. The model of independent potters serving a wider clientele seems to fit the evidence. A certain type of control may, however, have existed in the production of highly labor-intensive pithoi. The considerable technological skill required in the manufacture of these vessels, the investment of labor, and the patterns of consumption point to specialized potters responsible for the fulfillment of the needs of the elite. Different patterns of production, therefore, surely coexisted within the same cultural framework.

Consumption of pithoi with different morphological, stylistic, technological and functional attributes implies different meanings and intents. Pithoi, products of much labor and time, were manufactured primarily to meet the needs of elite groups. The acquisition and use of these pithoi would seem to be an aggrandizing vehicle, through which consumers could send and receive messages related to social significance and ranking. The more sporadic discovery of similar pithoi in private buildings is here interpreted as a marker of the wealth and cultural taste of the owner or as an indicator of a special connection with the central sector of the state organization.

Contextual associations of significance can also be observed in basic functional attributes such as capacity, accessibility and stability. Pithoi with high storage capacity and low transportability and accessibility were mostly used in palatial and elite contexts. The storage containers used in ordinary domestic units are readily transportable, highly accessible, comfortable to hold and have low or medium capacity. The use of pithoi with different functional attributes within the different social contexts of Minoan society highlights models of storage behavior and levels of subsistence autarky.

In conclusion, the present discussion has highlighted the complex patterns in the production, distribution and consumption of pithoi. Potters' choices were inspired from "potting vocabularies" deeply rooted in local traditions; consumers' choices from similarly embedded social and economic restrictions. Pithoi, a usually neglected ceramic category, have the potential to provide valuable information about the ever-changing economic and social relations within Minoan society.

WORKS CITED

Betancourt, P.P. 1983. *The Cretan Collection in The University Museum, University of Pennsylvania*. Vol. 1, *Minoan Objects Excavated From Vasilike, Pseira, Sphoungaras, Priniatikos Pyrgos, and Other Sites*. University Museum Monograph 47. Philadelphia: The University Museum.

———. 1990. *Kommos*. Vol. 2, *The Final Neolithic Through Middle Minoan III Pottery*. Princeton, NJ: Princeton University Press.

Betancourt, P.P. and C. Davaras, eds. 1995. *Pseira*. Vol. 1, *The Minoan Buildings on the West Side of Area A*. University Museum Monograph 90. Philadelphia: The University Museum.

Bosanquet, R.C. and R.M. Dawkins. 1923. *The Unpublished Objects from the Palaikastro Excavations 1902–1906*. *BSA* Suppl. 1. London: Macmillan.

Chapouthier, F. and P. Demargne. 1942. *Fouilles Exécutées a Mallia*. Vol. 3, *Exploration du Palais. Bordures Orientale et Septentrionale (1927, 1928, 1931, 1932)*. *ÉtCrét* 6. Paris: Paul Geuthner.

Christakis, K.S. 1996. "Craft Specialization in Minoan Crete: The Case for Itinerant Pithos Makers." *Aegean Archaeology* 3: 63–74.

———. 1999a. "Minoan Pithoi and Their Significance for the Household Subsistence Economy of Neopalatial Crete." Ph.D. diss., Bristol University.

———. 1999b. "Pithoi and Food Storage in Neopalatial Crete: A Domestic Perspective." *WorldArch* 31: 1–20.

Day, P.M. 1988. "The Production and Distribution of Storage Jars in Neopalatial Crete." In *Problems in Greek Prehistory. Papers Presented at the Centenary Conference of the British School of Archaeology at Athens, Manchester, April 1986*, edited by E.B. French and K.A. Wardle, 499–508. Bristol: Bristol Classical Press.

———. 1991. "A Petrographic Approach to the Study of Pottery in Neopalatial East Crete." Ph.D. diss., University of Cambridge.

———. 1995. "Pottery Production and Consumption in the Sitia Bay Area during the New Palace Period." In *Achladia: Scavi e ricerche della Missione Greco-Italiana in Creta Orientale (1991–1993)*, edited by M. Tsipopoulou and L. Vagnetti, 149–75. Incunabula Graeca 97. Rome: Gruppo Editoriale Internazionale.

Dobres, M.-A. and C.R. Hoffman. 1994. "Social Agency and the Dynamics of Prehistoric Technology." *Journal of Archaeological Method and Theory* 1: 211–58.

Earle, T. 1997. *How Chiefs Come to Power: The Political Economy in Prehistory*. Stanford, CA: Stanford University Press.

Evans, A. 1921. *The Palace of Minos at Knossos*. Vol. 1. London: Macmillan.

———. 1928. *The Palace of Minos at Knossos*. Vol. 2. London: Macmillan.

———. 1930. *The Palace of Minos at Knossos*. Vol. 3. London: Macmillan.

Godart, L. and Y. Tzedakis. 1992. *Témoignages Archéologiques et Épigraphiques en Crète Occidentale du Néolithique au Minoen Récent IIIB*. Incunabula Graeca 93. Rome: Gruppo Editoriale Internazionale.

Gosselain, O.P. 1998. "Social and Technical Identity in a Clay Crystal Ball." In *The Archaeology of Social Boundaries*, edited by M.T. Stark, 78–106. Washington, DC: Smithsonian Institution.

Halbherr, F., E. Stefani and L. Banti. 1977. "Haghia Triada nel periodo tardo palaziale." *ASAtene* 55 (n.s. 39): 1–296.

Hall, E.H. 1912. *Excavations in Eastern Crete. Sphoungaras*. University of Pennsylvania, The Museum Anthropological Publications 3.2. Philadelphia: The University Museum.

Hawes, H.B, B.E.W. Williams, R.B. Seager, and E.H. Hall. 1908. *Gournia, Vasiliki and Other Prehistoric Sites on the Isthmus of Hierapetra, Crete: Excavations of the Wells-Houston-Cramp Expeditions, 1901, 1903, 1904*. Philadelphia: American Exploration Society, Free Museum of Science and Art.

Hazzidakis, J. 1921. *Étude de Préhistoire Crétoise: Tylissos à l'Époque Minoenne*. Paris: Paul Geuthner.

Hendon, J.A. 2000. "Having and Holding: Storage, Memory, Knowledge, and Social Relations." *American Anthropologist* 102: 42–53.

Kanta, A. and L. Rocchetti. 1989. "La ceramica del primo edificio." In *Scavi a Nerokourou, Kydonias*, 101–279. Incunabula Graeca 91. Rome: Edizioni dell'Ateneo.

Knappett, C.J. 1997. "Ceramic Production and Distribution in Protopalatial Crete: Technological, Economic and Social Perspectives." Ph.D. diss., Cambridge University.

La Rosa, V. 2002. "Pour une révision préliminaire du second palais de Phaistos." In *Monuments of Minos: Rethinking the Minoan Palaces. Proceedings of the International Workshop "Crete of the Hundred Palaces?" Held at the Université Catholique de Louvain, Louvain-la-Neuve, 14–15 December 2001*, edited by J. Driessen, I. Schoep, and R. Laffineur, 71–96. *Aegaeum* 23. Liège: Universite de Liège.

La Rosa, V. and N. Cucuzza. 2001. *L'insediamento di Selì di Kamilari nel territorio di Festòs*. Studi di archaeologia Cretese 1. Padova: Bottega d'Erasmo.

Levi, D. 1976. *Festòs e la civiltà minoica*. Vol. 1. Incunabula Graeca 60. Rome: Edizioni dell'Ateneo.

Levi, D. and F. Carinci 1988. *Festòs e la civiltà minoica*. Vol. 2. Incunabula Graeca 77. Roma: Edizioni dell'Ateneo.

Michailidou, A. 1990. "The Settlement of Akrotiri (Thera): A Theoretical Approach to the Function of the Upper Storey." In *L'Habitat Égéen Préhistorique. Actes de la Table Ronde Internationale Organisée par le Centre National de la Recherche Scientifique, L'Université de Paris 1 et L'École Française d'Athènes (Athènes, 23–25 Juin 1987)*, edited by P. Darcque and R. Treuil, 293–306. *BCH* Suppl. 19. Paris: Boccard.

Niemeier, W.-D. 1985. *Die Palaststilkeramik von Knossos: Stil, Chronologie und historischer Kontext*. *AF* 13. Berlin: Gebr. Mann.

Nikolakopoulou, I. Forthcoming. "Μινωικοί πίθοι από το Ακρωτήρι Θήρας." In *Proceedings of the 9th International Congress of Cretan Studies, Elounda, 1–6 October 2001*.

Palio, O. 2001. *La casa tardo minoico I di Chalara a Festòs*. Studi di Archaeologia Cretese 2. Padova: Bottega d'Erasmo.

Pelon, O. 1997. "Le palais post-palatial à Malia." In *La Crète Mycénienne. Actes de la Table Ronde Internationale organisée par l'École française d'Athènes (Athènes, 25–28 Mars 1991)*, edited by J. Driessen and A. Farnoux, 341–55. *BCH* Suppl. 30. Athens: École Française d'Athènes.

Pernier, L. 1935. *Il palazzo minoico di Festòs*. Vol. 1, *Gli strati più antichi e il primo palazzo*. Rome: Libreria dello stato.

Platon, L. 2002. "The Political and Cultural Influence of the Zakros Palace on Nearby Sites and in a Wider Context." In *Monuments of Minos: Rethinking the Minoan Palaces. Proceedings of the International Workshop "Crete of the Hundred Palaces?" Held at the Université Catholique de Louvain, Louvain-la-Neuve, 14–15 December 2001*, edited by J. Driessen, I. Schoep and R. Laffineur, 145–56. *Aegaeum* 23. Liège: Université de Liège.

Platon, N. 1964. "Ανασκαφή Κάτω Ζάκρου." *Prakt* 1961: 216–24.

———. 1966. "Ανασκαφή Ζάκρου." *Prakt* 1962: 142–68.

———. 1971. *Zakros: The Discovery of a Lost Palace of Ancient Crete*. New York: Charles Scribner's Sons.

Popham, M.R. 1970. *The Destruction of the Palace at Knossos: Pottery of the Late Minoan III A Period. SIMA* 12. Göteborg: Paul Åströms.

———. 1984. *The Minoan Unexplored Mansion at Knossos. BSA* Suppl. 17. Oxford: British School of Archaeology at Athens and Thames and Hudson.

Rethemiotakis, G. and K.S. Christakis. 2004. "Cultural Interaction between Knossos and Pediada: The Evidence from the Middle Minoan IB Pottery." In *Knossos: Palace, City, State. Proceedings of the Conference in Herakleion Organised by the British School at Athens and the 23rd Ephoreia of Prehistoric and Classical Antiquities of Herakleion, in November 2000, for the Centenary of Sir Arthur Evans's Excavations at Knossos*, edited by G. Cadogan, E. Hatzaki and A. Vasilakis, 169–75. *BSA* Studies 12. London: British School at Athens.

Sakellarakis, Y. and E. Sapouna-Sakellaraki. 1997. *Archanes: Minoan Crete in a New Light*. Athens: Ammos.

Sapouna-Sakellaraki, E. 1988–1989. "Η κεραμεική του θαλάσσιου ρυθμού από τις Αρχάνες και η πιθανή ύπαρξη τοπικού εργαστηρίου." *CretChron* 28–29: 28–52.

Seager, R.B. 1909. "Excavations on the Island of Mochlos, Crete, in 1908." *AJA* 13: 273–303.

———. 1910. *Excavations on the Island of Pseira, Crete*. University of Pennsylvania, The Museum Anthropological Publications 3.1. Philadelphia: The University Museum.

———. 1916. *The Cemetery of Pachyammos, Crete*. University of Pennsylvania, The University Museum Anthropological Publications 7.1. Philadelphia: The University Museum.

Silverman, J. 1978. "The LM IB Painted Pottery of Eastern Crete." *TUAS* 3: 31–5.

Sklavenitis, C. 1996. "Κεραμικά κέντρα και λαϊκοί αγγειοπλάστες της δυτικής Κρήτης." In *Κεραμικά Εργαστήρια στην Κρήτη απο την Αρχαιότητα ως Σήμερα. Πρακτικά Ημερίδας Μαργαρίτες, 30 Σεπτεμβρίου 1995*, edited by I. Gavrilaki, 81–100. Rethymnon: Istorike Laographike Etaireia Rethymnis.

Soles, J.S. and C. Davaras. 1994. "Excavations at Mochlos, 1990–1991." *Hesperia* 63: 391–436.

Stark, M.T. 1998. "Technical Choices and Social Boundaries in Material Culture Patterning: An Introduction." In *The Archaeology of Social Boundaries*, edited by M.T. Stark, 1–11. Washington, DC: Smithsonian Institution.

Tsipopoulou, M. and E. Hallager. 1996. "Inscriptions with Hieroglyphs and Linear A from Petras, Siteia." *SMEA* 37: 7–46.

Van de Moortel, A. 2002. "Pottery as a Barometer of Economic Change: From the Protopalatial to the Neopalatial Society in Central Crete." In *Labyrinth Revisited: Rethinking 'Minoan' Archaeology*, edited by Y. Hamilakis, 189–211. Oxford: Oxbow.

van Effenterre, H. and M. van Effenterre. 1976. *Fouilles exécutées à Mallia: Exploration des maisons et Quartiers d'habitation IV (1956–1960). ÉtCrét* 22. Paris: Paul Geuthner.

SOUTHWESTERN ANATOLIAN POTTERY FROM LATE MINOAN CRETE: EVIDENCE FOR DIRECT CONTACTS BETWEEN ARZAWA AND KEFTIU?

JEREMY B. RUTTER

Having recognized ceramic imports from all over the central and eastern Mediterranean to the Late Minoan harbor town of Kommos on Crete's south coast, Watrous appropriately devoted a substantial portion of his volume on the Late Bronze Age (LBA) pottery recovered from the site between 1976 and 1983 to an investigation of the trade routes that these imports implied.[1] The culture areas represented by these foreign pots included Egypt, the Syro-Palestinian coast, Cyprus, various Aegean islands other than Crete, the Mycenaean Greek mainland, Sardinia, and unspecified portions of Anatolia.[2] Continuing excavations at Kommos in 1984–1985 and again in 1991–1995 resulted in the discovery of substantial numbers of additional imports.[3] A 1997 conference devoted to assessing the significance of the Cape Iria shipwreck provided an opportunity for an update on pottery imported to Minoan Kommos from outside Crete, although this interim report understandably, in view of the context in which it was presented, concentrated on finds of the fourteenth and thirteenth centuries B.C.[4] More re-

The subject of this paper, despite its comparatively late chronological focus, struck me as an appropriate choice for my personal tribute to Phil Betancourt at a colloquium celebrating his contributions to Mediterranean archaeology. His publication of the earlier Minoan pottery recovered during the first decade of excavations at Kommos (Betancourt 1990) has helped me enormously during my own work at that site since 1991; his interest in ceramic fabric analysis resulted in our fruitful collaboration on problems involving the Early Helladic pottery from Lerna (Betancourt et al. 1988; 1995).

1. Watrous 1992, 149–83. For the remarkably high number of foreign ceramic imports recovered at Kommos, see Knapp and Cherry 1994, 138–41; and Cline 1994, 106.
2. The bulk of the imports initially identified as "Italian" by Watrous (1992, 163–8, figs. 73–6) were shown by subsequently published petrographic and chemical analyses (Watrous et al. 1998) to come from Sardinia. For those few pieces he considered either certain or likely to have been imported from Anatolia to Kommos, Watrous sensibly chose not to insist upon any particular regions as probable loci of production within that large, but for the LBA archaeologically still quite poorly documented, landmass (1992, 156, 168).
3. For the most recent preliminary report on these excavations, see Shaw and Shaw 1993.
4. Rutter 1999. Ceramic imports to Kommos from Protopalatial contexts are presently being studied for publication by Aleydis Van de Moortel. Those from MM III–LM IIIB contexts at the site not included in Watrous 1992 will be published in Rutter 2006.

cently, visits to the storerooms of the Kommos Excavations in Pitsidia by ceramic specialists with particular expertise in Egypt[5] and on the island of Gavdos[6] have resulted in additional significant discoveries with regard to Kommos' overseas connections.

But by far the most numerous, and hence arguably most significant, additions over the past decade to the surprisingly broad range of off-island ceramic imports recognized at Kommos consist of a class of pottery that we initially termed simply "reddish-brown burnished" because we had no idea where it might have been made.[7] While it was always clear that this class consisted overwhelmingly of closed shapes, it took us some time to assemble a collection of diagnostic rims and handles, and thus to recognize that virtually all of the pieces we were inventorying could be assigned to a single shape. It likewise took us a while to recognize that the heavy ribbing characteristic of the interior lower body of this shape was the result of wheel-finishing but not of wheel-throwing.[8] The purpose of this short article is to describe this class of imports, to suggest where it may have been produced, and to explore briefly how and why it may be of considerable importance.

The clay body, or fabric, of this class may be characterized as "medium-coarse," with inclusions ordinarily ranging between 6 and 12% in total bulk and up to between 1.5 and 3 mm in maximum dimension. The fracture is typically red or yellowish-red in Munsell terms, the interior surface ordinarily a homogeneous red or sometimes reddish-brown (figs. 1–4 for fractures and exterior surfaces). Exterior surfaces exhibit a similar color range, but are often mottled and sometimes feature dark reddish-brown or even reddish-gray patches. The cores of fractures fire a somewhat darker color about half of the time, usually reddish-brown but occasionally grayish-brown or gray. There is enough variability in the grits visible with a ten-power hand lens to suggest that more than one clay source was used to produce these vessels, but we have not yet undertaken a full-scale program of petrological analysis to confirm this. Subangular or angular white grits are usually the dominant inclusions; dark gray and black, subrounded or subangular grits, usually smaller in size, are also typically present; equally frequent are reddish-brown or dark reddish-

5. David Aston and Bettina Bader (SCIEM Project, Austrian Academy of Sciences; during a visit to Pitsidia in July and August 2002) and Pamela Rose (Tell el-Amarna excavations; during a visit to Pitsidia in July 2003) have agreed upon the identification of two medium- to large-sized, red-slipped, carinated bowls in Nile silt fabrics from LM IIIA contexts [C7549, C10469] and of one flask fragment [C7550] in a Marl A4 fabric marking it as a product of Upper Egypt.

6. Katerina Kopaka and Christina Papadaki (University of Crete, Rethymnon; during a visit to Pitsidia in July 2001) identified a number of vessels from Protopalatial, Neopalatial, and LM II contexts at Kommos as Gavdiot imports. The pieces of LM II date were transport vessels (an oval-mouthed amphora [C11880] and a transport stirrup jar [C10258]), while the Neopalatial items included a large and deep convex-sided cup of early LM IA date [C9096].

7. Rutter 1999, 143, 153 n. 35, table 4, figs. 1–2. As of 1997, 16 examples of this class had been inventoried; that number has since grown to 44.

8. Hence my initial description of this class as "wheelmade jars" (supra n. 7) was erroneous with regard to both shape and technique of manufacture.

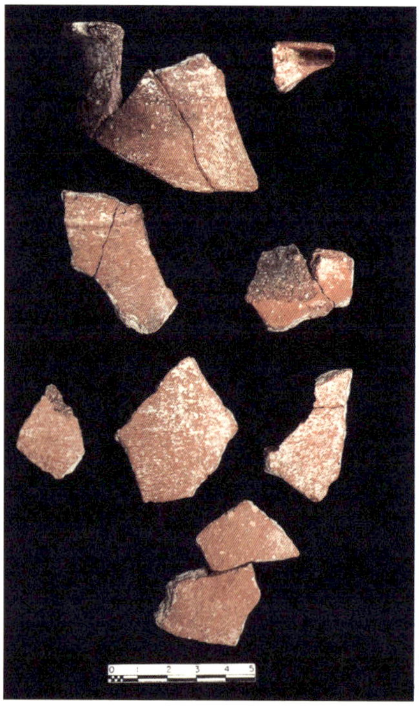

Fig. 1. C11835 (all sherds).

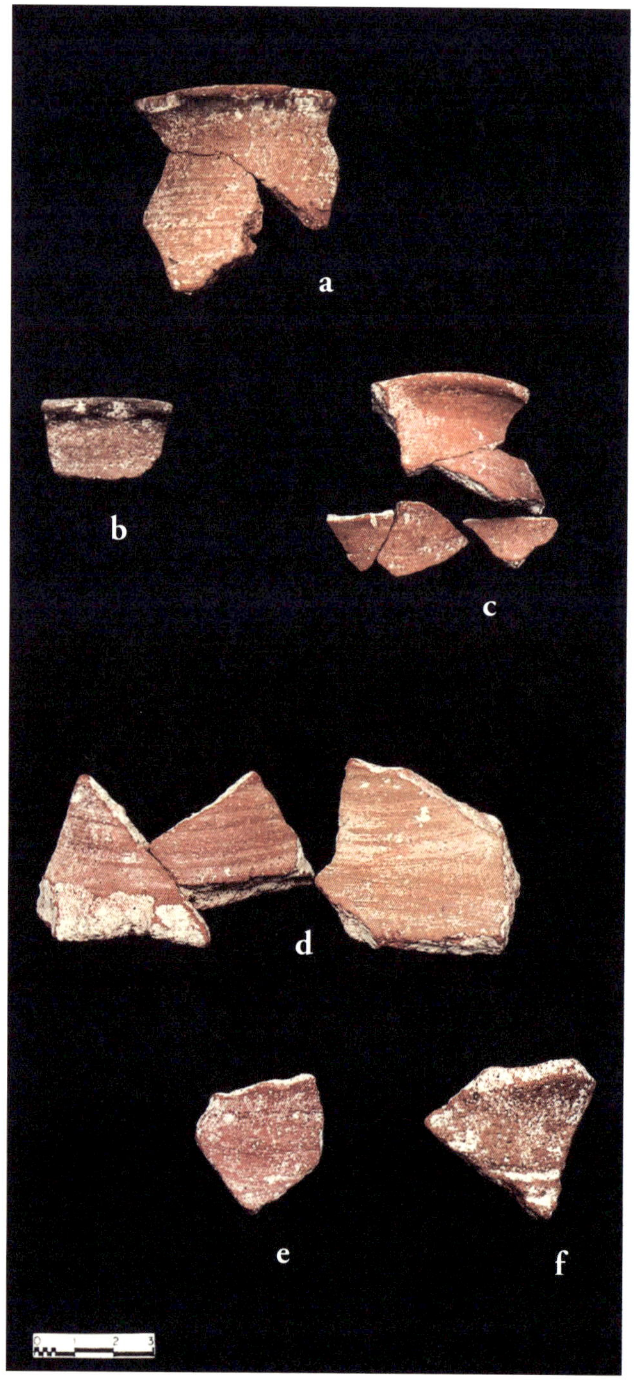

Fig. 2. (a) C10988, (b) C11216, (c) C9192, (d) C10685 (2 sherds), (e) C10850, (f) C8933.

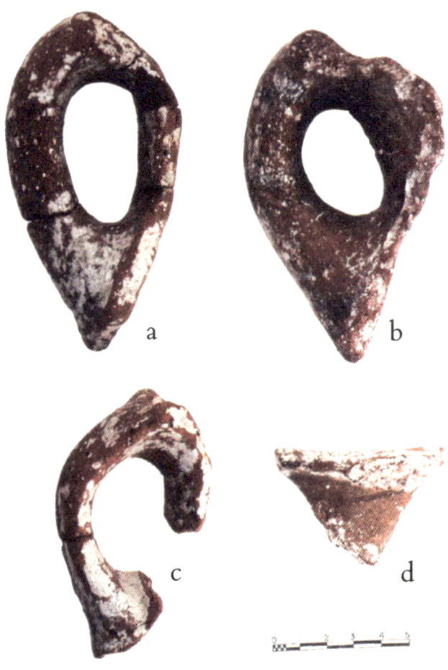

Fig. 3. (a) C7526, (b) C11296, (c) C7570, (d) C7619.

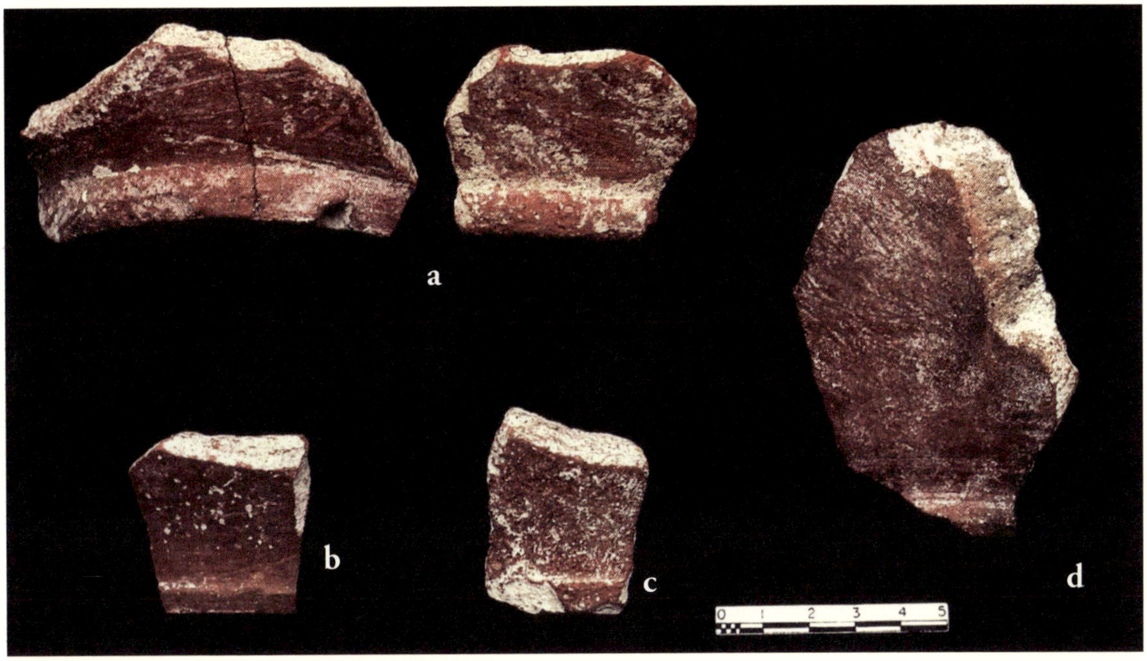

Fig. 4. (a) C9926 (2 sherds), (b) C9848, (c) C9863, (d) C9880.

brown subrounded grits or platelets. This array of inclusions is distinctively different from that of local fabrics in the western Mesara.[9] At first glance, fragments of this reddish-brown burnished fabric look quite similar to at least some examples of Minoan cooking pottery, but the two classes differ in two important respects. The fabric of the cooking pottery is coarser, with inclusion frequencies beginning at around 15% and reaching as high as 30%. And cooking pottery is virtually never burnished, at least in the Mesara; the few exceptions known to me have a burnish applied over a pale-firing slip on the interior only. So the thin, relatively long, and easily visible burnish troughs on the moderately lustrous exterior surfaces of this reddish-brown imported class make examples of it comparatively easy to identify.

Aside from these characteristics of fabric and surface treatment, the reddish-brown burnished imports at Kommos exhibit a number of morphological peculiarites. Of the more than forty different vessels now inventoried, all but two are closed shapes having distinct necks and varying comparatively little in size. Rim diameters range between 7 and 10

9. A single body fragment of this class [C5731], mistakenly identified in the 1980s as an "Italian" import (Watrous 1992, 164 no. 814, pls. 53, 56 [mislabeled "522"]), was sampled for petrological and chemical analysis. Day describes its fabric as follows: ". . . contains polycrystalline quartz, chert and rare schist in a red fabric. . . not incompatible with an origin in the Aegean" (Watrous et al. 1998, 339). In a visit to Pitsidia in July 2002, Jennifer Moody was kind enough to look at several other examples of this class. Notwithstanding her extensive experience in examining and describing the fabrics of pottery recovered by surface surveys in northwest, western south-central, and northeast Crete over the past three decades, she informed me that she could not remember ever having seen anything quite like the fabric of our "reddish-brown burnished" class at Kommos.

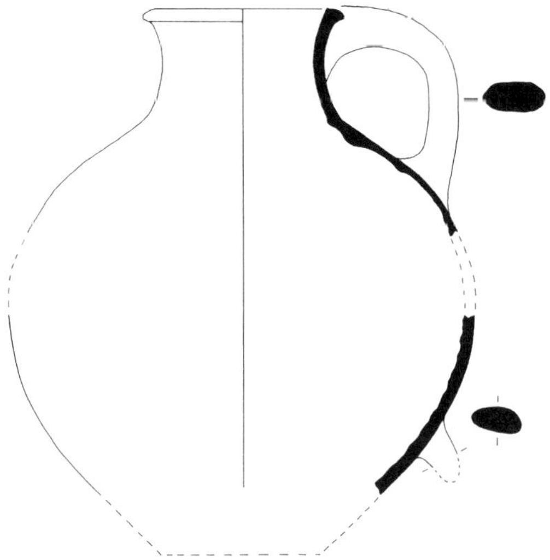

FIG. 5. Kommos C1174 (after Watrous 1992, fig. 31.740). D of rim: 9.6 cm.; est max D 21.5 cm.

cm, maximum diameters between 20 and 30 cm (with one exception at around 17 cm), and base diameters between 7 and 11 cm (with one exception at around 12.5 cm). The volumes of these vessels are estimated to range from 4.5 to 5.5 liters (fig. 5). Necks are of medium height and diameter, capped by markedly thickened and usually either horizontal (fig. 7a, c) or sloping (figs. 5, 6d, 7b, 8, 9b) lips, and ordinarily set off lightly from the convex shoulder below by a group of closely spaced, shallow grooves, rounded in section (figs. 2, 6a–b, d, 8).

Six examples of handles have now been found, all of them fairly broad and robust vertical straps attached at the top to the rim and at the bottom to the sloping shoulder (figs. 3, 5, 6d, 7–8). One rim and neck fragment (figs. 2a, 9b) preserves the remains of a small, circular perforation pierced vertically through the lip before firing and traces of a second such perforation pierced obliquely through the lower neck some 4.5 cm directly below. These holes may have been intended to facilitate the attachment of a lid; the surviving rim and neck profile of this piece looks very much like those of the jugs on which handles or handle scars survive, so this perforated fragment need not represent a different shape. Two fragments on which a semicircular lug projects prominently downward from the lower body have also been found (figs. 5, 10), in one case on a vase whose non-joining but fully preserved upper portion shows that it had a single vertical handle running from its rim to its shoulder (fig. 5). Comparanda from other sites on Crete (see footnotes 13–16) make clear that the lug was positioned directly below the vertical handle, presumably to facilitate both pouring and carrying when the vessel was full.

The bases of these reddish-brown burnished jugs are as distinctive as any of their other features and belong to two basic types (fig. 4). One is a raised base that features a biconical exterior profile and that has repeatedly broken at the point of junction between the flat bottom and the conical or convex lower body (fig. 6e–g). The second is also a raised base, but one with a smoothly rounded exterior profile at essentially the same level as a dramatic thickening on the interior profile (figs. 6h, 9a). On this second type, the bulges on both the interior and exterior profiles are evidently coils of clay added to strengthen the join of the base slab with the lowermost coil of the body. This alternative approach to

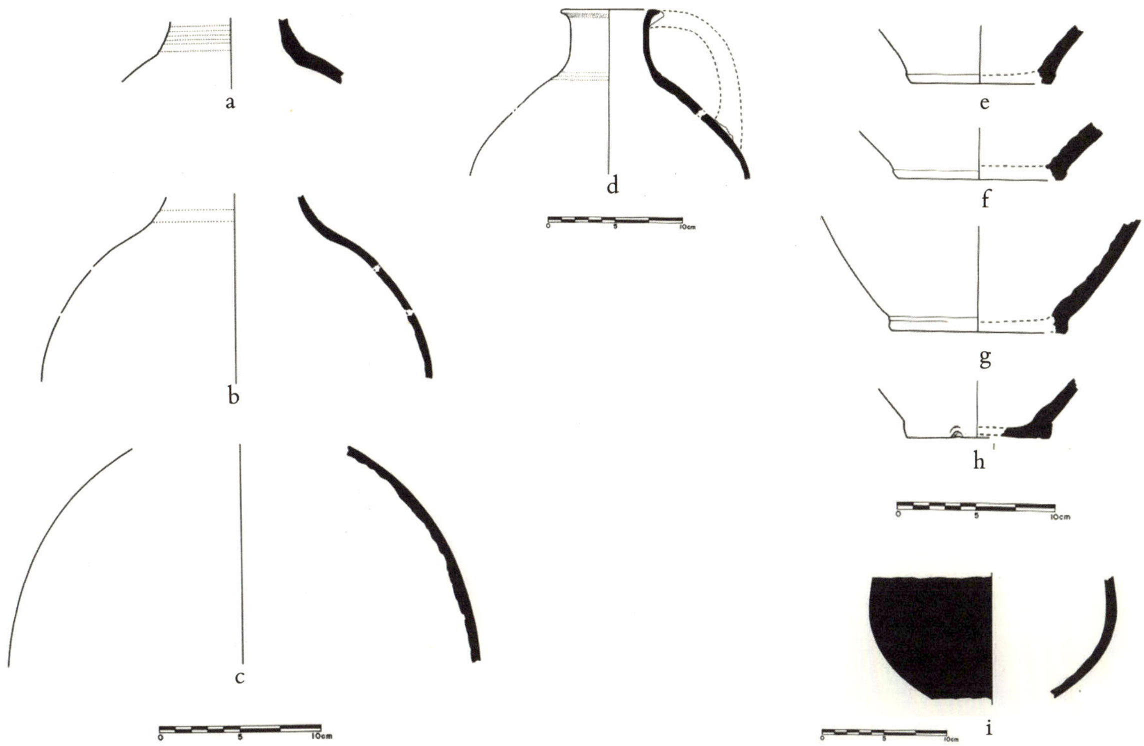

FIG. 6. Southwestern Anatolian jug fragments from Kommos: (a) C10685, (b) C11066, (c) C10743, (d) C11835, (e) C9848, (f) C9863, (g) C9880, (h) C9926, (i) C11133.

fashioning a raised base evidently accomplished its purpose since the two base fragments representing it are both broken at points nearer to the center of the bottom, where the vessel wall is substantially thinner. Yet a third technique that features a thicker-bottomed but also hollowed base, again with an added coil of clay on the interior, is represented by just one example (fig. 11); this appears to have been the most successful technique of all, since the base has survived intact, but perhaps this is simply because this base is smaller than any of the other six surveyed.

The interior profiles of these reddish-brown burnished jugs exhibit marked ribbing (figs. 5, 6c, f–g, 10, 11), as though from having been thrown hurriedly on a wheel, without any subsequent attempt made to scrape, pare, or otherwise thin the vessel walls. Yet careful study of the surviving fragments, especially of the bases and of vessels that exhibit sudden changes in wall thickness at various points in their elevations, reveals that these jugs were coil-built rather than wheel-thrown. They may, to be sure, have been finished on a wheel, either repeatedly at several stages in the building of the shape or else just once at the end of the shaping process. But they were certainly not wheel-thrown as complete shapes nor even pieced together from two or three major sections, as were quite a number of the

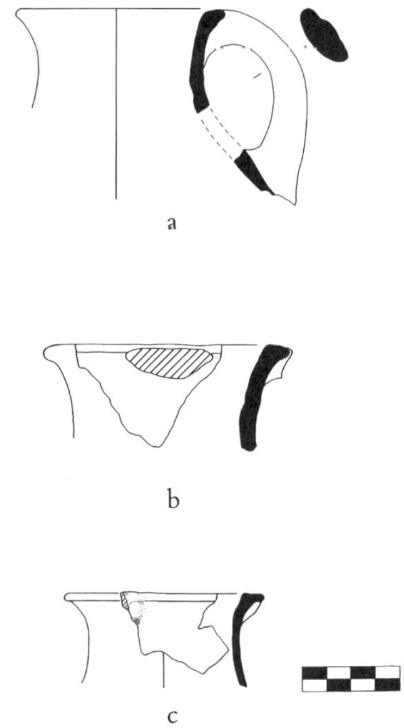

Fig. 7. Southwestern Anatolian jug fragments from Kommos: (a) C7570, (b) C7619, (c) C9192.

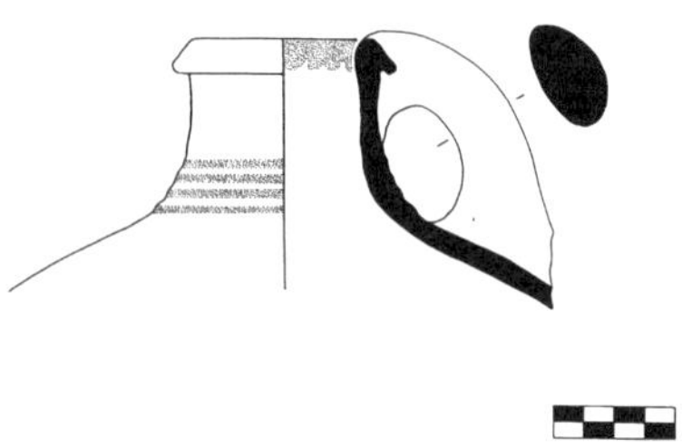

Fig. 8. Kommos C11296.

larger open as well as closed vessel forms produced in the Late Minoan Mesara. One of the surviving fragments preserved very clear evidence in its section for a series of at least three coil joints in its lower body.[10]

The reddish-brown burnished class of ceramic imports at Kommos differs from locally produced pottery in virtually every respect. The fabric and color of these vessels are non-local. By far the most common shape in this class, a rim-handled, very full-bodied jug sometimes with a subsidiary lug directly below the handle on the lower body, is alien to the local ceramic repertoire. Morphological features, such as the base types and the distinct profiles of the sloping lips, as well as decorative features, such as the grooving at the junction of neck and shoulder, are probably affected to some degree by a method of coil-built manufacture that may or may not include finishing on a wheel, but that is not at all characteristic of the local Minoan potting tradition in this period. Two pieces attributable to open shapes—a large body fragment from a deep, wide-bodied cup or bowl (fig. 6i) and a small rim sherd from a basin (fig. 12)—seem from their fabric and surface finish to belong to this same ceramic class. The cup has a red slip applied to the exterior only. The basin, possibly also supplied with a colored slip on the exterior only, was produced in a substantially coarser fabric and has two shallow concentric grooves in the upper surface of its flattened lip. By virtue of their uniqueness at Kommos, neither piece adds much to the larger picture, other than to suggest that a small number of open vessels, produced in the same region as the far more common rim-handled jugs, were for some reason also brought to Kommos. A third piece linked by its fabric and shape to the reddish-brown burnished class has an exterior covered with diagonal rows of applied circular knobs fashioned from a noticeably coarser clay than that of the vessel body (fig. 13). Perhaps because of its striking decoration, this jug lacks a burnish on its paler-firing, reddish-yellow exterior, but its interior surface closely resembles that of the typical reddish-brown burnished jugs.

Unfortunately, despite the frequency of these jugs at Kommos, not one has been found

10. The piece in question [C10975] is a lower body fragment rather than a feature sherd and is consequently not illustrated here.

complete as part of a floor deposit. The time of their initial introduction to the site is narrowly dated to the short-lived LM II period. Most were found in fills of LM II and IIIA date. About five examples come from LM IIIB contexts, but in all cases these could easily enough be earlier kick-ups or survivals. The *floruit* of this class at Kommos is thus predominantly the second half of the fifteenth and all of the fourteenth century B.C. Not surprisingly, the largest number of inventoried examples were found in and around the long-lived Neopalatial House X, where LM II through LM IIIA2 deposits are particularly abundant.[11] But it is clear that reddish-brown burnished jugs were in common use all over the site. The most fully preserved examples, in fact, come from the northeast corner of the pebble-covered court in front of the northernmost gallery of the shipshed Building P (figs. 1, 6d) and from a dumped fill in Room 26 on the Hilltop (fig. 5).[12]

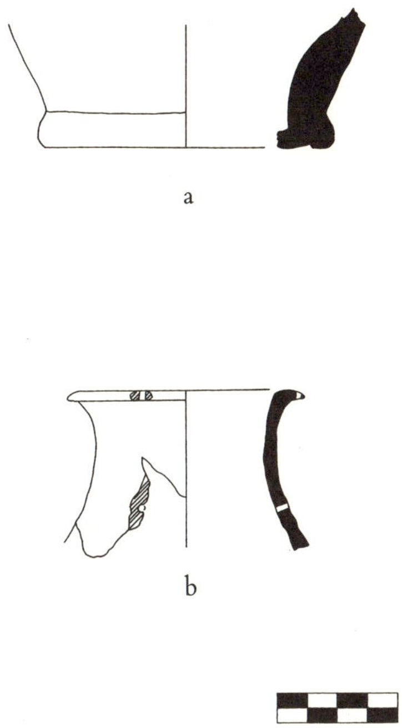

FIG. 9. Southwestern Anatolian jug fragments from Kommos: (a) C12063, (b) C10988.

The evidence from Kommos is largely corroborated by discoveries at a small number of other sites on Crete where closely comparable rim-handled jugs, often with a subsidiary horizontal handle or lug on the lower body, have been found. Evans found one in an LM IIIB context in the so-called Schoolroom of the palace at Knossos.[13] Alexiou found another in the LM II Tomb Zeta at Katsamba.[14] Popham found a pair of additional LM II examples in corridor L and room M of the Unexplored Mansion at Knossos.[15] A single example

11. For the most recent preliminary report on the excavation of House X, see Shaw and Shaw 1993, 131–61.

12. For Building P at Kommos, see Shaw and Shaw 1993, 166–77, 182, 187–8; for Hilltop Room 26, see Watrous 1992, 42–3, fig. 2; and Nixon 1996, 74–5.

13. Evans 1921, 369, fig. 279C; Popham 1964, 8, fig. 4, pl. 2b, lower right.

14. Alexiou 1967, 50 no. 3a, pl. 17b, left.

15. Popham 1984, 47 L43, 62 M105, pl. 86a–b. Thanks to the generous hospitality of Eleni Hatzaki and with the kind permission of the British School at Athens, I was able to examine one of the complete jugs from the Unexplored Mansion [M 105] in the summer of 2003, as well as to look through some of the unpublished sherd material retained from the excavation of that building. Among the latter were four rim and handle fragments, four rim and neck fragments, four neck and shoulder fragments, and two spouts, representing as many as twelve additional jugs of this type, all recovered from LM II destruction contexts in Room H, the pillared hall. All but one of the shoulder and neck fragments come from vessels of the same basic type as the jugs from Kommos but have been left unburnished, although seemingly coated on the exterior with a colored wash, often mottled from red to black. The fully preserved jug M 105 likewise lacks a burnished surface. One of the fragments from Room H, however, as well as a largely restorable example of the type from an LM II context in the Temple Tomb (TT/3 TV9 #1718; to be published by Hatzaki in her forthcoming full publication of the Temple Tomb) have the burnished exterior that is typical of this form of jug as it is represented at Kommos, together with a pronounced groove at the base of the neck.

from the Kephala Tholos near Knossos was originally dated to LM IIIC by Cadogan, but a recent, more comprehensive study of this tomb by Preston, along with the parallels from elsewhere in the Knossos area as well as from Kommos, suggest that an LM II date for this piece is more appropriate.[16] Platon found another pair in an LM IIIA1 context in room B1 of the settlement at Chondros Viannou.[17] Finally, Sackett and Popham report a single example lacking a lower body lug or handle from an early LM IIIC context on the summit of Kastri at Palaikastro.[18] Worth noting about these discoveries is the fact that all but two of these vessels come from settlement rather than funerary contexts (the exceptions being the LM II jug from Katsamba Tomb Zeta and the probably contemporary jug from the Kephala Tholos). The find circumstances at Chondros Viannou and the Unexplored Mansion at Knossos suggest that such jugs may have been used in pairs. Only the jugs from Chondros Viannou and the Kephala Tholos have the lug on the lower body that is attested twice at Kommos, those from the Knossos area typically being furnished with true horizontal handles in this position. Finally, the discovery of a complete jug from Kastri, notwithstanding such minor differences in shape as the absence of any lug or handle on the lower body, indicates that reddish-brown burnished jugs of this general sort continued in use on Crete until early in the twelfth century.

But are these jugs really imports to Crete from outside the island if they have been found at so many locales on it? It may be instructive to quote the late Mervyn Popham in this regard, since he certainly knew his Late Minoan pottery and had clearly handled a number of the vessels in question. He considered the fabric of these jugs to be a version of what he called "cooking pot ware," and termed the jug shape in question an "ewer."

> The ewer resembles very closely in shape and the placement of its handles a bronze type which it is likely to be imitating; its unusually sharply defined lip and pouring spout may reflect the same origin . . . This . . . is a long-lived type, perhaps originating in LM IA; it survives in less well proportioned shape into LM IIIC, and we may suspect the existence of a specialised centre of production for it.[19]

Although Popham evidently saw no reason to doubt this shape's Minoan pedigree, he clearly recognized some of its peculiar morphological characteristics and was prepared to view the ceramic type as a specialized imitation of a metallic model. Bronze proto-

There may well be fragments of a number of additional jugs of this type among the sherd material retained from the Unexplored Mansion; in the limited time available to me in 2003, I was able to examine only that recovered from Rooms H and P.

16. Cadogan 1967, 259, 265 no. 13, fig. 5, pl. 50. I am grateful to Laura Preston for bringing this piece to my attention and also for helpful discussion of its probable date.

17. Platon 1997, fig. 8.

18. Sackett et al. 1965, 298 no. KP16, fig. 16, pl. 75e.

19. Popham 1984, 175.

types for the shape in question are well known from LM I settlement contexts on Crete, from Shaft Graves IV–V at Mycenae, and from a single vessel found in the ruins of Akrotiri on Thera.[20] Popham was also able to cite a contemporary ceramic version of the form from the Volcanic Destruction Level of late LM IA at Akrotiri.[21] Thus the imitation of a metal form in ceramic that Popham envisaged was already underway at a comparatively early stage of the LBA, and the ceramic version of this distinctive type had a lengthy history of at least 350 years and possibly even longer, depending on the absolute date assigned to the Theran eruption.[22] The reddish-brown lustrous surface of the burnished ceramic versions of the form from LM II–IIIB Kommos and other sites on Crete make excellent sense as terracotta copies of copper or bronze originals. But why are there none of these ceramic imitations on Crete prior to the LM II period, particularly at a site like Kommos which has produced so many examples of the shape? And why are the fabric and production tech-

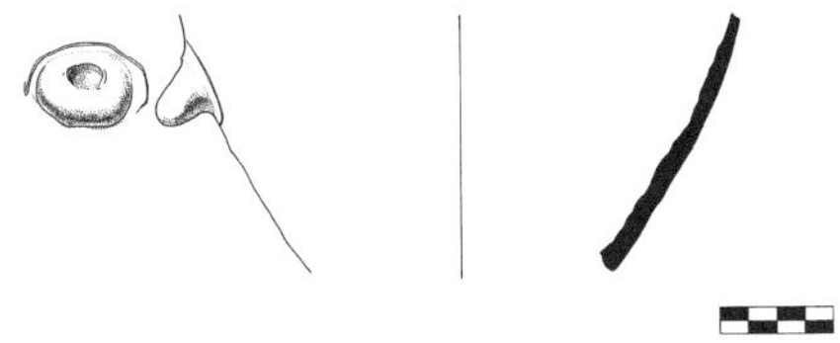

FIG. 10. Kommos C7976.

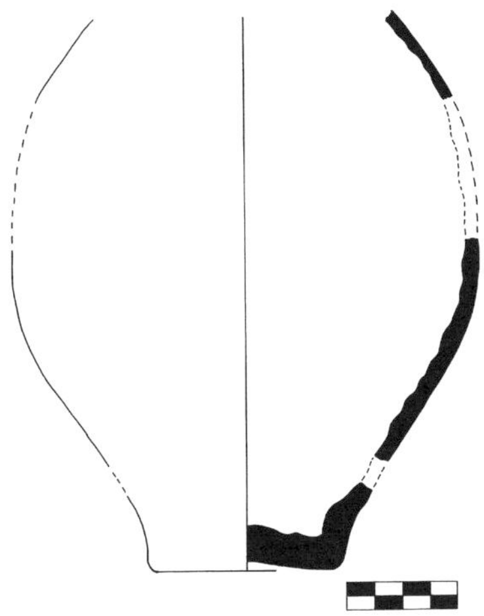

FIG. 11. Kommos C11912.

20. Matthäus 1980, 162–71 (shape 20).

21. Popham 1984, 277 n. 130; Marinatos 1974, pl. 5a, from Room 7 of the House of the Ladies. Marinatos illustrates another, somewhat slimmer example of the same shape in the same preliminary report (1974, pl. 71b). Both of these early examples feature the horizontal handle on the lower body typical of the metallic prototype as well as of the LM II ceramic versions of the form from the Knossos area; they also have the markedly raised bases which are such a distinctive feature of this ceramic type. With the very kind assistance and cooperation of Irene Nikolakopoulou and Christos Doumas, I have been sent color images of the two vessels in question (Akrotiri inventory nos. 2560 and 4099). Although they lack burnished surfaces and appear to be somewhat paler on the exterior than the reddish-brown burnished jugs from LM II–IIIA Kommos, they exhibit all the morphological features of the commonest versions of the type from LM II Knossos, but with a more pronounced trefoil mouth. In view of their significantly earlier date, such minor differences with respect to the examples of this shape so far identified on Crete are hardly surprising. In Nikolakopoulou's opinion, the two published jugs and an additional three specimens of the same type are all imports to Akrotiri. They were produced in a medium-coarse fabric ranging from reddish-brown to weak red in color, visually reminiscent of cooking pots considered by the excavators at Akrotiri to be likely imports from the northern Cyclades.

22. Matthäus (1980, 176 and n. 3) in commenting even earlier on the close connection between ceramic versions of this form and their metallic prototypes notes that the ceramic copies continued to imitate as late as the LM IIIB period the metal form in vogue during the Neopalatial era (his shape 20) rather than the more angular version popular both at Knossos and on the Greek mainland in the ensuing LM II/LH IIB–LM/LH IIIA1 periods (his shape 21: 1980, 171–6). The conservatism on the part of potters producing this form can be explained in any number of ways, including the failure of these potters to be exposed to metal examples of the form postdating those produced in the LM/LH I period.

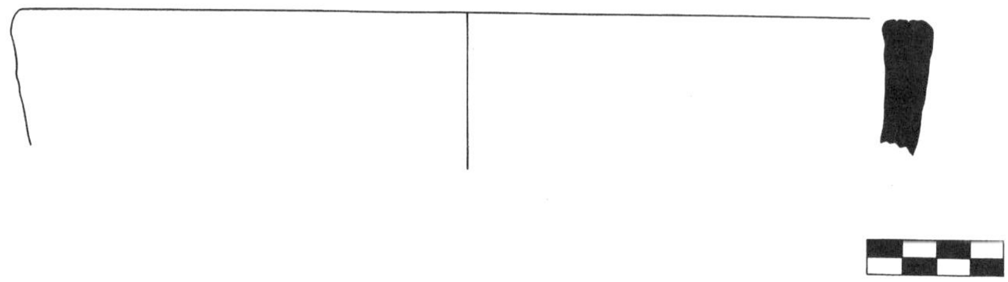

Fig. 12. Kommos C11911.

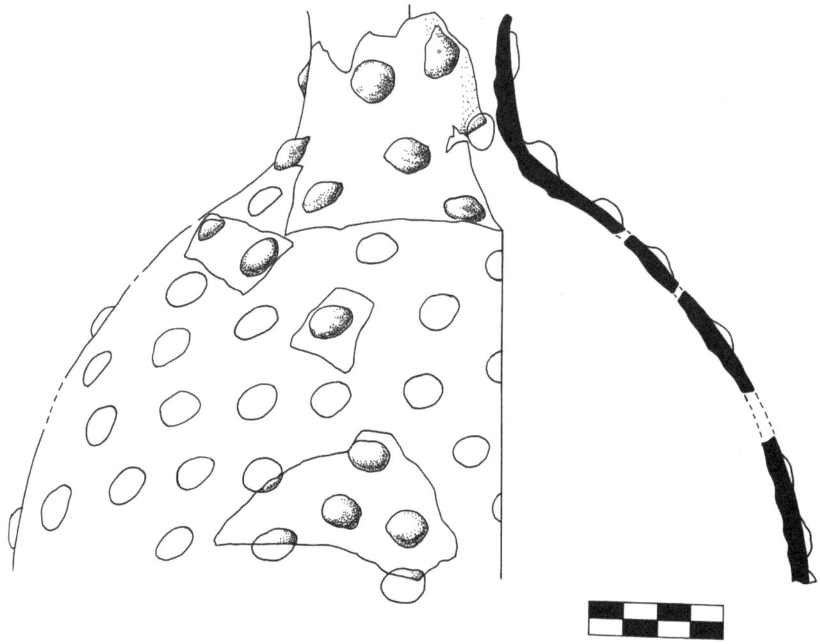

Fig. 13. Kommos C8689.

nique of these reddish-brown burnished jugs so different from those represented at the main centers of Minoan ceramic production?

A disparate set of site reports, most of them published within the past decade, suggest that the home of the reddish-brown burnished class of pottery under consideration here was located somewhere in southwestern Anatolia, in all probability at one or more coastal sites in the general vicinity of the Gulf of Izmir and the region to its immediate south that was known to the Hittites as the "Arzawa lands."[23] A number of the features typical of the reddish-brown burnished jugs from Kommos, especially the surface colors, the surface treatment, and the profiles of rims and necks on closed shapes, are common at sites such as Panaztepe, Bayraklı, and Limantepe toward or at the east end of the Gulf of Izmir.[24] Somewhat similar jugs, some of them featuring multiple grooves at the transition from

23. Hawkins 2002; Bryce 1998, 54–5, 78–9, 209–14, 230–4, map 3.

24. Surface colors: Günel 1999a, pls. 156.2, 162.1–2, 174.1–3 [Panaztepe]; 1999b, 59 [Limantepe]; Bayne 2000, 62, 68, 70 [Bayraklı]; rim and neck profiles: Günel 1999a, pls. 113.2–6, 114.7–8, 115.1–4, 117.1, 135.1–2, 136.1–3 [Panaztepe]; Bayne 2000, 77, fig. 18.1–4, 79 [Bayraklı].

the neck to the shoulder, are common in LBA levels at the inland site of Beycesultan, though these are regularly provided with either ring or flattened bases and have pronounced trefoil mouths.[25] Two examples of jugs closely resembling the larger reddish-brown burnished jugs from Kommos in fabric, profile, and size, although lacking either a lug or a handle on the lower body, were part of a ship's cargo recovered some 25 km east of Bodrum near the mouth of Şeytan Deresi (Devil's Creek) and provisionally dated to the early Shaft Grave period, or very end of the local Middle Bronze Age.[26] Finally, the very distinctive knobbed decoration of jug C8689 from Kommos (fig. 13) has distant parallels on large jars of shape 26 and cooking bowls of shape 31 from Beycesultan levels V and IVC, respectively.[27] Although the parallels so far published are by no means close enough to enable one or more specific southwest Anatolian production centers of the reddish-brown burnished jugs from LM II–IIIB contexts at Kommos and other contexts on Crete to be identified, in combination they serve to mark the coastal regions between the Gulf of Izmir and the Gulf of Kerme as the probable source area of these imports. Features such as the thickened horizontal or sloping lips, the burnished reddish-brown and often somewhat mottled exteriors, the emphasis on articulated bases, the distinct but usually not sharply offset necks on closed forms, and the penchant for multiple fine grooves at the transition from neck to shoulder are all aspects of the reddish-brown burnished jugs from Kommos that are very difficult to parallel in Minoan pottery but that seem quite common in that of west-central and southwest Anatolia at this time.

The unusually high frequency of jugs of a particular size in this reddish-brown burnished class as it is so far attested on Crete suggests that these vessels may have been used to transport a particular product from coastal Anatolia to Minoan ports.[28] The possible provision for the attachment of a lid on one of the jug necks from Kommos (figs. 2a, 9b) may be a further indication of such a transport function for these medium-sized vessels. They are nowhere near as large as the contemporary Canaanite jars of the Levant or the coarse-ware stirrup jars of the Aegean, much less of Cypriot pithoi. Indeed, they are even smaller than the transport container that Watrous christened the short-necked amphora, which was produced in large numbers at or around Kommos.[29] But their reduced size may be a

25. Mellaart and Murray 1995, 4, 7, 13, fig. P.5.1, 3, 8, pl. IIIb.4 [Beycesultan III], 24, 29, 41, fig. P.19.5–9, pl. VIb [Beycesultan II].

26. Bass 1976, 298–9, fig. 5B–C.

27. Lloyd and Mellaart 1965, 91, 98, fig. P.9.4, 7 [Beycesultan V], 115, fig. P.22.10, 116, fig. P.23.1, 117 [Beycesultan IVC]. I am grateful to Peter Pavuk for drawing these parallels to my attention.

28. Ceramic versions of the jug form thus far attested on Crete are noticeably smaller on average than copper versions of either LM/LH I or LM II/LH IIB–LM/LH IIIA date (Matthäus 1980, 163–8, 172–3).

29. Rutter 2000. The capacities of short-necked amphorae range from c. 9.5–10.5 liters, roughly twice those of the reddish-brown burnished jugs.

function of the product they were designed to carry, whatever that may have been. In any case, if the suggestion that these reddish-brown burnished jugs from Kommos and other Minoan sites are western Anatolian imports is correct, these vessels would at last provide evidence from the Anatolian side for the kind of intense interaction between the coastal regions of southwest Anatolia and Crete that sites such as Knidos, Iasos, and above all Miletos, to name but a few, have long provided from the Minoan side.[30]

The distribution of these imported, reddish-brown burnished jugs on Crete is rather unusual. Unlike the quantities of Egyptian and Sardinian vessels found at Kommos,[31] they are by no means peculiar to that site. At the same time, unlike both Cypriot and Syro-Palestinian imports, they are not limited to coastal sites on Crete.[32] Yet there are several well-explored Minoan sites that have produced substantial evidence for occupation during LM IIIA but no examples of either jugs or any other shapes in this reddish-brown burnished class. These sites include coastal locales in both western (e.g., Chania) and eastern (e.g., Mochlos, Gournia) Crete, as well as important centers at some remove from the sea (e.g., Hagia Triada, just an hour's brisk walk from Kommos). So why do these jugs turn up where they do?

Moreover, in view of how little is known of the LM II period throughout the island of Crete, it is striking how many of these jugs appear for the first time at their respective sites in contexts of that period. This is, of course, precisely when copious artifactual evidence for Mycenaeans on Crete shows up for the first time. Is there some connection between reddish-brown burnished jugs and Mycenaean overlordship on Crete?[33] To my knowledge, nothing remotely resembling these coil-made, medium-coarse, burnished jugs has been found on the Greek mainland at the time in question. Nor is there anything similar from the richly furnished Mycenaean cemeteries on Rhodes. On Kos, however, there are a number of monochrome red-burnished jugs from the Langada tombs that seem broadly

30. Niemeier and Niemeier 1997; Niemeier 1999.

31. Watrous 1992, 162–8; Rutter 1999, 142–4, 173–5 table 3, 177–9 table 5; 2006.

32. Rutter 1999, 141–2, 147–8; 2006.

33. The more developed shape of the copper version of such jugs, Matthäus' shape 21 (1980, 172–3, pl. 68A), is above all characteristic of the so-called "burials with bronzes" on Crete (e.g., Zapher Papoura Tombs 14 and 36 at Knossos, Archanes Tholos A, and Kalyvia Shaft Grave 4 at Phaistos) that are often identified as the tombs of a Mycenaean ruling aristocracy (Popham et al. 1974, 253–4; Matthäus 1980, 68–74; Driessen and Macdonald 1984; Kilian-Dirlmeier 1985; Löwe 1996, 52–4; Whitley 2002, 222–3). Of the four examples of shape 21 published before 1980 from the mainland, at least two and perhaps three were found at Dendra, one at Asine. Although these later metal jugs, or hydrias, as Matthäus and Catling term them, are often smaller and exhibit more care in their manufacture than the earlier ones of Matthäus' shape 20 (1980, 174–5), they never feature a lug on the lower body as do ceramic versions of the type from Kommos, Knossos' Kephala Tholos, and Chondros Viannou. Contemporary examples of essentially the same shape from Sellopoulo Tomb 4 at Knossos that lack a horizontal handle on the lower body are described by Catling and Matthäus as jugs (Matthäus 1980, 196 [shape 26]; Popham et al. 1974, 236–8 nos. 31–2, 251).

similar.[34] Unfortunately, these have been published without profiles and exclusively in black-and-white photographs, so it is difficult to assess how closely they resemble the reddish-brown examples from Crete. The earliest of these jugs from Kos, however, is no earlier than LH IIIA, so they postdate the sudden appearance of reddish-brown burnished jugs at Kommos and in the Knossos area in LM II. If the presence of these jugs in LM II contexts marks a new stage in contacts between Crete and the Arzawa lands of western Anatolia at precisely the time when a Mycenaean administration came to power at Knossos, one may reasonably ask whether this new relationship might have any connection with the initial mention shortly thereafter of Ahhiyawa in the Hittite texts in connection with the activities of Madduwatta and Attarisiya, the "Man of Ahhiya."[35] Could it be, for example, that the name Ahhiya or Ahhiyawa was originally applied by the Hittites to the LM II–IIIA2 Early kingdom centered at Knossos, by far and away the most powerful polity in the southern Aegean during the period c. 1450–1375 B.C.?[36] If this had been the case, one might have expected the destruction of Knossos c. 1375 B.C. to have resulted in the disappearance of Ahhiyawa from Hittite documents. But perhaps the name was adopted by a successor power on the Greek mainland. Alternatively, the earlier term Ahhiya may have been applied to Mycenaean Knossos in LM II–IIIA2 Early, while the later term Ahhiyawa was used by the mainland Greek (probably Argive) successor to Knossian dominance in the Aegean during the period c. 1375–1200 B.C.[37]

Further speculation on historical questions of such potential importance is unquestionably premature in the light of our limited understanding at present of contacts between Crete and southwestern Anatolia during the fifteenth and fourteenth centuries B.C. But the recognition that the reddish-brown burnished class of pottery surveyed here is imported to Crete rather than locally produced, as well as being far more common at some key sites in LM II–IIIA1 central Crete than previously realized, may open up some interesting avenues of future research on several different fronts in the years to come.

34. Morricone 1965–1966, 107 no. 15, fig. 315.2 [Tomb 10], 124 no. 1, fig. 108.5 [Tomb 16], 151 no. 4, fig. 143.2 [Tomb 25], 202–3 no. 2, fig. 214.5 [Tomb 44], 209 no. 7, fig. 221.6 [Tomb 45], 271 no. 3, fig. 315.3 and 276 no. 1, fig. 314 [sporadic finds without context].

35. Bryce 1998, 59–63, 140–9; Cline 1994, 68–77, 121–5.

36. I owe this provocative suggestion to Sturt Manning, to whom I am also grateful for some intriguing initial discussions of this possibility.

37. For the notion that the name Ahhiyawa might have been applied to different regions within the Aegean at different periods, albeit with different candidates for those locations than those suggested here, see Cline 1994, 69. For two recent discussions of the "Ahhiyawa question," see Georgiadis 2003, 112–3 and Hope-Simpson 2003, the latter with a comprehensive bibliography.

WORKS CITED

Alexiou, S. 1967. *Υστερομινωικοί Τάφοι Λιμένος Κνωσσού (Κατσαμπά)*. Βιβλιοθήκη τῆς ἐν Ἀθήναις Ἀρχαιολογικῆς Ἑταιρείας 56. Athens: En Athenais Archaiologike Hetaireia.

Bass, G.F. 1976. "Sheytan Deresi: Preliminary Report." *IJNA* 5, 4: 293–303.

Bayne, N. 2000. *The Grey Wares of North-West Anatolia in the Middle and Late Bronze Age and the Early Iron Age and their Relation to the Early Greek Settlements*. Asia Minor Studien 37. Bonn: Rudolf Habelt.

Betancourt, P.P. 1990. *Kommos*. Vol. 2, *The Final Neolithic through Middle Minoan III Pottery*. Princeton, NJ: Princeton University Press.

Betancourt, P.P., G.H. Myer and J.B. Rutter. 1988. "The Ceramic Petrography of Early Helladic Pottery from Lerna." In *A Pot for All Reasons: Ceramic Ecology Revisited, Papers Dedicated to Frederick R. Matson, 1986*, edited by C.C. Kolb and L.M. Lackey, 73–80. Philadelphia: Laboratory of Anthropology, Temple University.

Betancourt, P.P., G.H. Myer and S.J. Vaughan. 1995. "Petrography." In *Lerna. A Preclassical Site in the Argolid*. Vol. 3, *The Pottery of Lerna IV*, by J.B. Rutter, 666–710. Princeton, NJ: American School of Classical Studies at Athens.

Bryce, T. 1998. *The Kingdom of the Hittites*. Oxford: Clarendon.

Cadogan, G. 1967. "Late Minoan IIIC Pottery from the Kephala Tholos Tomb near Knossos." *BSA* 62: 257–65.

Cline, E.H. 1994. *Sailing the Wine-Dark Sea: International Trade and the Late Bronze Age Aegean*. *BAR-IS* 591. Oxford: Tempus Reparatum.

Driessen, J. and C. Macdonald. 1984. "Some Military Aspects of the Aegean in the Late Fifteenth and Early Fourteenth Centuries B.C." *BSA* 79: 49–74.

Evans, A. 1921. *The Palace of Minos at Knossos*. Vol. 1. London: Macmillan.

Georgiadis, M. 2003. *The South-Eastern Aegean in the Mycenaean Period: Islands, Landscape, Death and Ancestors*. *BAR-IS* 1196. Oxford: Archaeopress.

Günel, S. 1999a. *Panaztepe*. Vol. 2, *Die Keramik von Panaztepe und ihre Bedeutung für Westkleinasien und die Ägäis im 2. Jahrtausend*. Ankara: Türk Tarih Kurumu.

———. 1999b. "Vorbericht über die mittel- und spätbronzezeitliche Keramik vom Liman Tepe." *IstMitt* 49: 41–82.

Hawkins, J.D. 2002. "The Historical Geography of Western Anatolia in the Hittite Texts," 94–101. In "Troy in Recent Perspective," by D.F. Easton, J.D. Hawkins, A.G. Sherratt and E.S. Sherratt. *AnatSt* 52: 75–109.

Hope Simpson, R. 2003. "The Dodecanese and the Ahhiyawa Question." *BSA* 98: 203–37.

Kilian-Dirlmeier, I. 1985. "Noch einmal zu den 'Kriegergräbern' von Knossos." *JRGZM* 32: 196–214.

Knapp, A.B. and J.F. Cherry. 1994. *Provenience Studies and Bronze Age Cyprus: Production, Exchange and Politico-Economic Change*. Monographs in World Archaeology 21. Madison, WI: Prehistory Press.

Lloyd, S. and J. Mellaart. 1965. *Beycesultan*. Vol. 2, *Middle Bronze Age Architecture and Pottery*. Occasional Publications of the British Institute of Archaeology at Ankara 8. London: British Institute of Archaeology at Ankara.

Löwe, W. 1996. *Spätbronzezeitliche Bestattungen auf Kreta*. *BAR-IS* 642. Oxford: Tempus Reparatum.

Marinatos, S. 1974. *Excavations at Thera*. Vol. 6, *1972 Season*. Βιβλιοθήκη τῆς ἐν Ἀθήναις Ἀρχαιολογικῆς Ἑταιρείας 64. Athens: En Athenais Archaiologike Hetaireia.

Matthäus, H. 1980. *Die Bronzegefässe der kretisch-mykenischen Kultur*. Prähistorische Bronzefunde. Vol. 2, Part 1. Munich: C. H. Beck.

Mellaart, J. and A. Murray. 1995. *Beycesultan*. Vol. 3, Part 2, *Late Bronze Age and Phrygian Pottery and Middle and Late Bronze Age Small Objects*. Occasional Publications of the British Institute of Archaeology at Ankara 12. London: British Institute of Archaeology at Ankara.

Morricone, L. 1965–1966. "Eleona e Langada: Sepolcreti della Tarda Età del Bronzo a Coo." *ASAtene* 43–44 (n.s. 27–28): 5–311.

Niemeier, B. and W.-D. Niemeier 1997. "Milet 1994–1995. Projekt 'Minoisch-mykenisches bis protogeometrisches Milet': Zielsetzung und Grabungen auf dem Stadionhügel und am Athenatempel." *AA*: 189–248.

Niemeier, W.-D. 1999. "Mycenaeans and Hittites in War in Western Asia Minor." In *POLEMOS: Le contexte guerrier*

en Égée à l'Âge du Bronze. Actes de la 7e Rencontre égéenne internationale Université de Liège, 14–17 avril 1998, edited by R. Laffineur, 141–55. *Aegaeum* 19. Liège: Université de Liège.

Nixon, L.F. 1996. "The Oblique House and the Southeast Rooms." In *Kommos*. Vol. 1, *The Kommos Region and Houses of the Minoan Town*. Part 2, *The Minoan Hilltop and Hillside Houses*, edited by J.W. Shaw and M.C. Shaw, 59–76. Princeton, NJ: Princeton University Press.

Platon, L. 1997. "Caractère, morphologie et datation de la bourgade postpalatiale de Képhali Chondrou Viannou." In *La Crète Mycénienne. Actes de la Table Ronde Internationale organisée par l'École française d'Athènes*, edited by J. Driessen and A. Farnoux, 357–73. *BCH* Suppl. 30. Paris: École Française d'Athènes.

Popham, M.R. 1964. *The Last Days of the Palace at Knossos: Complete Vases of the Late Minoan IIIB Period*. *SIMA* 5. Lund: Carl Bloms.

———. 1984. *The Minoan Unexplored Mansion at Knossos*. *BSA* Suppl. 17. Oxford: British School of Archaeology at Athens and Thames and Hudson.

Popham, M.R., E.A. Catling and H.W. Catling. 1974. "Sellopoulo Tombs 3 and 4, Two Late Minoan Graves near Knossos." *BSA* 69: 195–257.

Rutter, J.B. 1999. "Cretan External Relations During Late Minoan IIIA2–B (ca. 1370–1200 BC): A View from the Mesara." In *The Point Iria Wreck: Interconnections in the Mediterranean ca. 1200 B.C. Proceedings of the International Conference, Island of Spetses, 19 September 1998*, edited by W. Phelps, Y. Lolos and Y. Vichos, 139–86. Athens: Hellenic Institute of Marine Archaeology.

———. 2000. "The Short-Necked Amphora of the Post-Palatial Mesara." In *Πεπραγμένα Η' Διεθνούς Κρητολογικού Συνεδρίου. Προϊστορική και Αρχαία Ελληνική Περίοδος*, Vol. A3, edited by T. Detorakes and A. Kalokairinos, 177–88. Heraklion: Hetaireia Kretikon Istorikon Meleton.

———. 2006. "Ceramic Imports at Kommos." In *Kommos*. Vol. 5, *The Monumental Buildings at Kommos*, edited by J.W. Shaw and M.C. Shaw, 646–88. Princeton, NJ: Princeton University Press.

Sackett, L.H., M.R. Popham, P.M. Warren and L. Engstrand. 1965. "Excavations at Palaikastro VI." *BSA* 60: 248–315.

Shaw, J.W. and M.C. Shaw. 1993. "Excavations at Kommos (Crete) during 1986–1992." *Hesperia* 62: 129–90.

Watrous, L. V. 1992. *Kommos*. Vol. 3, *The Late Bronze Age Pottery*. Princeton, NJ: Princeton University Press.

Watrous, L.V., P.M. Day and R.E. Jones. 1998. "The Sardinian Pottery from the Late Bronze Age Site of Kommos in Crete: Description, Chemical and Petrographic Analyses, and Historical Context." In *Sardinia and Aegean Chronology: Towards the Resolution of Relative and Absolute Dating in the Mediterranean*, edited by M.S. Balmuth and R.H. Tykot, 337–40. Studies in Sardinian Archaeology 5. Oxford: Oxbow.

Whitley, J. 2002. "Objects with Attitude: Biographical Facts and Fallacies in the Study of Late Bronze Age and Early Iron Age Warrior Graves." *CAJ* 12: 217–32.

ELENI S. BANOU received her degree in History and Archaeology from the University of Athens and studied Classical Archaeology at the University of Pennsylvania where she received a Ph.D. Her dissertation is entitled "Pottery Groups from the West Side of Area A at Pseira, Crete." She was a staff member of the Pseira excavations and has contributed to many of the Pseira publications. Banou is a member of the Greek Archaeological Service and has been directing excavations since 1993 at the site of Pera Galenoi, located just west of Fodele on the north coast of Crete. [ebanou@freemail.gr]

KOSTANDINOS S. CHRISTAKIS studied Classical and Near Eastern Archaeology at the University of Rome "La Sapienza" and received his Ph.D. at the University of Bristol. He currently teaches in the Department of Education at the University of Crete. Christakis is collaborating with G. Rethemiotakis in the investigation of the site Galatas Pediados, Crete, and he is responsible for the publication of the stratified deposits from the sanctuary of Kato Simi Viannou. His published works (articles and two monographs) focus on staple storage, subsistence economy and the politics of the past. He is currently working on a book examining the storage technologies and the palatial and domestic economy of the settlement of Knossos. [christakis@her.forthnet.gr]

PETER M. DAY received his B.A. in Archaeology from the University of Southampton. After his introduction to Aegean archaeology as Research Fellow in Ceramic Petrology at the Fitch Laboratory, British School at Athens, he carried out doctoral research at the University of Cambridge, where his dissertation "A Petrographic Approach to the Study of Pottery in Neopalatial East Crete" was based on the archaeological and ethnographic study of pottery manufacture. His postdoctoral research at the MacDonald Institute of Archaeological Research, Cambridge, and at the Laboratory of Archaeometry, NCSR "Demokritos" in Athens, concentrated on the Early Bronze Age of Crete. Since 1994 he has taught at the Department of Archaeology, University of Sheffield, and is the author or coauthor of over 60 articles and monographs, many concerning the methodology and application of ceramic analysis. [p.m.day@sheffield.ac.uk]

EDWARD W. FABER was awarded a B.Sc. in Archaeological Science from the University of Sheffield. Following this he spent time as a graduate researcher in the Laboratory of Archaeometry, NCSR "Demokritos" in Athens, including participation in the European Union TMR project GEOPRO. He has recently submitted a Ph.D. thesis to the University of Sheffield entitled "Middle Minoan Polychrome Pottery: An Integrated Microstructural, Geochemical and Mineralogical Investigation of its Production Technology and Provenance." [edwardwfaber@yahoo.co.uk]

MARIA RELAKI was awarded a B.A. in Archaeology and Art History from the University of Athens, and an M.A. in Archaeology and Prehistory from the University of Sheffield. After having worked briefly for the Greek Archaeological Service in eastern Crete, she went on to gain her Ph.D. with a dissertation entitled "Social Arenas in Minoan Crete: A Regional History of the Mesara from the Final Neolithic to the End of the Protopalatial Period" from the University of Sheffield. She has used ceramic petrography to study ceramic assemblages from Mochlos, Kavousi and Poros in Crete and Rhodes in the Dodecanese, resulting in several publications. She is currently a Post-doctoral Research Associate at the University of Sheffield, working on ceramics of the Early Bronze II southern Aegean. [m.relaki@sheffield.ac.uk]

JEREMY B. RUTTER received his Ph.D. from the University of Pennsylvania and is now the Sherman Fairchild Professor of the Humanities, Dartmouth College. He is the author of *The Transition to Mycenaean* (1976, with Sarah H. Rutter), *Ceramic Change in the Aegean Early Bronze Age* (1979) and *Lerna*. Vol. 3, *The Pottery of Lerna IV* (1995), as well as numerous journal articles and reviews. [Jeremy.B.Rutter@Dartmouth.edu]

ELENI TSIVILIKA studied History and Archaeology at the University of Thessaloniki. She is a member of the Greek Archaeological Service and since 1993 has codirected, with Eleni Banou, excavations at the site of Pera Galenoi, Crete.

ALEYDIS VAN DE MOORTEL received an M.A. in Classics from the Catholic University of Leuven, an M.A. in Anthropology with a specialty in Nautical Archaeology from Texas A&M University and an M.A. and Ph.D. in Classical and Near Eastern Archaeology from Bryn Mawr College. Her dissertation was entitled "The Transition from the Protopalatial to the Neopalatial Society in South-Central Crete: A Ceramic Perspective." She is currently Assistant Professor of Classics at the University of Tennessee. From 1992–2003 she worked as a pottery analyst at Kommos in southern Crete, and she is publishing the Protopalatial pottery from the civic center. She is now codirector of the Greek-American excavations of the Bronze Age and Early Iron Age site of Mitrou, in East Lokris. [avdm@utk.edu]

MALCOLM H. WIENER has published numerous papers dealing with the Eastern Mediterranean world in the Bronze Age, focusing in particular on the external relations of Minoan Crete and the chronology of the Middle and Late Bronze Age. His publications include "Crete and the Cyclades in LM I: The Tale of the Conical Cups," "Trade and Rule in Palatial Crete," "The Isles of Crete? The Minoan Thalassocracy Revisited," "The Nature and Control of Minoan Foreign Trade," "Present Arms / Oars / Ingots: Searching for Evidence of Military or Maritime Administration in LM IB," "The White Slip I of Tell el-

Dab^ca and Thera: Critical Challenge for the Aegean Long Chronology," "The Absolute Chronology of Late Helladic IIIA2 Revisited," "Times Change: The Current State of the Debate in Old World Archaeology," "Time Out: The Current Impasse in Bronze Age Archaeological Dating," "Chronology Going Forward (With a Query about 1525/4 B.C.)" and "Egypt and Time." [mhwiener@villacandia.com]

Printed on Cougar Opaque paper
from Bembo types, with design
and typography by
Jerry Kelly.

NEW YORK · MMVI